ROUTLEDGE LIBRARY EDITIONS:
EDUCATION

SPECIAL EDUCATION AND SOCIAL INTERESTS

SPECIAL EDUCATION AND SOCIAL INTERESTS

Edited by
LEN BARTON AND SALLY TOMLINSON

Volume 210

Routledge
Taylor & Francis Group

LONDON AND NEW YORK

First published in 1984

This edition first published in 2012
by Routledge
2 Park Square, Milton Park, Abingdon, Oxfordshire OX14 4RN

Simultaneously published in the USA and Canada
by Routledge
711 Third Avenue, New York, NY 10017

First issued in paperback 2014

Routledge is an imprint of the Taylor and Francis Group, an informa company

British Library Cataloguing in Publication Data
A catalogue record for this book is available from the British Library

ISBN 13: 978-0-415-50691-5 (Volume 210)
ISBN 13: 978-0-415-75312-8 (pbk)

Publisher's Note
The publisher has gone to great lengths to ensure the quality of this reprint but
points out that some imperfections in the original copies may be apparent.

Disclaimer
The publisher has made every effort to trace copyright holders and would
welcome correspondence from those they have been unable to trace.

SPECIAL EDUCATION AND SOCIAL INTERESTS

**Edited by Len Barton
and Sally Tomlinson**

CROOM HELM
London & Sydney
NICHOLS PUBLISHING COMPANY
New York

© 1984 L. Barton and S. Tomlinson
Croom Helm Ltd, Provident House, Burrell Row,
Beckenham, Kent BR3 1AT

Croom Helm Australia Pty Ltd, First Floor,
139 King Street, Sydney, NSW 2001, Australia

British Library Cataloguing in Publication Data

Special education and social interests. —
      (Croom Helm series on special education needs:
      policy, practices and social issues)
      1. Exceptional children—Education
      2. Educational sociology
      I. Barton, Len   II. Tomlinson, Sally
      371.9   LC3969
      ISBN 0-7099-3243-X
      ISBN 0-7099-3252-9 Pbk

First published in the United States of America 1984 by
Nichols Publishing Company, Post Office Box 96, New York, NY 10024

Library of Congress Cataloging in Publication Data
Main entry under title.

Special education and social interests.
      1. Handicapped children—Education—Addresses, essays, lectures.
2. Minorities—Education—Addresses, essays, lectures. 3. Slow learning
children—Addresses, essays, lectures. I. Barton, Len. II. Tomlinson, Sally.
LC4015.S676 1984   371.9   84-4748
ISBN 0-89397-194-4

Printed and bound in Great Britain

CONTENTS

SERIES EDITOR'S PREFACE

'Special educational needs' or children with 'learning difficulties' are categories that are being used within recent government reports, circulars and legislation to describe certain types of pupils. Government-supported changes are taking place within the educational system that will have both an immediate and a long-term effect on the nature of the provision deemed necessary to cater for these pupils.

These categories are not applicable merely to children in special schools but are now being applied to an increasing number of pupils and young people, embracing a wide range of ideas, policies and practices. For example, they are used to describe pupils in disruptive units, remedial classes, those involved in programmes of social education, young people on youth training schemes and pupils from ethnic minorities.

Within the school system ability is very narrowly defined and success is still judged through individual merit and particularly the number, types and quality of the examination certificates that a person can gain. A common characteristic of all the young people described above is that they are seen as the low achievers, the failures of the system. Despite the rhetoric of equal opportunity and the central importance of education, these pupils experience low status within schools and limited life chances in the world outside.

In this new series of specially commissioned books, emphasis will be given to exploring some of the important political, social and educational issues involved in this significant movement. Specific topics will be examined, and current policies and practices will be analysed. The important aims of the series are to stimulate debate, to encourage reflection on practice and to introduce alternative ways of thinking and working. Priority will be given to considering the relationship between 'theory' and 'practice' and future trends and requirements will be identified and discussed.

This series will be of interest to teachers, students, lecturers, research workers, administrators, parents and members of all other professional groups associated with these pupils and young people.

Len Barton

ACKNOWLEDGEMENTS

We wish to express our appreciation of the support and sound advice that Peter Sowden has given us throughout the various stages of the production of this book.

Although they remain anonymous, we are grateful for the constructive criticism of two referees.

We would like to thank the editors of *Mental Retardation* for their permission to publish some brief extracts from a paper by Louis Rowitz.

GLOSSARY

In the Introduction, Chapters 2, 3, 5 and 8, analysis primarily relates to issues and practices in England and Wales. Chapters 2, 4, 6, 7, and 9 are primarily concerned with issues and practices within the United States. Chapter 1 offers an analysis of issues and practices in Sweden; in this chapter the label mentally retarded is used to cover both ESN(M) and ESN(S) groups.

It may be helpful to some of our readers to know the usage by the American contributors of the following terms:

caretakers: this refers to members of the caring profession;

gatekeepers: this refers to the mediating role of professional groups;

public school: this is the equivalent of the state school provision in England and Wales. In the United States private schools are the equivalent of our public schools.

FOREWORD

In the twentieth century the greatest stumbling-block to the explanation of educational achievement (or non-achievement) was the assumption that the factors responsible were properties of the individual pupil — whether these were psychogenic (intelligence, motivation or aspirations) or sociogenic (aspects of home background). Even social class was reduced to a personal membership characteristic: at a single methodological stroke classes were eliminated as active collectivities to be replaced by artificial aggregates of those similarly ranked on some occupational scale. Gradually this 'atomistic empiricism' receded in the face of a two-pronged critique.

On the one hand it became clear that pupils did not bring a clutch of discrete personal and membership characteristics into the school but rather a set of social relationships, value orientations and cultural patterns which in turn displayed a differential goodness of fit with teacher assessment and formal evaluation. On the other hand the definition of achievement itself became a crucial topic in need of explanation. Once it was no longer treated as an unproblematic 'given', this opened up the whole sociological issue of who defines it, through what processes and in whose interests. With the gradual abandonment of 'atomistic empiricism', the explanatory problem shifted from that of identifying key characteristics of individuals which accounted for how they fared on unquestioned criteria of achievement, to a question of specifying those social processes through which achievement was defined and delineating those social relations which determined performance *vis-à-vis* particular definitions.

Unfortunately, as the pioneering work of Sally Tomlinson and Len Barton reveals, most investigations of Special Education remained stuck in the ruts of the old explanatory model. The individual 'deficiencies' or 'deficits' of children undergoing Special Education are still the main reasons given for them being there. The resilience of this type of account derives from the enduring conceptualisation of a 'handicap' as a personal misfortune which all good humanists will recognise as requiring special individual attention. From this perspective the question of *cui bono* is redundant — obviously all right-minded people are disinterestedly and consensually promoting the interests of the particularly disadvantaged. Yet, as Tomlinson has demonstrated, we are in fact confronting a group phenomenon — a category of shifting composition, size and definition — never a determinate population of the self-evidently handicapped. Now if this category is subject to substantial social variations rather than reflecting small and random medical, biological or psychological fluctuations, then the answer to 'who benefits?' is not obviously 'those in manifest need'. Indeed, as the category enlarges and job opportunities shrink simultaneously, then receiving Special Education often becomes a matter of social penalisation rather than social welfare. Who now are the beneficiaries of this growth? Here Sally Tomlinson and Len Barton make a valuable sociological contribution by inviting us to address the vested interests of those professionally involved in extending their area of expertise, defending their institutional arrangements and creating their catchment population, in partial collusion with, for example, some ordinary teachers off-loading their problems and in partial opposition to others, for example the medics and the psychologists.

Thus the definition of the population 'in need' of Special Education has been shown to be largely at the mercy of social interests. Equally valuable is the Editors' recognition that the other side of the equation must be examined too, i.e. the processes involved in the social definition of Special Education itself. Here they laudably avoid the evergreen temptation of advancing either the 'Great Wave Account' (the spread of egalitarian values swept in these 'remedial' provisions) or the 'Obliging Plasticine Account' (problems of social control were met by adaptive institutional segregation). Neither of these will do because they lack any mechanism, grounded in social interaction, to explain these occurrences. Yet this part of education, like every other, only changes when (groups of) people do something to it — construct it, modify it or rebuild it.

Today what people confront when attempting to shape or change part of instruction, in conformity with their interests, are well-established state educational systems which can only be influenced by affecting the relevant decision-making processes. We cannot gain theoretical purchase on this decision-making by treating educational influence as the equivalent of osmosis, where the systemic boundaries are viewed as completely permeable membranes, where systemic responses are presumed to complement particular interests automatically, and where different systemic structures are held to be of no account in conditioning who can introduce change and how. Instead we need to locate social interest groupings, to specify their access to processes of educational negotiation and to analyse strategic power-play in these transactions. The punctilious analysis of educational politics is a precondition of understanding the precise changes in policies and provisions.

There are no short-cuts. We cannot move directly from what the (putatively) dominant want to the conclusion that they universally get it, for this involves slurring over the middle ground of negotiation, compromise and concession. Nor is it possible to by-pass educational politics by the opposite manoeuvre, namely construing the macroscopic features of Special Education as blown-up versions of microscopic practices. It is never enough to observe small-scale labelling procedures in classrooms, place a big etcetera after these case studies and then view Special Education in its entirety as these practices writ large. For such practices themselves take place within larger structures and are conditioned by them, since these influence the extent of discretion for labelling, the degrees of freedom for appeal, the range of provisions available and the means of expressing opposition to them. The politics of Special Education is clearly one of the next items on the research agenda — now that both its public and its profile have been acknowledged to be social products, thanks largely to the efforts of the Editors of this volume.

Margaret Archer
Deddington
May, 1984.

INTRODUCTION
Len Barton and Sally Tomlinson

This book is intended to contribute to the development of a model of special education in which social interests, rather than individual differences or deficits, come to be regarded as an appropriate mode of analysis. It expands the theme developed in Barton and Tomlinson (1981) and Tomlinson (1982) that there is currently a need to acquire wider social, political, historical and comparative perspectives on the policies and practices that make up special education: to widen debates about the kind of educational and social arrangements made for those variously termed handicapped, exceptional or in special need, and to begin to analyse special education as an integral part of the normal education system.

This need is becoming more pressing, as it is now clear that there are apparently parallel developments in special education and in beliefs about those deemed to be 'special', in all Western countries, particularly Scandinavia, Britain and the USA. There appears to be a major convergence of policy in that, although these countries now stress the integration or mainstreaming of pupils, in fact their special educational sectors are expanding and more and more of their children are receiving some kind of a 'special' education. Indeed, it is one of the most notable developments of education systems in twentieth-century technological societies that more and more children are now deemed to be candidates for a 'special' education whether offered in a segregated or an integrated setting. Since, in Western technological societies, adequate achievements in normal education are becoming more crucial to gaining *any* sort of employment and exerting *any* influence on the wider society, this expansion raises serious socio-political questions about the function and purpose of special education.

It is also becoming clearer that special education, albeit in changed forms, and rationalised by changing ideologies, is becoming a much more important part of education systems in advanced technological societies. It is now a more important mechanism than it has ever been for differentiating between children, and allocating some to a life-style that — if not as stigmatised as in the past — will almost certainly be characterised by dependence and powerlessness. In addition, the economic recession in these societies has brought into sharper focus a perennial question in special education: how much should be spent on groups who may not be economically profitable or 'useful' in the society?

In all the Western countries (and in Eastern-bloc countries too, although they are not considered in this book), the dominance of medical and psychological models and the emphasis on individual differences and deficits has precluded, until very recently, the development of models of special education which take account of the social interests served by its development and expansion, or which could provide an overview of changing social treatment of the 'handicapped' or 'special'. However, in all these countries there does appear to be a convergent recognition among some academics, policy-makers and practitioners that what is needed now is research which goes beyond traditional models and applied issues, to examine the social and educational structures, processes, ideas and relationships which shape and constrain developments in special education.

Practitioners in special education have, until recently, regarded themselves as a separate establishment, set apart from their colleagues in normal education, and have sometimes been regarded as less important by these colleagues. This neglect has also been apparent in academic literature, particularly that produced by historians and sociologists of education, who have not regarded special education as important when describing and theorising about the development of education systems. Theories specifically concerned with the expansion of education systems (see Archer, ed., 1982), ignore special education. Yet the emergence of state education systems in the nineteenth and twentieth century — which had an explicit aim of drawing all children (apart from elite groups who retained their own private arrangements) into a common public education — was paralleled by the systematic exclusion of a number of children and young people from this common education. This seeming contradiction continues to demand an explanation. In Western countries, ideologies of humanitarianism disguised the frequent 'non-educational' activities offered to handicapped children in special schools or classes, and obviated the need for explanation, but increasingly, as the purposes of education are being subjected to closer scrutiny and evaluation, so the nature and purposes of special education are being called into question. It is now becoming possible to move beyond rhetoric and ask why special education has developed and expanded in a similar manner in Western industrial countries over the past hundred years, what are the relationships between special and normal education, and how social interests affect developments and changes.

Sociological Perspectives

Within the discipline of sociology, there are a variety of theoretical and empirical approaches available, at both the macro and micro level, to begin to explore these questions. We wrote in an earlier volume that 'sociology can help clarify issues, stimulate debates, provide models and theories on which to base understanding, and thus render the moral and political judgements which people make, more informed' (Barton and Tomlinson, 1981, p. 14).

A major task of sociology is to demystify social processes and social situations. Much of what happens in social life is the product of power struggles and vested interests and special education is no exception. But it has long been an area in which the 'confidential' nature of files and information kept on children has compounded mystique and made processes in special education appear 'natural' rather than the product of negotiations between groups who have power and groups who are weaker. A crucial task in sociology is to help social participants move beyond 'taken-for-granted' assumptions and begin to question the interests and motives of those with the power to make decisions, in this case decisions in special education. The variety of sociological perspectives now available can illuminate the educational arrangements made in all societies. Structural-functional perspectives have long been useful to analyse the development and purpose of education in a wide variety of societies, and there is no reason why these perspectives should not further illuminate developments in special education. Conflict perspectives, whether centred around neo-Marxist views of education systems as the outcome of political and ideological class struggle, or Weberian notions concerning the development of dominant interest groups who are able to structure education systems as they wish, are of the utmost importance in explaining development perpetuation and change in special education. Phenomenological and interaction perspectives are also crucial. These perspectives stress the way in which social reality is a creation of social participants, and that social categories and assumptions are not given or natural, but are a product of conscious communication and action between people. The application of phenomenological perspectives to special education is proving particularly valuable, as researchers are now able to 'take as problematic' the processes of categorising, labelling, assessing and treating the 'handicapped' and the special.

These approaches correspond to what are generally known as macro- and micro-level analyses in sociology. Both large-scale macro and smaller-scale micro approaches are important in analysing special education and we would stress that the approaches are complementary. Thus, discussions as to why special education has expanded and changed its forms — for example, Sarason and Doris's (1979) study of the treatment of the mentally-retarded in the USA, or Booth and Potts' (1983) discussion of advances in integration in England, or Kirp's (1983) illuminating comparison between special educational policies in the USA and England — are all extremely valuable studies, allowing us to understand developments and processes in special education on quite a large scale. But equally, small-scale studies of interaction at the level of classroom, school, hospital or workshop are important. Indeed, it may be particularly important to understand more about how participants in special education actually do interact — for example, how do children actually acquire 'labels' or take on handicapped 'identities'. (The chapters in this volume by Rowitz and Gunn, and Goode consider these aspects.) Although relating macro and micro levels of analysis is a perennial problem for the sociology of education (see Hestor, 1982 and the introduction to Karabel and Halsey, 1977), we think that it may be more necessary in special education than in any other areas of study, to make such a synthesis. It is not possible to have an adequate understanding of wider social structures unless we understand how people interact within these structures.

While each particular sociological approach or perspective has a contribution to make in analysing social interests in special education, we tend to take the view that consensus perspectives have a limited value in analysing events in special education. Much of the writing on special education assumes that all are in agreement that developments and changes are 'progress' and are in the best interests of the children or young people in question, and that the only problems lie in implementing new developments. It may in future be more enlightening to analyse developments in special education in terms of conflicting interactions. In the social world, conflict is endemic and special education is not exempt. In education systems one or more groups — a religious order, a social class, a bureaucracy — usually comes to exercise power and authority over other groups and education is usually shaped in the interests of the dominant groups (Archer, 1979; Weber, 1972). In special education, in Britain, as Kirp (1983) has pointed out, it is professionals and administrators who have the power to shape and control through 'a model of social welfare which does not recognise conflict . . . it contemplates professionals and administrators working on behalf of an ever-expanding clientele towards an agreed-on common good' (p. 106). In terms of both the impact of management trends and the medicalisation of special

education, Bart's chapter in this volume discusses some of these issues with reference to the USA. We think it is important to analyse the ways in which powerful groups can impose their ideas of what the care and education of the handicapped or the special should be like. Thus it is essential to analyse the beliefs and ideologies that those in control of special education hold, the 'models' they work within and the decision-making processes through which they act. Quicke's chapter in this volume, for example, illustrates that the model within which many educational psychologists work still tends to be the traditional psychometric paradigm.

Comparative Perspectives

We also think that it is important to analyse changes and developments in special education in some kind of a comparative perspective, to avoid assuming that developments in one country are the 'norm', and to prevent social analyses of special education becoming nationalistic or ethnocentric. Comparative perspectives are also a necessary framework for enquiry as to whether different political and economic systems, and those with centralised or decentralised education systems, produce different ways of dealing with the care and education of the 'handicapped' or the special.

Official comparative literature (that produced by international organisations) is often couched within a rhetoric of humanitarianism and egalitarianism and the 'care' of the handicapped is equated with progress. For example, a UNESCO publication in 1973 stated that 'it is generally agreed that national policies should be directed to providing equal access for all to education, and with integrating all citizens into the economic and social life of the community' (UNESCO, 1973, p. 12). But how, or whether, this 'general agreement' is really reached or actually translated into practice is a matter for comparative research and debate. Information from international organisations, descriptions of special education in other countries (OECD, 1981; UNESCO, 1974) and statistical cross-cultural information (Werner-Putnam, 1979) may all provide a basic understanding of special educational developments in other countries, but they do not necessarily provide comparative perspectives, particularly comparative sociological perspectives. Comparative analyses need to review the characteristics of the whole education system in other countries as well as special educational characteristics and developments, and then make comparisons between countries. Booth (1982) noted after reviewing legal and policy developments in special education in Norway, Italy, the USA and Britain that

> to understand how changes are made and who has the power to make them, we need to know more than whether an education system is centralised or de-centralised. We need to know the official formal system, and the informal hidden one — the efficiency of communication between the centre and the regions, and how the system can be influenced (p. 44).

Comparative sociological perspectives on special education should make clear whether and how structures, processes and developments *are* different or similar in different countries. They should make clear whether different political and economic arrangements and ideological beliefs affect the care and education of the 'special' and they should raise particular cross-cultural and cross-national problems. For example, it is a sociological problematic that, in countries with widely different political systems, the people labelled as mildly retarded or subnormal and those labelled maladjusted are usually the poor and the non-white. Apart from Carrier's chapter, this volume is not comparative in the sense of comparing developments or social interests in different countries or educational systems, but the chapters do illustrate that in other countries those interested in special education are finding it useful and illuminating to analyse special education from sociological and social interest perspectives.

Social Theories

It may be useful at this point to consider what sort of social theorising has to date been found useful in analysing special educational activities. Tomlinson (1982) pointed out that there has long been an existing sociological tradition in special education in Western Europe and the USA, although many writers and practitioners would not recognise it as such. This is the structural-functionalist approach, epitomised by a concern for order, balance and equilibrium in a society.

> The dominant concern within this approach has been the 'fitting in' of the handicapped, adults and children, into society. Thus, there has developed a whole literature on the social problems created by defects or handicaps, and particularly on the families of handicapped

children, and the place of the handicapped in the community, especially the employment prospects of those who have passed through special education (Tomlinson, 1982, p. 13).

Within a functional approach, surveys have documented the extent and type of handicap, and in addition the management, provision for, and direction of the handicapped or special has been seen as a *social* problem. However, functionalist approaches are based on the notion that consensus in society is a normal state of affairs and, in much of the literature on special education, notions of conflict are absent. The ideology of 'humanitarianism' and 'doing good' to children, has fitted very well with functionalist approaches and still does. For example, beliefs that there is a 'consensus' over 'integration' in Britain are very strong in recent published work. Literature produced from consensus perspectives cannot handle or account for the growing conflicts in special education, as increasing numbers of interest groups attempt to affect its purpose and direction.

However, other kinds of theorising have been used to explain developments in the care and education of the handicapped, and some do so in a way which accommodates conflict. For example, Farber (1968) used organisation theory — popular in the USA in the 1960s — to develop the notion of the handicapped as a 'surplus population', whose level and amount of education was likely to be determined by the economic state of a particular society. Söder's chapter in this book develops Farber's argument and shows how ideologies about the 'mentally retarded' change as a country's economic situation changes. Far from there being a humanitarian consensus about the amount of money that should be spent on handicapped people, humanitarianism — or its absence — can be shown to depend on economics!

From conflict perspectives, Tomlinson (1981) and Lazerson (1983) have both used theories of social control to suggest that the smooth running of the normal education system depended in a large measure on the explicit control of potentially troublesome groups of children and young adults via 'special' education, and in this book Barton and Tomlinson suggest again that developments in special education cannot be understood without reference to the social control functions of the state education system. Lazerson (1983) particularly used historical evidence to demonstrate that in the USA a major incentive underlying special education was the control of the 'non-normal' population. Even post-war, he concluded, 'educators, special or otherwise, continued to assume that many handicapped children did not belong in public schools, and that the removal of the handicapped from regular schooling was essential if the normals were to receive adequate education' (p. 37).

Social control theories can appear simplistic however. Archer (ed., 1982) has noted that they often assume 'the victory of the dominant classes to be unproblematic', and ignore the complexity of social, political and professional vested interests. To explain further the way in which any group arrives at a position of dominance in any part of the education system, theories of social and cultural reproduction are available (see Bernstein, 1971-5; Bourdieu and Passeron, 1977), although they have not yet been used much in special education. Tomlinson (1982) used the work of Bourdieu and Passeron to suggest that professionals are part of a dominant group whose cultural definitions ensured that it was predominantly working-class children who became categorised as educationally subnormal (moderate) ESN(M).

In the USA there is a relatively well-entrenched tradition of analysing 'mental retardation' and other handicaps from social system and interaction perspectives. In 1958 Lewis Dexter had suggested, in an article in the *American Journal of Mental Deficiency*, that 'mental defectives' acquire negative self-images and 'social problem status' because of their perceived deviance from normal adult status (Dexter, 1958), and during the 1960s Scott (1970) used the concepts of deviance and stigma to explore the social construction of categories of handicap. Jane Mercer (1970), also a pioneer of alternative ways of analysing 'mental retardation' in the USA, was particularly interested in examining this state 'not as an individual pathology, but as a status which an individual holds in a particular social system, and a role which he plays as an occupant of that status' (p. 383).

Similarly, Tim Booth (1978) in England attempted to show how becoming a 'mentally-handicapped' person is an intricate social process leading eventually to the acceptance of a social role that cannot solely be defined in clinical terms.

The chapter by Rowitz and Gunn in this volume takes the view that 'labelling' children as mentally retarded 'is a process which needs to be viewed in the larger perspective of a community social system' (p. 155), and the chapters by Bogdan and Kugelmass and by Hurst demonstrate that studies from interaction perspectives are crucial to understanding wider structures.

All special educational programmes exist in a larger context — they are part of schools, school systems, states and nations. Definitions, ways of thinking, do not get formed in a vacuum, nor are they formed at random . . . To isolate education and the disabled from the context of the systems of which they are a part is to distort, leaving significant aspects unexamined (Bogdan and Kugelmass, p. 188).

Finally, recent commentaries about growth and developments in special education make use of what can be termed ideological diffusion theories. These theories assume that the spread or diffusion of particular beliefs or ideologies have a direct bearing on social events. This type of theorising can be seen most clearly in current explanations of integration. Ideologies of egalitarianism are invoked to explain why moves to dismantle segregated special educational provision have been instituted in industrial societies. For example, Vislie (1981), commenting on the establishment of integrated education in Norway wrote that 'policies for integration were initiated to achieve equalities of educational opportunity in all aspects of the education system' and noted that special education in Norway is not provision for particular groups of children by disability or deficiency, but simply different forms of organising provision and expenditure. However, Vislie (1982) commented in a lecture that some Norwegian parents were now beginning to worry that the presence of disabled pupils in comprehensive schools might affect their children's education — notions of egalitarianism may well be overtaken by perceived self-interest. In Britain proponents of integration assume that the ideological diffusion of egalitarianism is advanced and entrenched enough for comprehensive education to embrace all children and for mechanisms of allocation to different parts of the education system to be minimised in the case of the special. Thus, Booth and Potts (eds., 1983) write that 'we have defined integration to mean the same as the development of comprehensive education' (p. 24), and Sayer (1983), describing practices of integration in his comprehensive school, concludes that

what we are trying to do is to extend the meaning of the comprehensive school so that it becomes truly comprehensive in spirit and has a basic resource to enable it to make an increasingly comprehensive response to the needs of all children and families in the locality (p. 89).

However, if an ideological diffusion of belief in inequality becomes acceptable again and pressures are exerted towards the differentiation of pupils, it is not difficult to imagine yet more changes in the form and provision of special education.

Social Interest Models

It is now possible to observe that there has already been a considerable amount of effort devoted to viewing special education in terms of social interest rather than in terms of individual deficit or handicap. The latter have incorporated notions of the 'social' only to define the handicapped as a social problem, or as objects for social welfare.

It is particularly encouraging to realise that social interest perspectives on the care and education of those deemed in need of 'special' attention have emerged from various European countries, and from the USA. It is also encouraging that a variety of sociological perspectives should already have been used to examine special education as a social process which can be analysed in the context of wider education systems and the wider structures of society. However, it may not yet be possible to suggest how a synthesis of approaches could best be made, to create a 'social interest' model which would be enduring enough to stand against medical, psychological or administrative models of understanding special education. What we can do is to suggest where further research might help the development of such a model.

First, we need more critical analysis of policy developments in special education and attempts to understand the models and premises on which policies are based. It is interesting that a recent critical piece of work on British policies in special education has been produced by an American (Kirp, 1983). We also need more comparative research on the implications of specific social policies for the educational treatment of the 'handicapped'.

Allied to this there is a need for more research and thought about the ideological justifications used to rationalise the implementation of policies and the way the ideologies are linked to economic and political considerations.

Third, more research is needed into the structural expansion of education systems and the part special education has played in expansion. Theories of the growth and development of education systems, and of differentiation and allocation mechanisms within these systems, cannot afford to ignore the special educational sector in the future. Work of this kind will make it easier, for example, to understand the possibilities and limitations of the integration movement. Allied to this there is a need for a greater understanding of the part special education plays in culturally determining or 'reproducing' sections of society as relatively powerless or stigmatised groups and whether mechanisms really are at work to lessen stigma and give greater control of their own lives to the 'special'. This will necessitate closer examination of those who make decisions and are in charge of policies and practices directed towards the handicapped.

Fourth, there is a continuing need for micro-level studies of the way in which those considered to be special or handicapped actually do live in the social world, how they are treated and labelled and how they perceive and accommodate to their treatment.

The chapters in this book are intended to contribute to the development of a social interest model of the care and education of the special in Western technological societies. They also represent the 'social interests' of their authors, rather than being representative of all the research possibilities suggested above. They are an indication that the 'sociological imagination' is now being applied more intensively to special education and its social importance being more fully recognised.

References

Archer, M.S. (1979) *The Social Origins of Education Systems*, Sage, London.
—— (ed.) (1982) *The Sociology of Educational Expansion*, Sage, London.
Barton, L. and Tomlinson, S. (eds.) (1981) *Special Education: Policy, Practices and Social Issues*, Harper and Row, London.
Bernstein, B. (1971-5) *Class Codes and Control*, 3 vols., Routledge and Kegan Paul, London.
Booth, Tim (1978) 'From Normal Baby to Handicapped Child', *Sociology*, *12*, 2, 203-22.
Booth, Tony (1982) *National Perspectives*, Open University Course, E. 241 Unit 10, Open University, Milton Keynes.
—— and Potts, Patricia (eds.) (1983) *Integrating Special Education*, Blackwell, Oxford.
Bourdieu, P. and Passeron, J.-C. (1977) *Reproduction in Education, Culture and Society*, Sage, London.
Dexter, L.A. (1958) 'A Social Theory of Mental Deficiency', *American Journal of Mental Deficiency*, *63*, 920-8.
Farber, B. (1968) *Mental Retardation: Its Social Context and Social Consequences*, Houghton Mifflin, Boston.
Hestor, S. (1982) 'The Social Constitution of Educational Subnormality', *Research in Education*, *27*, 85-93.
Karabel, J. and Halsey, A.H. (eds.) (1977) *Power and Ideology in Education*, Oxford University Press, Oxford.
Kirp, D.L. (1983) 'Professionalization as a Policy Choice. British Special Education in Comparative Perspective' in J.G. Chambers and W.T. Hartman (eds.), *Special Education Policies*, Temple University Press, Philadelphia.
Lazerson, M. (1983) 'The Origins of Special Education' in J.G. Chambers and W.T. Hartman (eds.), *Special Education Policies*, Temple University Press, Philadelphia.
Mercer, J. (1970) 'Sociological Perspectives on Mild Mental Retardation' in H.C. Hayward (ed.), *Sociocultural Aspects of Mental Retardation*, Prentice-Hall Inc., New Jersey.

OECD (1981) *The Education of the Handicapped Adolescent – Integration in the School*, OECD, Paris.

Sayer, J. (1983) 'A Comprehensive School for All' in T. Booth and P. Potts (eds.), *Integrating Special Education*, Blackwell, London.

Sarason, S. and Doris, J. (1979) *Educational Handicap, Public Policy and Social History*, Free Press, New York.

Scott, R.A. (1970) 'The Constructions of Conceptions of Stigma by Professional Experts' in J.A. Douglas (ed.), *Deviance and Respectability*, Basic Books, New York.

Tomlinson, S. (1981) *Educational Subnormality: A Study in Decision-making*, Routledge and Kegan Paul, London.

—— (1982) *A Sociology of Special Education*, Routledge and Kegan Paul, London.

UNESCO (1973) *The Present Situation and Trends in Research in the Field of Special Education*, Paris.

—— (1974) *Case Studies in Special Education. Cuba, Japan, Kenya, Sweden*, Paris.

Vislie, L. (1981) 'Policies for Basic Education in Norway and the Concept of Integration' in *The Education of the Handicapped Adolescent*, OECD, Paris.

—— (1982) 'Comparative Perspectives', conference organised by the Association of Special Education Tutors, Manchester Polytechnic, 29 October 1982.

Weber, M. (1972) 'Selections on Education and Politics' in B. Cosin (ed.), *Education. Structure and Society*, Penguin, Harmondsworth.

Werner-Putnam, R. (1979) 'Special Education – Some Cross-National Comparisons', *Comparative Education*, *15*, 1, 83-98.

PART ONE: IDEOLOGIES, ISSUES AND PRACTICES

1 THE MENTALLY RETARDED: IDEOLOGIES OF CARE AND SURPLUS POPULATION
Mårten Söder

The public sector in most industrialised countries of the world has expanded considerably since the Second World War. One effect of this development has been the gradual transfer of responsibility for socialisation and care from informal primary groups, first and foremost the family unit, to the public sphere of formal organisations. The character of the relationship between many severely handicapped persons and their surroundings has therefore also changed. Previously they were dependent on family members and other close ties, whereas now they are more often dependent on public support. Their lives are therefore affected to a greater extent by the way this support is provided, and likewise more vulnerable to how their condition and needs are viewed by the society in which they live.

Against this background it becomes important to study and analyse the belief system that controls and legitimates the scope and direction of public support services. The term 'ideology of care' will be used to denote this set of beliefs, including conceptions, assumptions and evaluations.

Ideology is thus seen as containing both cognitive and evaluative elements. Ideology is linked to action. It often becomes explicit in programmes and goals. The function of ideology is to justify the choice between different alternatives of action. In social affairs one often lacks rational 'scientific' knowledge that is encompassing enough to guide the choice of action. The choice, therefore, has to be based also on values and assumptions. The ideology of care is thus a combination of scientific knowledge, subjective values and implicit assumptions.

Ideology can be analysed from at least two principally different perspectives. Using the first perspective the observer takes a *verstehende* position. Ideology is seen as the intentional expression of the goals of the actor. The ambition of the observer is to understand ideology in terms of the actor's own motives and his individual frame of reference or world view.

Using the second perspective the observer takes a transcendent position. The frame of reference of the actor is not taken for granted. His motives are interpreted in terms of a theory used by the observer. Most

15

often this means that ideology is seen as distortions of reality that have the function of masking and legitimising the real interests of the actor. This is the perspective often used in the sociology of knowledge and most notably in the Marxist tradition (Eriksson, 1975).

In this chapter the ideology of care for the mentally retarded will be analysed from both these perspectives. The first perspective is used to give a description of the development in Sweden over the last hundred years. The second perspective is used to relate the development of an ideology of care to broader economic and political factors. The theoretical concept developed in this analysis focuses on the role of the mentally retarded in the productive process of society. (See Söder, 1981, for a more in-depth discussion.)

Two dimensions are foremost in the description of the ideology of care. The first concerns the degree of optimism or pessimism expressed in the view of the possibilities the mentally retarded have for personal development. The second concerns how active or passive is the view of the public services (socio-political and the special pedagogic) provided for the mentally retarded. An active view regards the services as justified by their capabilities of influencing and altering the lives of the mentally retarded. The more passive view is characterised by resignation wherein mental retardation is regarded as a condition that is taken for granted and which is difficult to influence. Public services are viewed as passive adaptations to that situation.

The chapter opens with a short description of the development of the ideology of care in this sector in Sweden. This development is then ana- lysed from a frame of reference based on the affiliation of the mentally retarded to the 'surplus population'. Present-day developments in the ideology of care are then discussed from the same perspective. In this context the main hypothesis is that the optimistic and active ideology of the 1960s is changing as a result of economic difficulties into a pes- simistic and passive one which is contributing to making the need the mentally retarded have of special resources disappear from sight. A summary in general terms is presented in the last section.

Ideology of Care for the Mentally Retarded in Sweden

Charity and Pedagogic Optimism

The first initiatives in the care of the mentally retarded as a special cate- gory in Sweden were taken at the end of the 1860s. These initiatives were taken by private individuals and were financed through voluntary contributions. Relatively soon, however, the county councils started to set up similar institutions.

At the beginning of the twentieth century slightly over a thousand mentally-retarded residents were housed in 24 institutions. These were rather small homes (25-35 residents) and, even at that time, the largest institutions did not accommodate more than 100 persons. Activities concentrated on upbringing and education, modelled on the ordinary primary school curriculum and particularly on the mini-courses designed for the poor and persons of low intelligence. Towards the close of the nineteenth century emphasis was increasingly placed on the importance of practical subjects.

From the very start, activities were directed at the educable mentally retarded. This emphasis was linked to the pedagogic approach applied in working with the children. Subsequently this requirement created the need to differentiate the educable from the uneducable. Places were needed for the uneducable, and for the educable who had gone through the 'schools for the mentally retarded' but who could not manage to live normally in society. Therefore asylums (for the uneducable) and workhouses (for educable adults) were started, either as special sections of the institutions or as independent institutions. The development of these institutional forms gathered considerable momentum when the government started to subsidise these programmes at the beginning of this century.

The ideology of care that dominated was rather diffuse and inarticulated. Three features were particularly prominent: a philosophy of compassion, a protective philosophy and optimism.

The philosophy of compassion was linked to the religious and philanthropic approach which typified the first pioneers in this area. It is difficult to make out any real target for the work during the first ten years or so. More was made of why the measures were one way of living up to the message of Christian love than what it was that they were really trying to achieve.

The protective philosophy was closely related to the philosophy of compassion. One wanted to take care of the mentally retarded in order to protect them from a cruel and uncomprehending world. It was easy to sustain this protective philosophy, as it was the philosophy of compassion, as the majority of the children were drawn from the lower social classes, often through the poor relief. The wish was to 'save' the children from the inferior environmental conditions in which it was felt they lived.

The third prominent feature was a substantial degree of optimism. A

proper upbringing and specially-designed education was going to equip
the children to manage in society. This optimism and a target-orientated
pedagogic ambition were expressed particularly during the 1870s and
1880s. Often quotes were cited from the psychiatrist C.U. Sondén who
as early as 1857 stated in an essay that providing the mentally retarded
with loving care would change a large number of them 'from incapable
consumers to active producers . . .' (Sondén, 1857).

Resignation and Social-Darwinism

However, this optimism started to lose ground towards the end of the
last century. The optimistic targets proved difficult to achieve. Eight
years in a school for the mentally retarded did not enable the students
to manage out in society. At the beginning of this century there was
talk of a target crisis and it was from this that the concept of lifelong
institutional care and a rationally organised system of institutions grew.

By the First World War this resignation turned into a repressive
Social-Darwinistic view. The retarded was seen as a threat to society.
He was regarded as a eugenic threat (a threat to the quality of society's
'aggregated germ plasm'), a moral threat (mental retardation, particularly its milder forms, was thought to be associated with moral defects)
and an economic threat (a financial burden without returns). In this
atmosphere laws allowing for sterilisation were passed, large state institutions were established and the number of asylums (for uneducables)
as well as workhouses (for adults) grew rapidly.

The eugenic argument came to the fore particularly in connection
with legislation on sterilisation. Sterilisation laws were introduced in
1934 and 1941 and debate around them was lively. A number of arguments were presented by legal experts for and against sterilisation. But
on one point there was widespread agreement — it was important to
protect society from 'physically and mentally inferior human beings',
and it was the mentally retarded as a group who were most often referred to as examples of such inferiority.

The Social-Darwinistic philosophy was also used to justify the establishment of special state-run hospitals. These were established in the
inter-war years for 'degenerate boys and girls', 'asocial imbecilic adults'
and 'uneducable mentally-retarded persons requiring special care'. The
majority were housed in military barracks that were vacated as a result
of a decision taken in 1925 to reduce the armed forces. The primary
task of the special institutions was to look after those mentally-retarded
persons who could not be taken care of by other means, or who were

not to be placed in the ordinary institutions for the mentally retarded. Right from the start the goals were passive and of a safe-keeping nature. The need to protect society was an explicit justification particularly at the institutions for asocial adults. At the beginning of the 1940s there were about 2,700 mentally-retarded persons in these institutions.

The number and size of asylums and workhouses increased considerably during this period. Private institutions, run by private individuals, were responsible for most of the increase. On the other hand, the number of places at the educational institutions did not increase notably. Only a few of these institutions were established between the wars.

The optimistic, pedagogically-orientated tradition from the nineteenth century was not evident during this period. But this tradition was shown to be still alive at a seminar for teachers of the mentally retarded started by the Association for the Care of Mentally Deficient Children at the end of the nineteenth century. A certain amount of pedagogic development was performed there and during the 1930s the influences on the work included reform-pedagogic elements.

Active Optimism

New principles concerning the ideology of care for the special service sector for the mentally retarded were formulated towards the end of the 1960s. The basic feature of the new principles was a criticism of the traditional care provided by the institutions. The mentally retarded were no longer to be looked after in that way. Instead the fundamental principle was to be their right to live under conditions that were as normal as possible. They were no longer to be separated from society but were to live among us under normal conditions. These concepts were formulated in the principles of normalisation and integration. (For a discussion of these concepts, see Wolfensberger, 1972.)

It is easy to regard the introduction of these principles as something radically new. However, in this section it will be shown that what happened in the 1960s was a consequence of a continuous, long-term, post-war development.

Perhaps the most striking feature of the post-war period is the increase in the number of registered mentally-retarded people. During that period the number has increased threefold (from about 12,000 at the end of the 1940s to approximately 36,000 today). There are several reasons for this. The life expectancy of the mentally retarded has increased, but that is only a contributory cause. The most important reason is that more people with inhibited intellectual development have been provided with public care.

A reconstruction and expansion of the service system has occurred simultaneously with this increased influx. This is not solely due to the pressure exerted by the greater numbers and legislation. After the war many of the institutions were in very poor physical condition. Attention was also drawn to the activities performed at the institutions by several 'scandals' reported in the press at the beginning of the 1950s. It can be said that the results of the institutional philosophy of the inter-war years were then starting to manifest themselves. A pro-reconstruction public opinion was created. Making education compulsory meant that new groups of parents became involved. Many of these were middle-class families that had kept their children outside the public service system. Once their children were included they made demands concerning both the external standard and the content of the care provided. The reconstruction demands were especially articulated when, in the mid-1950s, parents organised themselves into a central parent organisation.

The reconstruction involved widespread new construction at the end of the 1950s and during the 1960s. The new institutions were of a higher physical standard than the older ones. At the same time the shortage of places resulted in a start being made in the development of alternative forms of care. Day-schools were established in order to rectify the shortage of places in the special schools. Work homes for the daily employment of mentally-retarded adults living at home were started. Work activities also started to appear in the institutions. Against the background of the increasing criticism of the pacifying effect of the institutions, the possibilities for stimulation provided by even relatively simple work were discovered.

The whole of this development marked a change in the ideology of care. The Social-Darwinistic ideas, at least in their most extreme form, disappeared rather rapidly after the war. What remained was a medical-psychiatric approach which in principle had the same passive, pessimistic outlook that had dominated between wars. Mental retardation was regarded as a static condition that could not be influenced. According to this approach the mentally retarded should be taken care of in large, state-run institutions and in this way one wished to create sufficient basic data for differentiation and other specialities. The mentally retarded were to be committed for passive safe keeping.

When education was made compulsory by law in 1944, the pedagogic groups started to have more to say on the content of the ideology of care. These groups possessed a more optimistic outlook of development.

It can be said that the optimistic ambitions from the end of the nine-teenth century survived the pessimistic outlook of the inter-war years in some pedagogic circles. This pedagogic approach came into open confrontation with the medical-psychiatric outlook in conjunction with the debate on the application of the new law in the 1940s. The pedagogues believed that the mentally handicapped were capable of development although they required specially-designed education. The problem was pedagogic and would best be solved if instruction was provided in a form as closely related to other instruction as possible.

The pedagogic approach was 'victorious' both in the immediate issues and in the 1940s' discussion on the long-term ideology of care. The optimistic ideology of care increased in strength throughout the 1950s and 1960s. Relatively early on it came to encompass those who were only slightly mentally retarded. The possibilities of coming out into society and becoming self-supporting were regarded with optimism.

The more severely mentally retarded were not immediately viewed with the same optimism. But eventually even their right to high-standard care in a physically suitable environment was expressed.

Eventually a more optimistic outlook pervaded the care of the more severely mentally retarded. This was noted in the latest piece of welfare legislation (from 1967) which entitled every mentally-retarded person, regardless of the degree of handicap, to the right to education.

It was this optimistic outlook that was formulated into the principles of normalisation and integration in the 1960s. To a great extent it was these ideas that lay behind the 1967 Social Welfare Act for the mentally retarded. This act was an important factor behind the developments of the 1970s — developments which have meant that more mentally-retarded persons than previously have been taken care of in other forms than those provided by the traditional institutions. The number of children living at home or in hostels integrated into normal buildings has increased. Even if the number of adults living in mental institutions has not dropped more than marginally, the number in state-run psychiatric hospitals has fallen and the number in integrated boarding houses has increased. At the same time staff density, counted as an average of all forms of care, has increased. The increase of various 'specialist groups' (psychologists, counsellors, recreational leaders, etc.) has been particularly noticeable.

The Mentally Retarded as Surplus Population

One of the most important, and most general, observations made in conjunction with the historical studies is the rapid and substantial change that has taken place in the ideology of care. One such change at the turn of the century has been described, where the optimistic, philanthropic pioneer ideology changed to a resigned pessimism which in a short time developed into the Social-Darwinistic philosophy of the protection of society. A similar change occurred during the period immediately after the Second World War. The passive ideology aimed at protecting society changed to one of pedagogic optimism and socio-political activity. In order to understand the causes and driving forces behind such changes we need a theoretical perspective that links the ideological changes to the overall political and economic situation of a given society.

The Concept of Surplus Population

The 1960s and 1970s saw the emergence of a rather substantial amount of behavioural science literature on the subject of mental retardation, the majority of which was socio-psychologically orientated. Attention was focused on the relative nature of the criteria used to demarcate the group. Jane Mercer attracted a particular amount of attention. She criticised the traditional clinical approach which regarded mental retardation as a personal characteristic, the existence of which in a population can be determined using a normally distributed intelligence curve. In opposition to this approach she advocated a social system perspective where mental retardation is determined by the demands and the role expectations existing in the social system (Mercer, 1973, 1975).

However, the socio-psychological approach has only resulted minimally in investigations of the elements in the environment and society that demarcate the group and govern the lives its members lead. Instead there has been a tendency to turn back the relativistic approach to elements centred on individuals. Studies of the adaptive behaviour of the mentally retarded have been more usual than studies of the characteristics of the social system (see, for example, Leland, 1973 and Nihira, 1973). We have been given more of a broader clinical perspective than a developed perspective of the social system (Granat, 1981).

One exception is Farber's work. In a book published at the end of the 1960s, he broadens the perspective by regarding the mentally retarded as a part of society's surplus population. This surplus population comprises 'that segment of the total population exceeding the number of individuals needed to fill the slots in a social organization' (Farber, 1968, p. 19).

In Farber's opinion, surplus population has, in principle, been dealt with from two different perspectives. The first is ecological:

> Briefly, the ecological view of a surplus population is concerned with matters of consumption . . . The ecological surplus population refers to that portion of the population which exceeds the number that the subsistence base will support at a given level of standard of living (Farber, 1968, p. 9).

This includes Malthus and the view influenced by him. The other perspective regards surplus population as an organisational surplus. Surplus population is determined in relation to the available positions in social organisations. As can be seen from Farber's definition of surplus population, this is the perspective that he himself represents.

In a modern society surplus population comprises a heterogeneous group of people. Farber provides as examples the old, sick, deviants and various categories of people outside the mainstream of society. In his opinion this surplus population is necessary. A residual population, from which recruitment can be made for the various positions in the organisations, is necessary for social reasons. Thus he adopts a functionalistic position which he develops further in a later essay (Farber and Royce, 1977). He regards surplus population as a necessary pre-condition for stratification in society and thereby for social order on the whole.

Farber feels that this perspective provides a better understanding of the social situation of the mentally retarded than both the theories that assume that the mentally retarded are incompetent and those that are based on labelling theories. From a sociological perspective it is their position as an organisational surplus that is central.

However, his way of talking about social organisations is not without ambiguity. What are the organisations in society that are fundamental to the demarcation of surplus population? Without exaggerating too much one could envisage two different interpretations. The first is a broad one. Social organisations can be understood as a category including formal organisations, social institutions as well as informal groups with a certain degree of stability. Some of Farber's arguments make such an interpretation the most likely. But such an interpretation creates problems in determining what surplus population is: it becomes a group that to a considerable extent lies outside ordered social life. The other interpretation is that social organisations primarily mean organisations that in some sense work to produce different utilities. Farber (1968) touches this interpretation when he says that 'the organizational view of a surplus population pertains to matters of production and the division of labour . . .' (p. 9). Surplus population would then be determined in relation to the production apparatus in society.

Farber is not clear on this point. It seems reasonable, though, to adopt the second point of view, that the surplus population be determined in relation to the production apparatus in society. In this way it is possible to discuss the social situation of the mentally retarded on the basis of the criteria that directly or indirectly form the foundation for the majority of theories on sociological classes and stratification (Korpi, 1978).

In the following discussion the mentally retarded are regarded as a part of the social population that is characterised by not playing a role in the social division of labour. Elements from both the ecological and organisational perspectives will be used to support the arguments presented.

There are two aspects of the position of the mentally retarded as surplus population that influence the ideology of care. The first is the part they play as producers. The ideology of care can be related to the possibilities that the mentally retarded have on the labour market. The other aspect is their role as consumers. Without resorting to a pure ecological perspective (which means that surplus population is determined in relation to the available subsistence space), the assertion to be made here is that the position of the mentally retarded as consumers of care and welfare is of significance to the ideology of care.

The Mentally Retarded as Producers

Sometimes in discussions on the ideology of care one comes across explicit references to the possibilities that the mentally retarded have on the labour market. These references usually date from the times when the ideology of care was undergoing change. In conjunction with these changes, motivation for 'new' approaches can be gathered from the assessments made of the possibilities that the mentally retarded had on the labour market. When the change was from an optimistic to a pessimistic ideology of care, the inability of the mentally retarded to support themselves and contribute to the production in society was a reason for pessimism. When the ideology of care was changing from a pessimistic to an optimistic outlook, then the opposite point of view was held to be true — it is their possibility of entering the labour market and supporting themselves that justifies the optimistic position.

With this as a background it is possible to formulate the following hypothesis, supported by historical data: in periods of economic expansion the ideology of care tends to be optimistic and positive, while in periods of economic stagnation it tends to be pessimistic and defensive. The position of the mentally retarded in relation to the labour market and their possibilities of entering it constitute the real mechanism behind this correlation.

The major social problem in the middle of the nineteenth century was the large propertyless surplus population in the rural areas. This surplus population is usually presented as one of the conditions behind industrialisation. But investments were required to facilitate mobility in order to meet the needs of expanding industry for labour. It was necessary to convert the agrarian surplus population into an industrial labour force. It was in this light that a number of optimistic ideas and new care principles appeared in the care sector. The optimistic view of the mentally retarded is one part of the investment in rehabilitation measures.

The defensive and pessimistic approach of the inter-war years developed in a society in which the first stage of industrial expansion had been arrested by the First World War. It was deepened during the economic crisis experienced between the two world wars. Even during the periods between the crises of the 1920s and 1930s unemployment levels were high. The driving force behind an optimistic and active ideology of care which is created by a shortage of labour in an expanding labour market was missing.

The post-war development of the care of the mentally retarded occurred in a society in which active efforts were made in a number of socio-political sectors. The basis of this development was a boom period and need for labour. The interest in 'those partially capable of working' and the possibility of putting them into the labour market increases sharply during this period. The optimistic outlooks concerning the mentally retarded also emerge as a result of the need for labour.

Perhaps the brief example of the content of the hypothesis given above should be outlined in more detail.

1. The economic expansion/stagnation categories do not refer to short-term changes in the economy. The ideology of care remains relatively stable for long periods of time. It is longer periods of economic development and structural change that have an effect. The optimistic ideology of care was formulated in situations where a large surplus population can certainly be found, but this exists in sectors or regions where no employment opportunities were created while at the same time the economy expanded in other regions/sectors. The defensive ideology of care dominates in periods when we lack the need an expansive economy

has of labour or where a specific expansion can utilise an available surplus population which already exists in the sector that is expanding.

2. The ideology of care that dominates is not just that pertaining to care of the mentally retarded. It is a part of a more general optimism/pessimism that applies to the entire surplus population.

3. The ideology of care described applies first and foremost to the mentally retarded that are receiving public services. These were not recruited, at least not prior to the post-war period, directly from the labour market. Instead recruitment was mainly from other care organisations. The pressure on care organisations created during periods of economic stagnation and by the needs that occur during expansion is thus to a certain degree indirect. It is channelled through other forms of care.

4. Changes in the ideology of care do not always occur simultaneously with changes in the economic situation. Not least does the situation in the 1970s show how other factors (pressure groups, legislation) can impede such changes.

These specific points mean that the formulated correlation is not direct and pragmatic. It is not the case that one suddenly notices that the possibilities that the mentally retarded have on the labour market have changed and this results in adaptations in the ideology of care. The link between social economy and the ideology of care is affected by the general view of surplus population and by the situation in other forms of care.

The Mentally Retarded as Consumers

The argument concerning the part played by the mentally retarded as producers primarily refers to those who are not so severely handicapped as to be directly excluded from entering the labour market. The mentally-retarded group that is so severely handicapped that it is not feasible for them to perform such work will also be viewed in different ways depending on society's economic situation. There is a tendency for care ideologies established for groups that are positioned relatively close to the labour market to spread to include other groups. Care ideologies founded on the basis of the situation of people who are only slightly retarded will in this way come to apply as well to the severely mentally retarded, although with some delay.

But the ideology of care for the severely mentally-retarded groups is influenced to an even greater extent by their position as consumers. Surplus population is taken care of by society in one way or another. They consume care and welfare. This consumption of care does not need to occur in the form of publicly provided care. For a long time it occurred mainly by the mentally retarded being cared for in informal social institutions, primarily the family. One cause for the steadily growing numbers of registered mentally-retarded people during this century is that society has increasingly assumed the responsibility for the provision of this care. The position of the mentally retarded as consumers of publicly financed and planned care has become increasingly prominent.

Even as consumers the mentally retarded are viewed in the light of care ideologies which vary with the economic situation. In times of economic expansion the state has more resources for investment in care. At these times the ideology of care tends to be generous, optimistic and active. In times of stagnation, with less economic resources for care, the ideology of care conversely tends to alter towards the pessimistic and passive.

During the nineteenth century the care of the mentally retarded was aimed at the educable, those who were thought to have a chance of managing to live an adult life as self-supporting citizens. It is difficult, at least with the available data that has been gathered from publicly-run care institutions, to determine how the more seriously mentally retarded were regarded, those who then were mainly taken care of within the framework of the family. There is, however, no doubt that the pessimism expressed during the inter-war period applied to the entire group of mentally-retarded persons. This pessimism was infected by the lack of economic resources. Prevention in the form of sterilisation and incarceration was justified at that time with reference to the state of municipal finances. The same argument was also used for the severely mentally retarded who were committed to the increasing number of asylums.

During the post-war period, with its economic growth, the optimism that was initially reserved for those in close proximity to the labour market increasingly came to be applied to groups of more severely mentally-retarded persons.

The position as consumer of public care is today shared both by the slightly and severely mentally retarded. Today their situation is particularly sensitive to the economic climate, because they are totally dependent on public measures that are governed by care ideologies which in their turn are linked to the economic condition of society.

Integration as an Ideology of Care

In recent years the world has been undergoing a widespread economic crisis. The belief held in the 1960s of constant economic growth now appears to be increasingly utopian. The entire Western world is fighting inflation, falling production, reduced investments and rising unemployment.

The number of jobs in industrial production will probably drop even more in the future. The increasing use of computers and industrial robots will reduce the number of jobs. The new jobs that technological development will create will hardly be those suitable for the mentally retarded. An OECD report comments on this development as follows:

> While micro-electronics will create new jobs (although the extent to which this is the case cannot yet be accurately predicted) most of these are likely to demand a higher level of education than did the jobs that will be lost: there will, for example, be greater opportunities for those with skills in mathematics, the physical sciences, and craft, design and technology. Unfortunately most of these subjects are ones which the majority of multi-handicapped youngsters, especially those with neurological and physical abnormalities and with mental retardation, find particularly difficult (Anderson and Tizard, 1979, p. 6)

Another aspect of the crisis includes cuts in public sector expenditure. A growing number of countries are trying to combat inflation by cutting back on public sector consumption.

If the general hypothesis developed above is correct, then this means that changes are taking place in the ideology of care for the mentally retarded. Today the mentally retarded are further from the labour market than ever before. They are less attractive as producers than the large numbers of young people who are unemployed. As consumers of public care they have been hit by cuts in public sector expenditure. It should therefore be possible to observe a change in the ideology of care which is as drastic as that described as occurring at the turn of the century and at the end of the 1940s.

Undoubtedly such a change is underway. But it is not clearly articulated in new concepts and ideological expressions. Instead it is creeping up on us as the optimistic and positive ideological orientation from the 1960s is being watered down and its content dissipated. The ideas that at one time were fundamental to give the mentally retarded the right to a life in society on the same conditions as other people now run the risk of being transformed into ideologies that cloak the need the mentally retarded have for supportive measures. This process of making their needs invisible consists of the ideology focusing on problems other than the fundamental ones: the requirement to satisfy the need of the mentally retarded for supportive measures in order to be able to live among the rest of us.

When the principles of integrating the disabled were first accepted, the ideology was ambitious and active. Measures which caused segregation were to be avoided. The disabled should have the same rights as other people to participate in community life. The task of social policy and special pedagogics was therefore to get them into the community and take the measures required to enable them to remain there.

In practice this resulted in many disabled persons being introduced into, or retained in, ordinary environments. To a greater extent they received their schooling in ordinary classes or ordinary schools, living at home with their parents or in apartments integrated into ordinary residential areas. Initially integration was mainly directed at people with minor disabilities whose integration required only minimal extra support resources. This was also one of the explanations behind the more telling arguments supporting the integration policy: it was cheap.

However, once integration became official policy, the content was increasingly reduced to just physical and technological aspects. In practice integration came to mean the physical placement of the handicapped in ordinary environments. But the social integration, the entrance into community life, which was the fundamental philosophy behind the original ideology, tended to disappear. The ambitious ideology came to be a physical and technological integration of the disabled with other people.

But a functioning integration of the severely disabled and the development of social integration requires more resources. However, the acquisition of the additional creativity and resources that this requires was halted by another element that had become common in the ideology of care. The various measures taken to assist the disabled started to be regarded as segregation. The special organisational solutions, special staff and the special pupil care teams for the disabled were regarded as facets of segregation.

There is consequently a risk here that the integration philosophy contributes to the denial of requests for investments which require substantial resources. The content of integration is reduced to physical placement. The disabled are considered to be integrated once they have been placed in an ordinary environment. Behind this reasoning is the notion that ordinary environments are one large all-embracing community into which the disabled are automatically absorbed once they have been positioned there. But this romanticises reality. Ordinary environments are often filled with social tensions, rejections and evaluations which accentuate and mark out different disabilities. Therefore, in order for integration to be meaningful, it is necessary to have the resources necessary for supporting the disabled person in the ordinary environment and to adjust and change this environment. Romanticising ordinary environments often results in these needs disappearing from sight.

A new approach to the handicapped was closely linked to the development of the integration ideology. Previously a handicap was regarded as one of the characteristics of an individual. It was a defect; different types of measures were justified by the incurability of the handicap. Nature was cruel enough to create some people who lacked all their faculties. What we could do was to adapt to that situation and let handicapped people live in a separate, peaceful environment.

In contrast to this, an approach was promulgated in the 1960s which emphasised that a handicap developed in relation to the surroundings. There were no characteristics that could be said intrinsically to constitute a handicap. The handicap first occurs when people are placed in a certain environment and certain demands and expectations are made of them. Under these circumstances certain characteristics appear as a handicap because they mean that individuals cannot satisfy the demands made of them. Thus a handicap is not solely limited to the individual, it occurs in relation to the environment.

But it is dangerous to apply this relativistic assumption, despite its apparent advantages, too uniformly. It gives the impression that handicaps can be rectified by measures directed at the environment – the problems associated with the handicapped persons can be alleviated if we can eliminate the handicapping characteristics in our surroundings.

Assuming this view can mean that there is a tendency to forget all too easily that there are individuals whose disability is so severe and affects functions that are so central that they will be handicapped in just about all environments that can be envisaged in today's society. In such cases talk about the relativity of a handicap can easily become cynical. We run the risk of losing sight of those who need help the most. In the same way as there is a risk of romanticising the environment in the integration philosophy, there is a risk here of romanticising the disability. Many people are so severely disabled that the handicap cannot be alleviated by measures aimed at manipulating the environment. This is a tragic truth that can easily be forgotten if excessive emphasis is placed on the part played by the environment.

Decentralisation is a consequence of the integration philosophy and the understanding of the relativity of handicaps. If a handicap is due to a situation, so that a person can be handicapped in one situation but not in another, the support resources used must be flexible. The resources cannot be tied to specific individuals, they must be adapted to the circumstances in question. The need for support occurs in certain situations. The resources must be disbursed by someone close to the situation who can identify the needs. This indicates there is a lot to be said for giving priority to resources at the local level. State control results in resources being linked to certain individuals. Flexibility requires that priority be allocated at the local level.

Moreover, measures decided centrally are often of a static nature. They run the risk, by tying the resources to specific individuals with special needs, of singling them out and segregating them – another reason why the resources should be allocated by people close to the problem.

But at the local level small groups of disabled persons are often particularly vulnerable. They are not many and they often have difficulty making their voices heard. They are prone to be on the losing side in the fight for limited resources. The local system of giving priority to resources is unfair to them, the tendency being to give priority to problems that produce quick results. Neither are resources spent on measures that can be expected to produce immediate effects other than support to those with non-rectifiable disabilities. Furthermore, priority tends to be given to problems that threaten the system. It is, for example, important that schools perform their duty: providing the pupils with education in established forms. The extra measures that are therefore given priority are those that rectify threats to these established forms. It becomes more important to maintain the established structure than to provide a severely disabled person, who sits in a corner and does not understand anything, with help. Decentralisation can result in these non-acute disabled persons, who do not pose a threat to the system, being forgotten. The risk of people disappearing when using this system of distributing resources is manifest.

Conclusion

In previous sections an attempt has been made to describe and analyse how the ideology of care for the disabled in general and the mentally retarded in particular is influenced by economic changes in society.

This influence is not simple and uncomplicated. Often it is passed on through a number of intermediary stages so that the actual correlation can be difficult to find without in-depth analysis. Basically there are two factors that create and maintain this influence. The first is the labour market policy situation. Specialist pedagogic and social policy measures have nearly always been aimed at making the clients capable of entering the labour market. The targets, conceptions and evaluations that are used as a basis are therefore coloured by the objective possibilities offered by the labour market in question. The second factor is the amount of resources that it is felt can be allotted to rehabilitation and socialisation measures. The 'economic margin' determines what resources are made available. This also governs and influences how the disabled and their capabilities are regarded in these sectors. Put simply, one can expect that the ideologies in specialist pedagogics and social policy will change with the economic situation.

It could be felt that in many ways this statement is simple and trivial. If there is a shortage of jobs and a lack of resources a number of social activities must make adaptations to take this into account. The state of the economy also sets the limits into which the measures of support for the disabled must be fitted. The ideology must be realistic, it must take account of the material preconditions.

But ideological changes are not open and deliberate in that way. Ideology adapts to a changed reality insidiously. It affects our most basic evaluations in a way which is difficult to recognise. It is as much a question of rationalising economic changes through ideology as consciously adapting to them.

Ideological changes can be described in another way. The ideologies we have are based on a programme. Ideology defines certain ways of acting. When the programme is to be put into practice the simplified assumptions of reality embedded in the ideology must be adapted to reality. An ideological programme is often found to be unrealistic when confronted by a recalcitrant reality. It is not possible to put the programme into action, or it is implemented but the final result is not what was expected. Reality involves both inertia and resistance. Forces act to adapt the intended changes so that our intention is lost. The reforms are adapted to the structural preconditions. (For an interesting discussion on these questions, see Hirschman, 1982, pp. 92-102.)

Often ideology is adapted to reality at the same time, even if it is often at the cost of the loss of the fundamental goals and values upon which the original ideology was based.

When the mentally retarded were first looked after in 'institutions for educable mentally retarded children' this service was provided in a spirit of religious philanthropy and optimism. The pedagogic optimism did not survive the confrontation with the hard social reality of the first years of the twentieth century. Instead the ideology was changed. Care in institutions came to be justified by Social-Darwinistic ideology and the ideology of protecting society.

The form (the institution) remained, but the content and the ideology were changed. Forms that were initially linked to pedagogic ambitions and a love of human beings came to represent society's safeguards against socially dangerous people.

In this chapter an attempt has been made to show the risk of a similar change occurring today. An ambitious and optimistic ideology has created new forms of support for the disabled, but in the future these forms can be used for purposes other than those for which they were intended. But changes creep up on us. They grow from starting-points in those ideologies that we have learned to comprehend. The invisibility of the needs of the disabled does not occur through radical changes in the formulation of ideology. They are expressed in terms of integration, relativity and decentralisation. One could say, without putting too fine a point on it, that the ideology itself bears the seeds of the process of making the needs of the disabled disappear from view.

Making the needs of the severely disabled invisible fills an economic function. The present economic crisis has created strong political pressure for cuts in public sector expenditure. Cuts in a sector that is primarily constructed to meet the needs of groups of less fortunate individuals will naturally affect these groups the most. There is therefore every, and serious, reason to look closely at the ideological reasons for cuts. That these motives are clothed in 'progressive' words concerning integration and normalisation possibly makes a critical inspection more difficult, but no less necessary.

References

Anderson, E. and Tizard, J. (1979) *The Education of the Handicapped Adolescent. Alternatives to Work for Severely Handicapped People*, OECD, Paris.

Eriksson, B. (1975) *Problems of an Empirical Sociology of Knowledge*, Acta Universitatis Upsaliensis, Studia Sociologica Upsaliensia 10, Uppsala.

Farber, B. (1968) *Mental Retardation, Its Social Context and Social Consequences*, Houghton Mifflin, Boston.

—— and Royce, E. (1977) 'The mentally retarded — valuable individuals or superfluous population' in Mittler (ed.), *Research to Practice in Mental Retardation.*

Vol. I: Care and Prevention. Proceedings of the fourth congress of the International Association for the Scientific Study of Mental Deficiency, University Park Press, Baltimore, Maryland, 45-51.

Granat, K. (1981) 'Utvecklingsstörning i ett socialt perspektiv' in Kebbon *et al.*, *Evaluering av öppna omsorgsformer*. Delegationen för social forskning, Socialdepartementet, Stockholm, 7-14.

Hirschman, A. (1982) *Shifting Involvements. Private Interest and Public Action*, Princeton University Press, Martin Robertson, Oxford.

Korpi, W. (1978) *The Working Class in Welfare Capitalism. Work, Unions and Politics in Sweden*, Routledge and Kegan Paul, London.

Leland, H. (1973) 'Adaptive behaviour and mentally retarded behaviour' in Richard K. Eyerman, Edward C. Meyers and George Tarja (eds.), *Sociobehavioral Studies in Mental Retardation*, Monographs of the American Association on Mental Deficiency, Washington DC.

Mercer, J. (1973) 'The myth of 3% prevalence' in Richard K. Eyerman, Edward C. Meyers and George Tarja (eds.), *Sociobehavioral Studies in Mental Retardation*, Monographs of the American Association on Mental Deficiency, Washington DC.

―――― (1975) *Labeling the Mentally Retarded: Clinical and Social System Perspectives on Mental Retardation*, University of California Press, Berkeley, California.

Nihira, K. (1973) 'Importance of environmental demands in the measurement of adaptive behaviour' in Richard K. Eyerman, Edward C. Meyers and George Tarja (eds.), *Sociobehavioral Studies in Mental Retardation*, Monographs of the American Association on Mental Deficiency, Washington DC.

Sondén, C.U. (1857) 'Om idioters uppfostran och vård', *Hygeia*, 229-310.

Söder, M. (1981) *Vårdorganisation, Vårdideologi och Integreri g. Sociologiska perspektiv på omsorger om utvecklingsstörda*, Acta Universitatis Upsaliensis, Abstracts of Uppsala Dissertations from the Faculty of Social Sciences, 25. Almqvist & Wiksell International, Stockholm.

Wolfensberger, W. (1972) *Normalization. The Principle of Normalization in Human Services*, National Institute of Mental Retardation, Toronto.

2 COMPARATIVE SPECIAL EDUCATION: IDEOLOGY, DIFFERENTIATION AND ALLOCATION IN ENGLAND AND THE UNITED STATES*
James G. Carrier

In this chapter I want to address the place of special education — the provision of special curricula or pedagogies for children judged relatively unable to benefit from mainstream education — in education and society in England and Wales, and in the United States. While sociological studies of special education are beginning to appear in both countries (e.g. Carrier, 1983b and Milofsky, 1976, for the United States; and Barton and Tomlinson, 1981; Ford, Mongon and Whelan, 1982; and Tomlinson, 1981, 1982, for England), generally sociologists of education neglect special education, limiting themselves at most to discussions of intelligence and its social bases (e.g. Bowles and Gintis, 1976; Dale, Esland, Fergusson and MacDonald, eds., 1981; Dale, Esland and Mac-Donald, eds., 1976; Karabel and Halsey, eds., 1977). In part, this general sociological neglect may be the result of the absence, until quite recently, of any substantial effort to show how the study of special education can bear on important social, and hence sociological, concerns. While sociological studies of special education are rare, comparative and historical sociological studies are even rarer. This is unfortunate, because the analysis of similarities and differences between countries and across time can help to raise important sociological points which may not occur to those whose attention is focused on contemporary practice in a single country.

Since the Second World War, but especially since 1960, England has experienced an increase of interest in and placement of pupils in special educational programmes. During this time a large number of reports, commissions and the like considered special educational needs and provisions (cf. Warnock, 1978, pp. 25-35), and in 1974 the Warnock Committee was established to enquire into the education of handicapped

* I am grateful to Peter Smith for his help with historical information, and to Graham Vulliamy, Stewart MacPherson and Len Barton, and to their students, who listened to an earlier draft of this chapter and made helpful comments, not all of which I have followed. This project never would have begun without the encouragement and support, in their different ways, of Len Barton and Achsah Carrier.

children generally, the first such enquiry in this century. The material extent of this boom is impressive. Between 1960 and 1970 the number of full-time pupils in special schools increased by more than a third, from 61,099 to 83,342, and from 1970 to 1978 the figure rose to 122,484 (of which 22,653 were educationally subnormal (severe) (ESN(S)) children not included in the 1970 figures) (Ford, Mongon and Whelan, 1982, p. 24). One must, of course, add to this the growing informal provision outside of special schools, such as disruptive pupil units (cf. Tattum, 1982). Figures provided in the Warnock Report (1978, pp. 37-8) indicate that in 1976-7 about 6.5 per cent of school children in England and Wales were receiving special education of some sort or another.

The experience of the United States has been similar. In the 1957-8 school year, 2.4 per cent of primary and secondary school pupils were receiving special education. By 1967-8 this was about 4.5 per cent, rising to 7.4 per cent in 1970-1 and 8.2 per cent in 1978 (Chandler, ed., 1981, p. 102; and from various Federal reports summarised in Carrier, 1977, p. 198). This was accompanied by a tremendous increase in Federal support for the training of special educators, from $1 million supporting 177 trainees in 1960, to $35 million supporting 22,000 in 1972 (Carrier, 1977, p. 304). And in addition to this growth in special educational pupils and staff, the 1960s and 1970s saw a great deal of judicial and legislative action on special education (cf. Kirp, 1974, 1977).

For both countries, then, there has been a boom in special education. My task in this chapter is to try to account for these two booms. It is tempting to explain their co-occurance by referring to broad factors affecting both countries at about the same time, such as the general prosperity following the Second World War, and a growing concern for educational excellence in the 1960s, and other factors that any careful reflection certainly would reveal. However, such an approach misses the point of comparative studies and the insights they can provide, because it assumes that 'general prosperity', 'growing concern for excellence', or any other of these factors meant the same thing in the two countries, as well as assuming that the two countries responded to these things in the same way. This ignores the fact that educational practices and policies spring from the interaction of those common factors with the very different pre-existing educational institutions, values and practices of England and the United States, and thus ignores the importance of the different social and cultural arrangements which shape education in these two countries.

Differentiation and Allocation

My basic approach is to see special education as a form of educational differentiation and allocation on a par with others. Like streaming, tracking, racial segregation and a host of other intentional and unintentional educational practices, special education, together with educational psychology, is a device which differentiates children into different sorts, and allocates them to different forms of educational treatment. Regardless of the scientific validity of the educational psychology theories which guide special education, and regardless of the empirical and theoretical adequacy of special educational practices, differentiation and allocation result from it and need to be seen to result from it. This point may not be particularly novel, but it does not seem to be the case that sociologists and others studying education have made what seems to me to be the next logical step, and compared special education with the other forms of differentiation and allocation, or tried to see how they might be related.

I will assume for the purposes of this chapter that all systems of education are selective, that all use one or more forms of differentiation and allocation. This may seem a pessimistic assertion, but I see no substantial evidence which refutes it. If my generalisation is valid, then we have two basic alternatives, which grade into each other in specific cases. The first alternative, historically the more common by far, has been systems which make no effort to teach all children. Here the differentiation and allocation take place prior to entry, with a substantial proportion of school-age children never going to school. In this situation, common schooling (which I take to mean teaching all pupils the same thing) is relatively easy to achieve, at least in principle, though this is just another way of saying that relatively little differentiation and allocation goes on within the school system. Children who, because of race, religion, language, nationality, class or anything else, are judged not suited to the common curriculum do not enter school in the first place, and the schools can operate quite comfortably teaching a relatively homogeneous curriculum to a relatively homogeneous body of pupils.

However, it appears to be the case that with the onset of mass schooling this placid state of affairs must yield, or at least has in fact yielded, in the face of the growing diversity of pupils who must be taught. At this point, differentiation and allocation shift their places, occurring after entry into education rather than before it. This suggests that, while mass schooling (teaching all children) and common schooling (teaching a single curriculum) are quite possible, mass common schooling (teaching a single curriculum to all children) is not.

The fact that common schooling seems to exist only in the absence of mass schooling fits the general view I take in this chapter, that education is an important mechanism for reflecting, reproducing and justifying inequalities in social status, for reproducing the social order, and becomes more so as schooling spreads (cf. Althusser, 1972; Bourdieu and Passeron, 1977). Reproduction theory suggests that the education system is a biased mechanism, the operation of which turns out to benefit overall the children of higher social status and penalise those of lower social status, though of course it may not produce these results in any given case (cf. Parkin, 1979, pp. 54-66). And my point here is that differentiation and allocation reflect this reproductive role and the bias it entails.

If it is to proceed smoothly and peacefully, educational differentiation and allocation need to be legitimate, justified by being seen to be based on what the society, or the significant elements within it, takes to be unproblematic facts and values. This is particularly pertinent in special education, which historically has based itself on the two 'objective sciences' of medicine and educational psychology, but the point is applicable more generally. And to the degree that these legitimating elements are accepted broadly and incorporated into the culture, they shape individuals' aspirations, bringing them into some agreement with their objective life chances, producing a 'sense of limits, commonly called the sense of reality' (Bourdieu, 1977, p. 164, emphasis omitted), so that differentiation and allocation proceed without demur.

Of course, the fact that differentiation and allocation are legitimated by being seen to be based on medicine and educational psychology does not at all prevent the schools from maintaining the biases which are part of their reproductive task, for two reasons. First, those biases are built into the very fabric of those facts and values on which differentiation is based; and second, the prominence given to those facts and values diverts attention away from the sorts of questions which may cast doubt on their own legitimacy and the legitimacy of the reproductive process (for a fuller discussion of this see Carrier, 1983b).

Although differentiation and allocation are related to each other, they differ in important ways. Differentiation is the identification of children as being of different sorts, more or less suited to the sort of education that can lead to high social status. It can take place either formally as an official act of the school system, for example when a child is classified as retarded, or informally by classroom teachers based on their own judgements, for example when a teacher decides that a child is dull or bright. Differentiation can be based on many different factors, ranging from ephemeral and seemingly subjective grounds like the child's appearance, accent or even the ways he or she establishes eye contact or nods in a sign of silent agreement and comprehension, to more permanent and seemingly objective grounds like a formal assessment of the child's intelligence, sensory abilities or physical coordination. In any case, differentiation is an identification or typification of the child, one which provides those who make it with a sense of the child's capabilities.

Allocation, on the other hand, is best thought of here as the practical pedagogic and curricular consequences of differentiation. Like differentiation it can occur formally, as when a child is officially placed under a separate curriculum (usually, in fact, a reduced curriculum), and it can occur informally, as when a teacher encourages one child more than others, looks at one child more than others, or gives one child more benefit of the doubt than others (for discussions of this sort of allocation, see Keddie, 1971; Rist, 1970). Also, the degree of allocation can vary. Minor allocation occurs when the child remains in the main classroom and receives only a slightly different curriculum or pedagogy, while major allocation occurs when the child is put in a special place away from the regular classroom and receives a very different curriculum or pedagogy. There are, of course, positions between these extremes. Although a thorough discussion of the point is beyond the scope of this chapter, it might be better to define allocation as the assignment of pupils to different educational treatments. Thus, for example, the fact that different school districts in the United States historically have had different resources and educational programmes of different qualities (cf. Kirp, 1968, 1977) has led to a form of geographical allocation which takes place without educational differentiation; just as, theoretically, differentiation can take place without allocation, though it is difficult to see just how it could do so in practice.

The final element I need to present in this introductory discussion is educational ideology, which, while it does not cause differentiation and allocation, is important in shaping the forms they take in any given system, as well, of course, as justifying the inequalities they produce. Educational ideologies include a number of different elements. The element which is most important in this chapter is whether it is thought that the educational system should be egalitarian or inegalitarian. Historically there have been basic differences between England and the United States on this issue, and, while it is quite clear that differentiation and allocation existed regardless of these differences, I argue in this chapter that they affect the forms these things take.

My concern in the main part of this chapter is to compare changes over time in English and American education in terms of the handful of basic variables which I have discussed already. The first of these is the degree to which there is mass education. I do not think it necessary to define this precisely. Instead, I assume that mass education at the primary level began in both countries relatively late in the nineteenth century. The second variable is the extent to which the prevailing educational ideology is egalitarian. Roughly, I take this to mean a denial of fundamental social class or other ascriptive differences between pupils, while an inegalitarian ideology would be one which asserts the existence of such differences. As I shall argue, English educational ideology was essentially inegalitarian until about the Second World War, after which it became increasingly egalitarian, though I make no judgement about absolute levels. The situation in the United States, on the other hand, is rather less straightforward. It is true that since before 1800 American educational ideology generally was egalitarian, but equally it was only as of 1954 that this officially embraced blacks as well as whites. The last variable is the form of educational differentiation and allocation, the variable which, if you will, I am trying to explain.

Briefly, I want to suggest that, with mass education, an egalitarian ideology, at least as it has existed in the United States, leads to differentiation and allocation being couched in terms of what is conceived of as the pupil's more or less unique constellation of personal attributes. This has led to two sorts of differentiation and allocation: those based on the pupil's personal, psychological make-up, and those based on the pupil's choice of different courses of study. In such circumstances, educational psychology and guidance services will flourish, though of course they will be less likely to do so if pupils have the 'sense of limits' to which I already referred, for the stronger this sense of limits, the closer the fit between individual aspirations and objective chances, the more likely pupils are to differentiate and allocate themselves spontaneously in the way the education system wants, however that may be defined. On the other hand, in an inegalitarian system, particularly as it existed in the early years of English mass education, differentiation and allocation are couched in terms of the ascribed group or class attributes of pupils. In such circumstances, mass formal forced selection and streaming can be expected to flourish. As should be obvious, these differences parallel what Ralph Turner (1960) described as the difference between contest and sponsored mobility systems.

Anticipating the points I will bring out in my more detailed discussion of English and American education, it appears that the boom in special education in England reflected a fundamental shift in educational ideology toward egalitarianism and a single curriculum in comprehensive schools. On the other hand, the boom in American special education was not the consequence of such a change, for an egalitarian ideology was already firmly established. Rather, the American boom seems to have been the result of at least two events of less global significance. One was a modification and extension of American egalitarian ideology: the civil rights movement and the ending of formal racial segregation in the schools. The other was a rising demand for education. No doubt other factors were at work in these two countries, but I do not think one can understand special education in England and America, especially in the post-war period, by ignoring the general points I have laid out here.

What I want to do now is turn to a closer look at the educational histories of first England and then the United States, to see how the key variables and processes I have mentioned in this introductory discussion have operated.

Education in England and Wales

Although I have said that English mass education was established late in the nineteenth century, its beginnings existed well before then. Substantial state involvement began one year after the Reform Act 1832 (this link between reform and education recurs in the nineteenth century). At that time Parliament granted £20,000 to charity organisations to assist in building elementary schools. After 1846 this grant could be used to cover operating as well as capital costs, and it rose to £800,000 by 1861 (Evans, 1975, pp. 19-21), when the Newcastle Commission reported that about 2.5 million children were in some sort of school. Early parliamentary support for education was, among other things, intended to reduce working-class agitation, some of which centred around the demand for schools (Johnson, 1976), and to provide a training which would, it was hoped, make workers less receptive to radical ideas. At its inception, then, parliamentary support for education was shaped at least in part by the desire to provide a training particularly suited to the labouring classes which would help support the existing stratified English social order.

The next important stage in the history of English mass education was sparked off by another Reform Act, this one in 1867. It gave workers at least numerical dominance in certain urban electorates, and increased the likelihood of more reform and eventual working-class control of Parliament. At this point, education reform, to tame and instruct the newly enfranchised groups, became more popular. Illustrative of this attitude was Robert Lowe, Chancellor of the Exchequer in the Gladstone government formed in late 1868. He argued that the lower orders, now on the road to political power, had to

> be educated that they may appreciate and defer to a higher cultivation when they meet it; and the higher classes ought to be educated in a very different manner, in order that they may exhibit to the lower classes that higher education to which, if it were shown to them, they would bow down and defer (quoted in Simon, 1974c, p. 356).

Thus, the premises of early mass education differed fundamentally from what I shall show underlay early American education. With the strongly inegalitarian English ideology, differentiation was based on social class, while internal allocation was by formal streaming, with different curricula for different sorts of people.

The upshot of all this was the Education Act 1870, which laid the basis for mass state schooling. It established locally-elected school boards and empowered them to levy a tax to raise revenue to run local schools, called Board Schools. This Act laid the basis for free, compulsory, universal childhood education, a basis which was extended by later legislation, notably a compulsory attendance law in 1880. Thus, by the 1880s the 'great majority' of children were being taught in these Board Schools (Simon, 1974a, p. 113).

The overtly class nature of education is highlighted by the juxtaposition of the 1870 Act with the Endowed Schools Act 1869. While the former dealt with working-class children's education, the latter allowed the restructuring of endowed grammar schools, so alienating them from the poor local scholars their founders often endowed them to serve (cf. Simon, 1974a, pp. 97-112), and helping some of them to become the great Public Schools thereby.

These two Acts, a year apart and aimed at opposite ends of the social scale, emphasise the way that education was being formed in the second half of the nineteenth century. Board Schools were established for the workers and Public Schools for the elite. In the middle, of course, were the Grammar Schools, themselves divided into first, second and third grades by the Taunton Report, in 1868: one for the children of the leisured class and top professionals; one for the children of other professionals, the military and the established merchants; and one for the children of farmers, traders and superior artisans. As Brian Simon (1974a, p. 97) sums up this period, its educational policies 'had been consciously designed to establish different types of schools for different social classes'. This fundamental division persisted in education until the Second World War, and even beyond.

To go back to the variables which are central to my discussion, in nineteenth-century England there was a strongly inegalitarian ideology and expanding pupil enrolments. The result was differentiation in terms of ascriptive, social class criteria, and major allocation through forced streaming. The different educational strata were explicitly matched with different social strata, so that both schools and society were constituted of fundamentally different sorts of units.

In the twentieth century this structure was extended as secondary education grew. As pressure for increased access to secondary education increased, so too did differentiation and allocation at secondary level, with Grammar Schools being the most prestigious sort of publicly-supported schooling. The Hadow Report in 1926, the Spens Report in 1938 and the Norwood Report in 1943 all advocated both an expansion of secondary schooling and an increase in the sorts of schooling provided, so extending differentiation and ramifying the system of allocation. By the Education Act 1944, then, a clear tripartite system of state schooling was in place, even if the middle part had not been established broadly. Grammar Schools, Technical Schools and Secondary Modern Schools offered their fundamentally different curricula for the children of gold, the children of silver and the others.

This was not, however, a simple replication of the earlier divisions in English education, for after the First World War there began to appear a shift in the bases of differentiation. Briefly, the older differentiation by social strata began to give way to one based on individual merit, as assessed by a measure of general intelligence, the 11+ examination (cf. Quicke, 1982, chapter 1). I am not concerned here with either the extent to which merit is a social construct, or the extent to which assessed merit correlates with social class. Rather, what is important here is the fact that this marked what strikes me as a fundamental shift in educational ideology, away from a social criterion of differentiation to an individual one. Of course this change did not take place all at once, and its consequences were not straightforward, but the change remains important.

At the risk of over-simplification, I would define the significance this way. In the nineteenth century the established educational ideology indicated that there were qualitatively different sorts of people, who were to be offered qualitatively different sorts of education. Although the labouring poor may have been undesired and undesirable in practice, at the same time it equally strikes the casual observer of nineteenth-century English history that in established ideology there was also a strong belief in (or, perhaps, wish for) the honest labouring poor, who went about their business quietly and well. (This appears in the growing popularity of functionalist views of English society, put forward most notably by Herbert Spencer, and in the pastoral element in English literature, which portrayed the humble nobility of honest craftsmen and workers.) It seems, then, that in some sense qualitatively different standards could be, and to some degree actually were, applied to different sections of society. The farm worker could, in his own way, be as good as the local gentry, and both were seen as necessary for the prosperity of society.

With the change to individual merit, however, this disappeared. Whatever the relationship of ideology to social reality, the newly developing educator's notion of merit — the 11+ examination — applied a single standard to all; a standard which, moreover, spoke of a person's fundamental worth, naturalistically conceived. Permissable, even laudable, social differences became tainting natural deficiencies. Ideologically speaking, those who failed the 11+ had nowhere to hide.

Paralleling this change in differentiation was a restructuring of allocation. Because merit was, under this ideology, a single variable of which people had more or less, so education needed to become a single process of which pupils had more or less. Curricula had to converge in the sense that the bright and the dull had to get more or less of fundamentally the same education, rather than fundamentally different educations. And this, of course, is what has been happening in English education since the Second World War.

It was in the early post-war period that significant support for comprehensive secondary schooling began to appear. Thus, for instance, in 1948 the National Association of Labour Teachers urged a policy under which 'all . . . pupils . . . pursue in common, without more than an unavoidable minimum grading of ability, many of the activities which are included in the curriculum' (quoted in Banks, 1955, p. 134). Except in a few areas, however, substantial support for comprehensive education was fairly short-lived, and by the fall of the post-war Labour government in 1951, the party, the unions and teachers were all having second thoughts (Banks, 1955, pp. 142-3). When Labour returned to power in 1964, however, they renewed pressure for comprehensive secondary education, most notably through the Ministry of Education's Circular 10/65 in 1965, urging though not requiring comprehensive schooling, and refusing to finance building projects which clearly were anti-comprehensive (cf. Bellaby, 1977, pp. 62-5).

Even before the Labour government, however, there was some movement to comprehensive schools. In 1960, 4.7 per cent of children in maintained secondary schools in England were in schools their local authorities called 'comprehensive'. This rose to 8.6 per cent in 1965, after which change became much more rapid. In 1968, 20.9 per cent were in such schools, and the half-way mark was reached in 1973. By 1979, 85.9 per cent were in comprehensives (Bellaby, 1977, pp. 11-12; Rogers, 1980, pp. 13-14). Of course, labelling a school 'comprehensive' does not make it so, and the definition of the term has been a slippery one. For example, in 1971, 36.5 per cent of pupils were in schools called comprehensive, but in that year the Campaign for Comprehensive Education, using their own narrower definition, claimed that only about 12 per cent were in comprehensives (Bellaby, 1977, p. 12). Indeed, some commentators argued that, if 'comprehensive' meant 'the absence of selection by academic ability', then very few children indeed were in comprehensives by the late 1970s (Bellaby, 1977, p. 12; cf. Riseborough, 1981).

Along with the growth in comprehensive education came another shift in educational ideology about differentiation and allocation. Where the Spens Report in 1938 marked official support for intelligence as a basis for differentiation, the Newsom Report in 1963 and the Plowden Report in 1967 marked the official rejection of innate intelligence as the significant source of differences between pupils, or at least made the argument that social advantage and disadvantage played important supplementary roles. While this did not mark a change in differentiation as profound as that entailed in the shift from a social to an individual criterion, it remains quite important, for it would seem to mark a move to the belief that differences between pupils are ephemeral or contingent on social events, rather than being substantial (e.g. Bernstein, 1971). This reflected the growing egalitarian ideology in England generally, and in English education in particular, the belief that underlying the apparent divergence between children is a more fundamental identity, which would be revealed if the schools could only be brought both to resist and to compensate for the transient and somewhat artificial social forces which hide it.

Paralleling this egalitarian belief that the criteria for differentiation do not reflect permanent, fundamental differences between children, there has been an increasing uneasiness about forms of educational allocation in special education, the feeling that these may be illegitimate, more for educational and administrative convenience than for the benefit of the pupil. This has resulted in growing pressure to do away with the old categories of educational exceptionality, which were criticised as classifying children in terms of rigid categories which improperly saw the exceptionality as residing within the child, while ignoring the part played by the rigidities and biases of regular classroom practice. In other words, it was objected that regular teaching should take more cognisance of the individual constellation of attributes of the child, rather than presenting a lock-step pedagogy (e.g. Galloway and Goodwin, 1979; Hegarty and Pocklington with Lucas, 1981). (This position parallels the dominant American educational ideology of the twentieth century, closely related to the growth of educational psychology and guidance counselling services in that country, a point I elaborate later in this chapter.)

These so-called 'integrationist' ideas, identified by one set of commentators as 'an extension of the comprehensive idea' (Hegarty *et al.*, 1981, p. 20), were given official expression in the Warnock Report, which advocated the abolition of the old categories of educational abnormality, and the process of ascertainment and the provision of segregated special schools which went with them, though it did not adopt the more extreme integrationist view that classroom practices are a significant source of the pupil's problems (cf. Lewis and Vulliamy, 1981, pp. 58-60). Integration became official policy first tentatively in Section 10 of the Education Act 1976, which never came into force, and then finally in the Education Act 1981. The practical consequences of this change in official ideology are uncertain, largely because the Act and its clarifying circulars are too recent. However, certain points can be made, based on the ideology behind the Act and reports of existing integration programmes (e.g. Hegarty *et al.*, 1981, 1982; Jones, 1981).

The most obvious point is that this egalitarian integrationist belief is in fact accompanied by a demand that more, not fewer, children be treated as educationally abnormal. For instance, the Warnock Committee said that some 17 per cent of pupils should be receiving special educational provision, almost a threefold increase of the 6.5 per cent who were receiving it in the mid-1970s. The Warnock Report itself, then, embodies the link that I argued exists between egalitarian ideology, mass education and substantial internal differentiation and allocation by educational psychology and special education.

Furthermore, given the existing distribution of educational performance and ability in England (e.g. Ford, Mongon and Whelan, 1982;
Tomlinson, 1981), a distribution which accords with the social reproduction argument I mentioned earlier in this chapter, it seems probable
that the results of this expansion, the results of extending special educational provision to more children who are seen to need it, would be to
increase the number of poor and immigrant children being differentiated
out and allocated to special educational programmes which legitimate
their poor performance.

This expansion in special education is facilitated by the integrationist
programme, under which assessment of the child as educationally abnormal does not have the extensive consequences that ascertainment
had under the 1944 Act, consequences which could forestall ascertainment, as when the lack of places in special classes or schools held up the
process (e.g. Woolfe, 1981). Alternatively, under integration the range
of special provision is to be greater and the consequences of assessment
are to be less profound, making the whole identification process easier,
and so facilitating an increase in the number of children allocated to a
special, modified curriculum.

In other words, although integrationist arguments, including the Warnock Report, have often focused on the task of getting the ascertained
child out of the special school and into the main school, it also appears
that the integrationist package would lead to an increased differentiation of pupils and their allocation to modified curricula. After all, an
important element of the integration programme is to see that 'the
education offered by ordinary schools becomes more differentiated'
(Hegarty *et al.*, 1981, p. 1). Unfortunately, there appears to be no substantial evidence that specially designed programmes, either in the main
school or in the special school, are of much benefit to the two sorts
of educationally abnormal children most likely to be the basis of the
growth in assessed pupils, the slow learners and the disturbed (cf. Galloway and Goodwin, 1979).

This view of the 1981 Act raises the distinct possibility that its practical effect would not be the reduction of differentiation and allocation,
but the legitimation of a more extensive grading of children. Unequal
educational performance would to some degree become institutionalised
in the expanded provision of educational programmes 'adapted' to the
pupil's needs, which in practice seems to mean reduced or truncated programmes (cf. Hegarty *et al.*, 1981, 1982). While an optimist might argue
that these adapted programmes would increase the educational performance of abnormal children, no one has suggested that they would allow

a significant number of the abnormal to return to the mainstream, to be de-differentiated and de-allocated. And because the assessment of a child as needing special educational provision is delivered by a 'multi-professional team' (Warnock, 1978, p. 45; cf. Department of Education and Science, 1983, pp. 5-6), it carries an authority that a more *ad hoc* or administrative judgement would lack.

In sum, my own rather pessimistic assessment of the integrationist programme as incorporated into official ideology, combined with what evidence exists on the directions in which school practice is heading, suggests that it will lead to increased differentiation and the institutionalisation of unequal educational performance in special programmes − most probably the unequally poor performance of the poor and immigrants − all made legitimate by the professional rhetoric and authority of medicine and particularly educational psychology.

To summarise, it would appear that there has been a fundamental change in the last 120 years of English educational ideology. This has been the slow but steady abandonment of the idea that there are qualitative differences between the different social strata, with qualitatively different curricula offered to them. Instead, as a part of a broader change in social thought, there has grown the idea that the only important differences between people, and thus between pupils, are quantitative: first, more or less intelligence, and later more or less socio-cultural advantage, or whatever social-psychological factors are considered significant. This shift has had effects on curriculum, leading to the comprehensive ideal: the unitary curriculum taught, ultimately, to mixed-ability classes.

In short, in the twentieth century educational ideology has become more egalitarian, undercutting the idea of differentiations based on ascriptive social differences between pupils and the allocation of different sorts of pupils to qualitatively different curricula. As my model presented at the beginning of this chapter suggested, however, this does not mean that pupils are not graded and sorted. Rather, this change to the idea that there are only quantitative differences between pupils has been accompanied by a growth in the rhetoric of deficiency, rather than difference; and educational psychology, with its practical arm of special education, has grown to satisfy the need to identify new parameters of deficiency (or educational need, if you prefer), to identify deficient pupils and to devise and present special curricula for them. The differentiating and allocating task of the schools has not changed, and the reproductive task of the schools has not changed either. While the bases of differentiation and allocation have changed with changing educational ideology, there remains a short end of the stick to be got, and those at the bottom continue to get it.

Education in the United States

I want to turn now to education in the United States. However, it will become clear quite quickly that, for most of its history, it is barely possible to talk about the American system of education. Even though in England there have been 'wide variations in terms of deference to or defiance of central directives' (Simon, 1974b, p. 11), the basic structure of education has included a central body which could and did issue those directives. On the other hand, historically in the United States there has been little central government involvement in education. Rather, until well after the Second World War education in the United States has been very much the concern of the separate states and indeed of the individual school districts themselves. In spite of this fragmentation, however, it is quite possible to see common patterns developing in American education, though they are tempered by regional and even local variations which can be, as will become clear, quite pronounced. This discussion of American education, then, will not be just a catalogue of particularities. However, more so than is the case with English education, the generalisations I make must be interpreted with caution, and not taken to deny the existence of substantial local variation.

The fundamental ideological divergence between American and English education that I want to bring out here is this: in the United States the ideal has been one of egalitarian education. As James Coleman (1968, p. 11) describes the egalitarian American educational ideology, it consisted of four basic elements:

> (1) Providing a *free* education up to a given level which constituted the principal entry point to the labour force. (2) Providing a *common curriculum* for all children, regardless of background ['a common curriculum that would not exclude [them] from higher education' (ibid, p. 12)] . (3) Partly by design and partly because of low population density, providing that children from diverse backgrounds attend the *same school*. (4) Providing equality within a given *locality*, since local taxes provided the source of support for schools.

Although American educational ideology is and has been egalitarian, 'egalitarian' has not meant the same thing at all times, as I shall show, and Coleman's summary seems to be more applicable to nineteenth-century than to twentieth-century American education. Also, the egalitarianism was contradicted by the education, or non-education, of blacks, particularly in the South. Racial segregation obviously complicates my presentation of American education. However, I do not think it invalidates the general points I will make in this section of my chapter, and for this reason I reserve the discussion of racial segregation until I finish my history of American education.

I said that egalitarianism is and has been fundamental in American educational ideology. This reflects, perhaps, the mass American electorate. After all, as early as 1791 some states had universal white male suffrage, as had all states joining the Union after 1817. And this was converted into mass political power in 1828, when the election of Andrew Jackson to the Presidency broke the political power of the old aristocracy.

Egalitarianism runs particularly deeply in the history of Puritan New England, especially Massachusetts. By 1789, towns in that state with at least 50 families were required to provide children with at least six months' education each year (Butts and Cremin, 1953, p. 246). In 1827 the state compelled school districts to levy taxes to support these schools, and in 1834 it established a fund to subsidise school districts.

New England, and particularly Massachusetts, led the rest of the nation. In the Mid-Atlantic states, roughly from New York down to Maryland, the move to mass common education came more slowly. For example, in 1849 New York State required direct taxation to support schools, and it abolished all school fees in 1867. In Pennsylvania there was state support for local schools in 1834, and by 1837 over three-quarters of the state's school districts had tax-supported common schools. In the South movement was even slower, with no substantial public schooling until after the end of the Civil War in 1865. Virginia is illustrative. In 1846 the state passed a law permitting, but not requiring, free schooling, and there was no other important legislation there before the Civil War (Butts and Cremin, 1953, pp. 250-1). The frontier states moved to free common schools fairly quickly: Wisconsin in 1848, Indiana in 1852, Ohio in 1853, Illinois in 1855, Iowa in 1858 and Michigan in 1869. This had been encouraged by the Land Ordinance of 1785, regulating the old North-west Frontier region (now the upper Midwest), which set aside public land in each township 'for the maintenance of public schools' (quoted in Butts and Cremin, 1953, p. 245).

Compulsory attendance, and hence universal education, was a different matter. Although the first compulsory attendance law was passed in 1852, in Massachusetts, legal and political challenges to these laws were not overcome until the 1890s. By 1900 32 states had effective compulsory attendance laws, and the last of the continental 48 states to pass such a law was Mississippi, in 1918. (As a sign of regional variation, the last ten states to pass these laws were all in the old South.)

It should be clear from this brief summary that in most parts of the United States common schooling has long been an integral part of educational ideology. And as secondary school enrolments increased, the ideal was applied to them as well. Though private academies were the first to supply the growing demand for secondary education, they failed to meet that demand, and public high schools began to appear in the second quarter of the nineteenth century, Massachusetts again leading the way. The academies maintained their dominance through the Civil War, but after about 1870 public high schools began to challenge them. The public schools achieved their dominance in the period from 1880 to 1930, when secondary school enrolments doubled every decade, reaching 4.5 million at the latter date, when more than half of all children between 14 and 17 were in school, and by 1940 this had risen to almost three-quarters (see generally Good, 1956, p. 253; Trow, 1977, pp. 107-8).

This growth in secondary education, and particularly in public secondary education, reflected the ideal that secondary education ought to be free for all, and that all should be able to attend the local high school. However, as enrolments increased and mass secondary education became a reality, internal differentiation and allocation began to appear. By the time of the Civil War many urban high schools were offering three different courses: Classics for those intending to go on to a college; English, by far the most popular, for those intending to leave school after receiving a high school diploma; and a normal or teacher training course. By the turn of the twentieth century this list had expanded in line with increasing enrolments, as business and commercial courses began to appear, and by 1920 home economics, science and industrial arts courses, as well as many others, were established (Butts and Cremin, 1953, p. 443; Cohen and Lazerson, 1977, p. 376).

Although this growing system of internal allocation and differentiation did perform the same general reproductive function as the English education system (cf. Karier, Violas and Spring, 1973), the two systems differed in important ways. Most importantly, in the United States, barring racial segregation, differentiation was never conceived of in terms of the child's social class or other ascriptive attributes, as it was in early English mass education. Rather, in the first half of this century in particular, American education came under the sway of the Progressive Movement, as close to an official ideology as was possible in so fragmented an education system. And it is important to note that Progressivism developed very shortly after the onset of mass education in the United States.

Progressivism replaced the older educational ideology to which, I said, Coleman's description (quoted above) applied. This ideology was starkly egalitarian and, my theoretical argument suggests, was only suited to a situation in which mass education did not exist, in which differentiation and allocation took place in the society prior to enrolment, rather than in the schools after enrolment. This older ideology held that all pupils should receive exactly the same treatment in exactly the same courses, a curriculum which many linked explicitly to a radical republican political ideology. Replacing this older ideology, Progressivism attacked its lock-step approach, and argued instead for a more child-centred education. Progressivism, led by the philosopher and psychologist John Dewey, argued that children were all different, and needed to set their own pace and learn on their own, so that their education needed to reflect their unique constellation of individual attributes (Trow, 1977, p. 109), attributes which included their future place in society. Thus, in 1908 the superintendent of schools in Boston, Massachusetts, argued:

> Until very recently [the schools] have offered equal opportunity for all to receive *one kind* of education, but what will make them democratic is to provide opportunity for all to receive such education as will fit them *equally well* for their particular life work (quoted in Kirp, 1974, p. 11).

Progressivism had an important impact on the processes of differentiation and allocation, an impact which survived the demise of the Progressive Movement itself to shape post-war American education as well. First, and perhaps most obviously, it focused attention on the individual attributes of the child, and so encouraged the development of ways of assessing those attributes: educational psychology developed as a framework justifying differentiation and allocation, and educational psychology techniques, especially intelligence tests, were used to differentiate pupils. Second, and somewhat less obviously, the Progressive idea that children should set their own pace allowed for and even encouraged self-selection: self-differentiation and self-allocation, though much more so at secondary than primary schools. As one might expect, under the system of contest mobility and the ideology of achievement which characterised the United States, this self-selection did not always reflect the sense of limits, the sense of reality to which I referred in the introduction to this chapter. Guidance and counselling services developed, then, which helped assure that pupil choices were 'realistic', strengthening reproduction under the guise of informed pupil choice (cf. Cicourel and Kitsuse, 1963).

It is worth digressing for a moment here. I said at the beginning of this chapter that it is incorrect to see parallel or similar educational changes in England and the United States as being simply unproblematic reflections of broad factors affecting the two countries at about the same time. The use of IQ testing illustrates this. Differentiation of pupils by IQ testing became widespread in both countries at roughly the same time, yet it is not correct to say that the social meaning or use of these tests were the same in both countries. In England, as I showed earlier in the chapter, the introduction of IQ tests in the form of the 11+ examination marked a weakening of inegalitarianism, a move away from differentiation based on and conceptualised in terms of ascriptive social differences, a move leading ultimately to the idea of common curriculum schooling. In the United States, on the other hand, the introduction of the IQ test did not mark a weakening of an inegalitarian ideology. Rather, it marked a change in the conception of egalitarianism, and was associated with the abandonment of common curriculum schooling. As this illustrates, the same historical event can have very different meanings in different social contexts.

I said at the beginning of my discussion of American education that an ideology of common schooling always has been important, but that this has meant different things at different times. The important shift in its meaning was brought about by the rise of Progressivism. Here the idea that all children should receive the same education was replaced with the idea that all children were entitled to an education properly suited to their needs and desires. The former, as I have noted, is an ideology which would not countenance internal educational allocation, and hence would be unsuited to mass schooling. And indeed, when mass schooling developed, this older ideology gave way to the newer one, Progressivism, which permitted and even encouraged internal allocation, albeit within an overall rhetoric of equality, common schooling and pupil choice.

Thus it appears that by the early part of this century there existed in the United States the sort of educational ideology which, I argued, did not flower in England until the 1950s and even later. While I suggested that this English flowering was associated with the move to comprehensive education and the boom in special education, the same connection cannot be made in the United States: the important elements of this ideology were in place well before the Second World War, and hence even further before the boom in American special education. The same mechanism, then, cannot account for the boom in both countries.

Before trying to account for the American boom, I want to deal with two important aspects of American education which would seem to require me to qualify substantially my overall assertion of the importance of the ideal of common schooling. These are: first, the persistence of private schooling, and second, racial segregation.

An adequate discussion of private schooling would take more time than the topic merits, so I will dispose of it briefly. The most important point to make is that, while private education has flourished in the United States, the vast majority of it consists of parochial (i.e. church-related) schools, primarily Catholic (e.g. Good, 1956, p. 379; for a discussion of some of the differences between public, parochial and other private schools, see Coleman, Hoffer and Kilgore, 1982). Adequate historical data is difficult to locate. However, in 1965, just under 13 per cent of pupils in day-schools in the United States were in non-public schools, and in that year just under 87 per cent of pupils enrolled in non-public schools were in Catholic schools. The corresponding figures for 1976 were just over 10 per cent and just over 70 per cent (*Standard Education Almanac*, 1975, p. 25; 1978, p. 164; 1979, p. 226). With the exception of religious instruction, the curricula of these schools, as well as the children attending them, did not differ markedly from public schools. Historically, many of the remaining, non-parochial private schools have been racially segregated schools in the South. Again, and again with the obvious qualifications, these did not differ markedly from public schools.

There remains a residuum of private schools in the United States, a number of them expensive, elite institutions, and to some degree their existence does contradict the egalitarian American ideology. However, in no way have these schools constituted a state-supported and officially sanctioned sector in the same way that English Grammar Schools have. Their curriculum is more intense than that of the academic programmes in public schools, but I do not think it is fair to say that it has been radically different. What is equally important is the fact that public schools were neither intended to fit nor seen to fit their pupils for a different social existence from the private schools. Pupils in the public and private schools could realistically aspire to broadly similar occupations and social standing. Public school pupils may, overall, have been less successful in gaining entry into universities and elite occupations, but their schooling did not disbar them in the same way that, for example, attendance at a Secondary Modern School would have done in England.

The other important aspect of American education which would seem to challenge the picture I have presented of an egalitarian ideology is racial segregation. This does conflict with the ideology, and I do not think I need to dwell on the conflict. Rather, what I want to present here are the ways in which this egalitarian ideology permeated even racial segregation. The basic point is that, at the level of official ideology, the belief in the twentieth century was that blacks could be segregated but should be treated equally: 'Separate but equal.' Thus, egalitarian beliefs appeared even in the centre of the most inegalitarian feature of American education. And it is important to remember that 'separate but equal' was not merely an ideological legitimation of inequality, but was the basis of a series of court decisions which outlawed racial segregation in growing areas of education in the twentieth century, by arguing that in specific cases separate was not equal. Even though the Supreme Court decision in *Brown* v. *Board of Education* in 1954 declared that separate never could be equal, the doctrine itself had been applied to undercut a great deal of segregation in higher education, just as it continued after 1954 to be applied to undercut discriminatory practices in all areas of education (see generally Kirp, 1968).

Egalitarian beliefs were strong in many parts of the country, were embodied in American law, and were eroding racial segregation, so that a picture of unrelieved and unchanging institutional racism is simply inadequate. Though segregation, in law or in fact, violated American egalitarianism, its existence did not disprove the existence of egalitarian beliefs. Thus, while segregation, and especially the history of its eradication, is important for understanding American education, it does not, I would suggest, invalidate the basic framework as I have sketched it in this section.

Racial segregation, or more accurately its ending, does, however, help explain important changes in differentiation and allocation in American schools, including the boom in special education. Some of these changes resemble changes in English education in the early part of this century. Most striking of these is the fact that, after racially segregated schools were abolished, forcing blacks and whites into the same schools, certain school systems introduced extensive tracking (ability grouping), including an expansion in programmes for the mildly retarded and to a lesser degree the emotionally disturbed. This resembles somewhat the shift in

England to the 11+ examination as a basis of differentiation, part of the gradual move to an egalitarian ideology. The most famous case of this in the United States was the Washington DC school system, which introduced IQ-based tracking 'shortly after it was ordered to dismantle its dual school system' (Kirp, 1974, p. 38). (Washington's tracking system was outlawed in 1969 by a federal court, in *Hobson* v. *Hansen*, on the grounds that it was racially discriminatory.) Just as the ending of segregation increased differentiation based on IQ in certain districts, so also it led to the search for new and legitimate differentiation devices which would both explain blacks' poor school performance and justify their allocation to special programmes. The most notable example of this sort of device is cultural deprivation theory (cf. Carrier, 1977, chapter 8).

One other factor is also important in explaining the special educational boom. It was in the late 1950s and early 1960s that educational expectations rose in the United States (cf. Milner, 1972). I can only speculate on why this took place when it did, but it seems likely that it was influenced by the general wave of upward occupational mobility following the Second World War. In any event, more and more parents expected their children to go to a college or university (cf. Cicourel and Kitsuse, 1963). This made parents more concerned with their children's education, and less tolerant of school programmes which did not give them what they wanted. This, coupled with the realisation, springing from the history of the civil rights movement, that the schools were vulnerable to political and legal pressures, led to a host of legal actions, lobbying efforts and new legislation in the 1960s and 1970s, as various public pressure groups sought to mould special education to suit their image of what it ought to be.

Some of these groups wanted an extension of special educational services and others wanted a contraction, always in the name of equality. Broadly speaking, parents of severely retarded and learning disabled children wanted an extension. Parents of the severely retarded agitated to end the exclusion of their children from school on the grounds that they were ineducable, culminating in a consent decree in the case of *Pennsylvania Association for Retarded Children* (PARC) v. *Commonwealth of Pennsylvania*, issued in 1972 (cf. Kuriloff, True, Kirp and Buss, 1974), which required the state to accept severely retarded children, a legal principle which was extended shortly thereafter, in *Mills* v. *Board of Education*, to include all handicapped children (cf. Kirp, 1977, pp. 130-1). The Federal government responded with Public Law 93-113, the Rehabilitation Act of 1973, which stated that no handicapped person could be discriminated against in any federally-supported activity or programme, which included all public schooling (cf. Abeson, 1974). Parents of the learning disabled, on the other hand, argued that the inclusion of their children in the mainstream classroom amounted to a failure on the part of the schools to recognise the condition and offer adequate educational treatment. This culminated in federal legislation in 1969 which bestowed official government recognition on learning disability and provided financial support for research and programme development (cf. Carrier, 1983a).

Those who wanted a contraction of services were concerned primarily with the mildly retarded, and they argued that existing practices stigmatised those so labelled, while failing to provide any educational benefit, and furthermore that the application of the label was biased against the poor and black, and was in many respects arbitrary. These arguments were aired in *Hobson* v. *Hansen*, already mentioned, in which the judge was told that two-thirds of those placed in special classes in the Washington DC public schools were incorrectly placed (Kirp, 1974, p. 13). These arguments also blended naturally with arguments for the integration of the handicapped, or mainstreaming, as it is sometimes called, for both pointed out that labelling the child is stigmatising, and that segregation into special schools or special buildings compounds the problem.

As a result of these and other pressures, in 1975 Congress passed the Education for All Handicapped Children Act, Public Law 94-142. This had three important effects. First, it capped the handicapped pool, stating that no more than 12 per cent of the school-aged population could be so designated. Second, it required that handicapped children be taught in the 'least restrictive environment' possible, given the needs of the child, of other children in the class with whom the handicapped child might be placed, and the competence of the teachers involved. While obviously this did not force total mainstreaming, it did put pressure on schools to move in that direction. Third, it required handicapped children to get Individual Education Programmes (IEPs): written assessments of the child's attainments, and statements of annual and short-term educational objectives, the need for special educational services, the duration of the special programme, and the criteria for evaluating the child's progress (cf. Reid and Hresko, 1981, pp. 178-96).

While this would seem to make it more difficult to place children in special education, or to increase the degree to which they are segregated from the mainstream, it is not at all clear that the Act has this effect. Most notably, the 12 per cent limit is a substantial increase over the percentage of children previously in special education. The figures I gave previously in this chapter showed that in 1978 only 8.2 per cent of pupils were in special education. The Act, then, envisaged a substantial increase in the assignment of children to special educational provision.

The Act is so recent that substantial assessments of its practical effects have yet to appear. However, indications of its likely effects can be gathered from the analysis of similar state programmes. The best documented of these is the Massachusetts Comprehensive Special Education Law of 1972, which anticipated most aspects of the Federal Act (cf. Budoff, 1975; Weatherley and Lipsky, 1977). Apart from leading to a great increase in cost and staff workloads, this law, in spite of all its safeguards and its strong mainstreaming bias, led to increased segregation of handicapped children in the schools: 'In part, this shift probably reflects increased use of resource rooms . . . school systems *decreased* the proportion of fully integrated children by sending them out of the regular classrooms for special help.' Further, the changes the law entailed resulted in 'a wholesale shifting of responsibility for troublesome children from the regular-class teacher to a specialist or resource-room teacher' (Weatherley and Lipsky, 1977, p. 183).

Recent reforms in American special education, then, have been intended to reduce the bias against the poor and blacks, as well as other minority groups, and to make provision of special education more equitable, and less stigmatising and segregating. In spite of this, however, there is reason to believe that these reforms, like recent English reforms, will serve to increase the number of children in special education, so strengthening and formalising differentiation and allocation in the schools.

To summarise: the picture of special education, and allocation more generally, in American education is more complicated than is the case in England. American education never underwent the fundamental change from an inegalitarian to an egalitarian ideology which characterised English education, though, as I noted, the position of blacks in American education complicates the picture. The main change appears to have been in the nature of American egalitarianism in the early part of this century, which reflected the move away from common schooling to mass schooling, and which facilitated differentiation and allocation. Just as, to some degree, subsequent changes in English education can be said to reflect the logic of that country's emerging egalitarianism, so to some degree the changes in American education can be said to reflect the logic of the change in American egalitarianism, coupled with the incorporation of blacks into the main educational establishment in the last quarter century. For the United States the use of special education and pupil guidance and counselling appeared rather early in this century as part of the dominance of the Progressive Movement, with its child-centred orientation. On the other hand, a different set of changes, which fed into the pre-existing educational ideology and practices, produced the boom in special education in the last 20 years.

Conclusion

In this chapter I have laid out a fairly simple model of education systems and the place of special education in them, and applied it to the history of mass education and special education in England and Wales, and in the United States. In a sense, then, the chapter has been comparative in two dimensions: I have compared countries, and within countries I have compared different historical periods. Other places and other times may not appear to have much immediate importance for those concerned with problems in the here and now, for those concerned with what part special education plays in England or the United States. The difficulty is, of course, that an exclusive concentration on the here and now leads one unknowingly to ignore certain questions or certain relationships which are more apparent in the context of comparative studies.

For instance, in the report of her excellent study of the ascertainment of children as educationally subnormal (moderate) (ESN(M)) in a large English city, Sally Tomlinson (1981, p. 18) points out that 'categorising children as ESN . . . has the function of controlling a potentially troublesome section of the population, and of "reproducing" a particular section of the class structure'. This is an important point to make, one which is essential for anyone trying to understand special education in England or the United States. But the very intensity of focus which allowed Tomlinson to illuminate in such detail the process of ascertainment did not really leave room for a very different question: why special education and not something else? A broader comparative perspective, on the other hand, encourages one to ask such questions, for it helps to make problematic the sorts of things that tend to be taken for granted in a narrower study, and indeed almost have to be taken for granted by anyone wishing to do a detailed analysis of the operation of an education system.

Comparative studies are also valuable for those with more immediate practical concerns: teachers and policy-makers. As the movement to integrate the handicapped illustrates, educational reforms can become emotive issues, attracting uncritical and even unreasoning support: 'Like

motherhood and democracy, integration is a good thing and no right
thinking person who cares for children should be against it' (Hegarty *et
al.*, 1981, p. 14). Anyone who wants educational changes to be humane
improvements rather than ill-conceived offspring of moral crusades
must view this state of affairs with some misgivings. While a comparative perspective cannot damp moral fervour, it can at least lead people
to pause, to see what has been tried elsewhere. An awareness of what
other countries or areas are doing, and of the consequences of their
doing it, can make us aware of potential difficulties, and benefits, of
policies which would not otherwise be apparent.

Moreover, those closely involved with only one educational system
are likely to see its faults but not its benefits, and equally are likely to
see only the supposed benefits and not the faults of other systems. The
grass on the other side of the fence does appear greener to those who
have no chance to look closely. English special educators, looking wistfully to the United States as a source of reform and new ideas, might
be surprised to know that some of their American cousins were looking
back, and just as wistfully. For example, in the early 1970s Lloyd Dunn
(1973, p. 67), an American special educator, said that 'more than 25
years [after the Education Act 1944], it is time the United States . . .
followed the lead of Great Britain' and adopted the category of ESN,
despite the fact that criticism of ESN and other categories in England
paralleled quite closely Dunn's own criticism of American categories
of educational abnormality. A better awareness of English education
would have made Dunn aware that ESN was no panacea.

I have argued in this chapter that all educational systems in industrial
societies are characterised by differentiation of pupils into different
sorts or types, and their allocation to different pedagogies or curricula.
This, I said, springs from the basic task of social reproduction, and the
consequent tendency of schools to favour children of the higher classes
and award them access to pedagogies and curricula more likely to lead
to higher educational attainment, or at least not to foreclose that attainment. This much is fairly unexceptional, being little more than a statement of the basic social reproduction model. To the degree that this
chapter has interest, it lies in applying this idea to forms of differentiation and allocation generally, of which special education is one, but
only one, example.

This step has allowed me to argue that, at least in England and the
United States, special education as a significant differentiating and allocating device is not a random occurrence, but appears only when mass
education occurs in conjunction with an egalitarian ideology, though,

as the American case indicates, this conjunction may not be a sufficient condition for a substantial growth in special education, as opposed to the other aspects of educational psychology. Mass education obliges schools to differentiate and allocate pupils – that is to say, children who have already entered the school system. And an egalitarian ideology renders illegitimate differentiation on the basis of ascribed social attributes. Thus, under English mass education until around the Second World War, the predominantly inegalitarian ideology led to and supported differentiation on ascriptive criteria, though as I noted there was an increasing egalitarian influence and an increasing use of educational psychology, in the form of the 11+ examination, as at least the formal mechanism of differentiation. The egalitarian social 'neutrality' of this instrument was, of course, vitiated by the extensive streaming which occurred in English primary schools (cf. Jackson, 1964).

With an egalitarian ideology, ascriptive criteria are not an acceptable basis for differentiation, which instead rests on the pupil's constellation of individual attributes. As I showed, egalitarianism was a strong element in American educational ideology as early as the beginning of the nineteenth century. With the onset of mass education, and especially mass secondary education, in the United States, Progressivism began to take hold, the significant tenets of which justified differentiation based on just that constellation of attributes. While this did not lead to the installation of extensive special education, it did encourage the development of ability-grouping based on IQ tests, and self-differentiation by pupils, as well as guidance and counselling services to encourage pupils to make 'realistic' choices. It helped establish educational psychology.

From this perspective, then, special education becomes one of a number of systems of differentiation and allocation which have flourished at different places and different times for different reasons. Special education thus is revealed to be a very social phenomenon in significant ways. In other words, while it may base itself on discoveries in the fields of medicine and psychology, it cannot be explained solely, or even primarily, in this way. Rather, it makes as much sense to say that educationally-pertinent research in medicine and psychology is itself motivated by a growth in the importance of special education, as is particularly clear in research on cultural deprivation and minimal brain damage. And the arguments I have made in this chapter suggest that this growth can be explained reasonably well by reference to the nature of the educational system and its accompanying ideology.

I want to close by considering one factor on which I have been able to touch only briefly in this chapter. As should be fairly clear, I have looked at special education in particular, and at differentiation and allocation more generally, as devices used to discourage and exclude children from the lower classes of society. And given the class constitution of much of special education in England and the United States, this is a reasonable perspective to take. However, exclusive concentration on this aspect of special education, this exclusionary aspect if you will, leads to only a partial understanding of the phenomenon. Generalisations which may hold for the mildly retarded and the disturbed, under whatever euphemisms are current, need not, and almost certainly do not, hold for the severely retarded, the learning disabled and probably some other categories as well.

This suggests the need to bring to bear yet another comparative perspective on special education, one which compares the different sorts of special educational categories, investigating their different histories and uses in order to discover the different sorts of social forces which have shaped them and which, therefore, they necessarily reflect. Indeed, as I have argued elsewhere (Carrier, 1983a), even a single category of educational abnormality can be shaped by and reflect different and even conflicting social forces. So it is that an adequate comparative sociology of special education must await new research, extending our knowledge of particular places and particular times.

References

Abeson, A. (1974) 'Movement and momentum: government and the education of handicapped children – II', *Exceptional Children*, *41*, 109-15.

Althusser, L. (1972) 'Ideology and ideological state apparatuses' in B. Cosin (ed.), *Education: Structure and Society*, Penguin, Harmondsworth, 242-80.

Banks, O. (1955) *Parity and Prestige in English Secondary Education*, Routledge and Kegan Paul, London.

Barton, L. and Tomlinson, S. (eds.) (1981) *Special Education: Policies, Practices and Social Issues*, Harper and Row, London.

Bellaby, P. (1977) *The Sociology of Comprehensive Schooling*, Methuen, London.

Bernstein, B. (1971) 'Education cannot compensate for society' in B. Cosin, R. Dale, G. Esland and D. Swift (eds.), *School and Society: A Sociological Reader*, Routledge and Kegan Paul, London, 61-6.

Bourdieu, P. (1977) *Outline of a Theory of Practice*, Cambridge University Press, Cambridge.

—— and Passeron, J.-C. (1977) *Reproduction in Education, Society and Culture*, Sage, London.

Bowles, S. and Gintis, H. (1976) *Schooling in Capitalist America*, Routledge and Kegan Paul, London.

Budoff, M. (1975) 'Engendering change in special education practices', *Harvard Educational Review*, *45*, 507-26.

Butts, R. and Cremin, L. (1953) *A History of Education in American Culture*, Holt, Rinehart and Winston, New York.

Carrier, J. (1977) 'Social Influence on the Development of Scientific Knowledge: The Case of Learning Disability', Doctoral Thesis, University of London.
—— (1983a) 'Explaining educability: an investigation of political support for the Children with Learning Disabilities Act of 1969', *British Journal of Sociology of Education*, *4*, 125-40.
—— (1983b) 'Masking the social in educational knowledge: the case of learning disability theory', *American Journal of Sociology*, *88*, 948-74.
Chandler, B. (ed.) (1981) *Standard Education Almanac 1981-1982*, Marquis, Chicago.
Cicourel, A. and Kitsuse, J. (1963) *The Educational Decision-Makers*, Bobbs-Merrill, Indianapolis.
Cohen, D. and Lazerson, M. (1977) 'Education and the corporate order' in J. Karabel and A.H. Halsey (eds.), *Power and Ideology in Education*, Oxford University, New York, 373-86.
Coleman, J. (1968) 'The concept of equality of educational opportunity', *Harvard Educational Review*, *38*, 7-22.
——, Hoffer, T. and Kilgore, S. (1982) *High School Achievement: Public, Catholic and Other Private Schools Compared*, Basic Books, New York.
Dale, R., Esland, G., Fergusson, R. and MacDonald, M. (eds.) (1981) *Education and the State*, two volumes, Falmer, Lewes.
Dale, R., Esland, G. and MacDonald, M. (eds.) (1976) *Schooling and Capitalism*, Routledge and Kegan Paul, London.
Department of Education and Science (1983) *Assessments and Statements of Special Educational Needs*, Circular 1/83, HMSO, London.
Dunn, L. (1973) 'Children with moderate and severe general learning disabilities' in L. Dunn (ed.), *Exceptional Children in the Schools*, Holt, Rinehart and Winston, New York, 65-123.
Evans, K. (1975) *The Development and Structure of the English Educational System*, University of London, London.
Ford, J., Mongon, D. and Whelan, M. (1982) *Special Education and Social Control*, Routledge and Kegan Paul, London.
Galloway, D. and Goodwin, C. (1979) *Educating Slow-learning and Maladjusted Children: Integration or Segregation?*, Longman, London.
Good, H. (1956) *A History of American Education*, Macmillan, New York.
Hegarty, S. and Pocklington, K. with Lucas, D. (1981) *Educating Pupils with Special Needs in the Ordinary School*, National Foundation for Educational Research (NFER)-Nelson, Windsor.
—— and —— with —— (1982) *Integration in Action*, National Foundation for Educational Research (NFER)-Nelson, Windsor.
Jackson, B. (1964) *Streaming*, Routledge and Kegan Paul, London.
Johnson, R. (1976) 'Notes on the schooling of the English working class 1780-1850' in R. Dale, G. Esland and M. MacDonald (eds.), *Schooling and Capitalism*, Routledge and Kegan Paul, London, 44-54.
Jones, E. (1981) 'A resource approach to meeting special needs in a secondary school' in L. Barton and S. Tomlinson (eds.), *Special Education: Policies, Practices and Social Issues*, Harper and Row, London, 212-34.
Karabel, J. and Halsey, A.H. (eds.) (1977) *Power and Ideology in Education*, Oxford University, New York.
Karier, C., Violas, P. and Spring, J. (1973) *Roots of Crisis*, Rand McNally, Chicago.
Keddie, N. (1971) 'Classroom knowledge' in M. Young (ed.), *Knowledge and Control*, Collier-Macmillan, London, 133-60.
Kirp, D.L. (1968) 'The poor, the schools, and equal protection', *Harvard Educational Review*, *38*, 635-68.

—— (1974) 'Student classification, public policy, and the courts', *Harvard Educational Review*, *44*, 7-52.

—— (1977) 'Law, politics, and equal educational opportunity: the limits of judicial involvement', *Harvard Educational Review*, *47*, 117-37.

Kuriloff, P., True, R., Kirp, D. and Buss, W. (1974) 'Legal reform and educational change: the Pennsylvania case', *Exceptional Children*, *41*, 35-42.

Lewis, I. and Vulliamy, G. (1981) 'The social context of educational practice: the case of special education' in L. Barton and S. Tomlinson (eds.), *Special Education: Policies, Practices and Social Issues*, Harper and Row, London, 53-70.

Milner, M. (1972) *The Illusion of Equality*, Jossey-Bass, San Francisco.

Milofsky, C. (1976) *Special Education: A Sociological Study of California Programs*, Praeger, New York.

Parkin, F. (1979) *Marxism and Class Theory: A Bourgeois Critique*, Tavistock, London.

Quicke, J. (1981) *The Cautious Expert*, Open University, Milton Keynes.

Reid, D. and Hresko, W. (1981) *A Cognitive Approach to Learning Disabilities*, McGraw-Hill, New York.

Riseborough, G. (1981) 'Teaching careers and comprehensive schooling: an empirical study', *Sociology*, *15*, 352-80.

Rist, R. (1970) 'Student social class and teacher expectations: the self-fulfilling prophecy in ghetto education', *Harvard Educational Review*, *40*, 411-51.

Rogers, R. (1980) *Crowther to Warnock*, Heinemann, London.

Simon, B. (1974a) *Education and the Labour Movement 1870-1920*, Lawrence and Wishart, London.

—— (1974b) *The Politics of Educational Reform 1920-1940*, Lawrence and Wishart, London.

—— (1974c) *The Two Nations and the Educational Structure 1780-1870*, Lawrence and Wishart, London.

Standard Education Almanac 1974-1975 (1975), Marquis, Chicago.

Standard Education Almanac 1978-1979 (1978), Marquis, Chicago.

Standard Education Almanac 1979-1980 (1979), Marquis, Chicago.

Tattum, D. (1982) *Disruptive Pupils in Schools and Units*, Wiley, Chichester.

Tomlinson, S. (1981) *Educational Subnormality: A Study in Decision-making*, Routledge and Kegan Paul, London.

—— (1982) *A Sociology of Special Education*, Routledge and Kegan Paul, London.

Trow, M. (1977) 'The second transformation of American secondary education' in J. Karabel and A.H. Halsey (eds.), *Power and Ideology in Education*, Oxford University, New York, 105-18.

Turner, R. (1960) 'Sponsored and contest mobility and the school system', *American Sociological Review*, *25*, 855-67.

Warnock Report (1978) *Special Educational Needs*, Report of the Committee of Enquiry into the Education of Handicapped Children and Young People, Cmnd 7212, HMSO, London.

Weatherley, R. and Lipsky, M. (1977) 'Street-level bureaucrats and institutional innovation: implementing special education reform', *Harvard Educational Review*, *47*, 171-97.

Willis, P. (1977) *Learning to Labour*, Gower, Aldershot.

Woolfe, R. (1981) 'Maladjustment in the context of Local Authority decision making' in L. Barton and S. Tomlinson (eds.), *Special Education: Policies, Practices and Social Issues*, Harper and Row, London, 175-93.

3 THE POLITICS OF INTEGRATION IN ENGLAND
Len Barton and Sally Tomlinson

In England the integration or mainstreaming of children previously categorised and transferred out of normal and into special education has currently created an important educational debate. In common with other Western industrial countries which initially developed segregated provision for those known as handicapped, exceptional or special, England now appears to be making moves to dismantle separate provision and educate both normal and special, if not in the same classroom, at least in the same building or on the same campus. The ideological justification for integration is, interestingly, exactly the same as the original justification for segregation — it is one of 'benevolent humanitarianism' or 'doing good to individual children'. Whereas only seven years ago the needs of handicapped children were apparently best served by separate provision (DES, 1975) now the children's needs are apparently best served by integrated provision (DES, 1980).

This chapter seeks to explore some of the motives behind the moves towards integration in England. It starts from the assumption that integration is not solely the product of benevolent and enlightened attitudes to children. The motives are rooted in economic, professional and political vested interests. The treatment meted out to those who, in post-1978 terminology, are considered to have 'special educational needs' (Warnock Report, 1978) may well be enlightened, but it also involves the social categorisation of a relatively weak or powerless social group whose lives are very much affected by professional and political decisions. The motives behind integration, just as those behind segregation, are a product of complex social, economic and political considerations which may relate more to the 'needs' of the wider society, the whole education system and professionals working within the system, rather than simply to the 'needs' of individual children.

This kind of analysis is currently not popular in England (see Warnock, 1982). There is considerable reluctance to examine special education as a social and political process rather than as an individualised process. But, more and more children will in the future be considered to have 'special needs'. The suggestion in the Warnock Report that in future some 20 per cent of school pupils may have 'special needs', rather than the 2 per cent officially in special education up to 1981, appears to have

65

become an accepted 'truism' among many policy-makers and practitioners. This means that, while in the past under 200,000 children were deemed suitable for a 'special' education, in the future some 1½ million children may receive some kind of 'special' education. So it is important to move away from the individual to social perspectives. Changes in the forms, organisation and provision in special education are not the result of mysterious processes of evolution nor benevolent adaptations; the changes in the law relating to special education (Education Act, 1981), and in moves towards integrated provision, are the result of decisions by government and by professionals who may, as in most educational processes, have other interests in mind than the 'needs' of the children and their parents. The early 1980s have seen considerable political manoeuvring between central and local education authorities and between different professional groups involved in special education (particularly medical, psychological and teaching personnel), and the forms the new integrated provision will take will be a product of these manoeuvres.

To assist understanding as to why an 'integration debate' is occurring in Britain, this chapter first briefly documents the emergence of segregated provision and the 'categories of handicap'. The second section documents some different and contradicting conceptions of integration. The third section points to the *naïveté* and ambivalence present in the debate, and points out that special education, like other parts of the education system, is about social control and social engineering, as much as about individual self-fulfilment. The final section argues the case that any pursuit of integration must also include an informed and sustained critique of those prevailing aspects of the education system that will impede the realisation of such goals.

Social Origins

The literature documenting the emergence of provision tends to stress the 'charitable' and the 'good' and often creates the impression of spontaneous development from humanitarian matters.

As with ordinary education, education for the handicapped began with individual and charitable enterprise. There followed in time the intervention of government, first to support voluntary effort and make good deficiencies through state provision, and finally to create a national framework in which public and voluntary agencies could act in partnership to see that all children, whatever their disability, received a suitable education (Warnock Report, 1978, p. 8).

In fact, the development of special education owed more to economic considerations, to professional vested interests and, from the beginnings of compulsory state education in 1870, to the needs of the normal education system to function unimpeded by 'troublesome' children (see Tomlinson, 1982, chapter 2).

Economic considerations have always been paramount in the development of special education. A permanent dilemma has been how to make sure that as many as possible of the handicapped grew up productive or, if that was not possible, to provide as cheaply as possible for their care. Thus, the first Commission of Enquiry into the education of the handicapped in England, The Egerton Commission, 1884-9, had a frankly economic purpose.

The blind, deaf and educable class of imbeciles, if left uneducated become not only a burden to themselves but a weighty burden on the State. It is in the interests of the State to dry up the minor streams which must ultimately swell to a torrent of pauperism (Egerton Commission Report, 1889, Introduction).

The move towards segregating children in special schools came during the 1890s, but the Chancellor of the Exchequer himself expressed fears that, if too much money was made available for 'defective' children, too many local authorities 'especially in Ireland' would discover large numbers of such children (quoted in Pritchard, 1963). The same economic considerations which governed segregated provision now constrain integrated provision. A government white paper on *Special Needs in Education* (DES, 1980) referred more often to 'present economic circumstances' than to special needs.

Professional vested interests have also shaped the development of special education in Britain. Its history is marked by professional rivalries and hostilities between medical, psychological, educational administrative and educational teaching personnel. The medical profession, struggling for recognition during the nineteenth century, enhanced its interests by claims to control the education of the 'defective'. The profession of psychology developed much of its professional mystique by claims to control the mental testing which developed post-1913 in Britain. Hostilities between medical and psychological personnel continued up to 1944, when medical officers were given, and still retain, the statutory right to 'diagnose' handicap and prescribe educational treatment, although under the 1981 Education Act educational psychologists now have statutory duties in the assessment processes. The various needs and interests of the plethora of professional groups involved in special education can be clearly seen to operate in the current integration debate. Particularly, the teachers' unions are keen to defend the interests of their members. The National Union of Teachers does not want its members to have to face children who 'present insuperable problems in the normal school' (NUT, 1978).

But the crucial underpinning to the development of special education was the need for normal schools to function unimpeded by children who would not, or could not, conform to the normal routines of the classroom. Special education became a 'safety valve' for the normal system. The method of 'payment by results' to teachers, in operation until the end of the nineteenth century ensured that children who could not or would not produce 'results' were excluded from normal schooling, and complex mechanisms of assessment and classification developed to rationalise the exclusion.

Table 3.1 illustrates the development of statutory categories of handicap from two in 1886, to eleven in 1945. The 1981 Special Education Act did officially abolish statutory categories, but the old labels appear to be remaining as descriptive categories. The Education Act of 1944 had, of course, enshrined the notion of selection by 'age, aptitude and ability' for particular types of schooling and this provided a continuing rationale for the segregation of handicapped children. During the period 1945-81 the numbers of children segregated in special schools increased dramatically. Booth (1981) provides an interesting discussion of this increase (from some 47,000 in 1950 to 135,000 in 1977), and points out the ambivalence of policy-makers, who could insist that the 'planned and sensible integration of handicapped children in ordinary schools should continue' (DES, 1980, p. 9), while at the same time publishing statistics which showed that placements in special schools and classes had increased. Booth also pointed to the considerable increase in 'special' provision, which until the 1981 Act did not officially fall within the 'special' remit – for example, the growth of disruptive units. Categorising more and more children out of the normal education system and into some form of special education is obviously functional for the normal education system and the question can be raised as to *why* an integration debate is taking place at all.

Table 3.1: Statutory Categories[a]

1886	1899	1913	1945	1962	1970	1981	Suggested Descriptive Categories
Idiot	Idiot	Idiot					Child with learning difficulties (severe)
Imbecile	Imbecile	Imbecile	Severely subnormal (SSN)	Severely subnormal (SSN)	Educationally subnormal (severe) (ESN(S))		
		Moral imbecile		Psychopathic			
	Blind	Blind	Blind		Blind		Blind
			Partially sighted		Partially sighted		Partially sighted
	Deaf	Deaf	Deaf		Deaf		Deaf
			Partially deaf	Partially hearing	Partially hearing		Partially hearing
	Epileptic	Epileptic	Epileptic		Epileptic		Epileptic
	Defective	Mental defective (feeble-minded)	Educationally subnormal		Educationally subnormal (mild or moderate) (ESN(M))	Special educational needs	Child with learning difficulty (mild or moderate)
			Maladjusted		Maladjusted		Maladjusted
							Disruptive
		Physical Defective	Physically handicapped		Physically handicapped		Physically handicapped
			Speech defect		Speech defect		Speech defect
			Delicate	Delicate	Delicate		Delicate
			Diabetic				
							Dyslexic?
							Autistic?

Note: a. Categories suggested but never adopted include: the neuropathic child, the inconsequential child, the psychiatrically crippled child, the aphasic child and others. Autism and dyslexia were recognised under the 1970 Chronically Sick and Disabled Persons Act.

Source: Tomlinson (1982).

Dilemmas of Integration

Central government, represented by the Department of Education and Science (DES), has always demonstrated considerable ambivalence towards the idea of integration in England. This ambivalence reflects the political nature of decisions to segregate some children away from mainstream education, and thus exclude them from even attempting the kind of credential-orientated education which brings occupational success, mobility and advancement in industrial society. After all, the result of a 'special' education is that children are destined for a 'special' life-career in terms of employability, self-sufficiency and dependence. The rise of comprehensive education in the 1960s brought the dilemma into the open.

DES ambivalence is illustrated in acts, circulars and recommendations over the past 30 years. A major claim in the recent integration debate is that 'integration is not new' – a clause in the 1944 Education Act enabled children to receive their special education in ordinary schools. However, as Parfitt pointed out in 1975, although 'the D.E.S. has always maintained that special education should be a second choice, . . . the chances are at present that ordinary schools will not provide satisfactory (special) education' (Parfitt, 1975, p. 12). A year later, in 1976, a Labour government included in the 1976 Education Act a clause requiring that pupils should only be given education in special schools in certain circumstances, but this clause was never implemented (Education Act 1976, Section 10). DES ambivalence was further reflected in the White Paper of 1980, which preceded the 1981 Act: 'The Government takes as its starting point the principle that children and young people who have such needs should be educated in association with those who do not . . .' (DES, 1980, p. 13). However, later on the same page, this 'starting point' is qualified: 'For some children with special needs association, or full association, with other children is the wrong solution, and to impose it would be unfair to the child, his parents, other children and the taxpayer' (DES, 1980, p. 13). This ambivalence results from contradictory educational, social and economic pressures. Egalitarian beliefs have, over the past 20 years, worked strongly in England towards the idea of educating all children within a common school – not selecting out for brightness or dullness, talent or handicap. Indeed, Mary Warnock herself was of the opinion that:

It will gradually come to be expected that ordinary schools must expect to cater for very many more special needs, and that the whole concept of children with peculiar needs (or indeed peculiar talents) must be a natural part of the comprehensive ideal (Warnock, 1980).

Lecturers who designed an Open University course on Special Educational Needs (E.241, 1981, see also Booth and Potts, 1983) are also strongly committed to the development of comprehensive schools in which *all* children are educated regardless of 'capabilities, background, interests or handicap' (Booth and Potts, 1983, p. 26). But these beliefs were equally counter-balanced by traditional pressures for selecting out an elite for high-status education, and later for selecting out those who were thought to impede the academic-type curriculum offered in comprehensive schools.

Similarly, the ambivalence can be traced to the familiar economic considerations that special education, whether offered in segregated or integrated provision, should not cost too much. There is certainly some indication, post-1981, that some local authorities are interpreting the 1981 Education Act as a licence to close special schools and place children in normal schools without offering money or resources, an 'integration on the cheap' feared by the teachers' unions (NUT, 1979, p. 12). The whole mechanism for the assessment of children with special needs — only children with severe difficulties being recorded via a statement — invites a rhetoric that the 'special needs' of large numbers of children are now being catered for in ordinary schools. The reality may be that no finance or resources are being offered to the schools either to 'discover' or to cater for these needs.

A further dilemma of integration which is implicit in the current debate at central and local level, and in the contributions by professionals and practitioners in both normal and special education, is that the old 'categories of handicap' and the new 'children with special needs' in fact include large numbers of children whom normal schools wish to exclude at all levels of integration. The NUT spoke of 'particular groups of pupils — particularly the severely maladjusted and those of extremely limited ability — who may present insuperable problems for teachers in the ordinary classroom situation' (NUT, 1979, p. 14).

The notion of 'children with special needs' conflates what we have here termed 'normative' conditions with 'non-normative'. That is, there can be some normative agreement about certain categories of handicap or need — such as blind, deaf, epileptic, severe mental handicap, etc. These conditions affect children in families from all social classes and occupational groupings. On the other hand, categories such as educationally subnormal, maladjusted, disruptive are not normative. There are no adequate measuring instruments or agreed criteria to decide on these particular categories — for example, the inclusion of children in a category of 'disruptive' depends on value-judgements, and there can be legitimate arguments between professionals, parents, etc., as to what constitutes the category. Kennedy (1980) has pointed out that 'the normal state against which we measure abnormalities is a product of social and cultural values'.

In England these non-normative categories have always included the largest numbers of children in special education, and the important point is that these children are predominantly of working-class origins, and, since the settlement of West Indian immigrants, have also included large numbers of black children. Thus, a major dilemma in the integration debate is that it is predominantly about the 'integration' of children who in England were known in the 1930s as 'the social problem class' (Burt, 1937), and this raises questions about the nature of special education — how far is it 'education', and how far is it 'social control'? The literature produced so far documenting 'integration' in England gives little indication that there are wider social and political implications. A visitor from abroad, coming uninformed, would receive the impression that an unproblematic, humanitarian process was taking place in the education system which was solely about provision and resources.

Underpinning the dilemmas as to whether and why integration is taking place, how expensive it will be, and who is being integrated or segregated, are debates about the actual meaning of integration. Definitions of the term are numerous, but most recent ones start from the assertion in the Warnock Report that integration is 'directly in line with the principle that handicapped and non-handicapped children should be educated in a common setting as far as possible' (Warnock Report, 1978, p. 100), and that there are 'three main forms of integration'. These forms are locational integration (special units or classes on the same site as an ordinary school, or in the same building); social integration (where locational integration takes place plus social interchange); and functional integration (in which special children join their peers on a part- or full-time basis). The Warnock Report was, of course, accepting the humanitarian assumption that integration *per se* is a 'good thing' and the major discussion should concern implementations, and indeed the Report described a range of alternative forms of provision ranging from complete segregation to short periods of 'exclusion' in ordinary schools.

Taking their cue from this assumption, two major recent research studies funded by the government have focused on optimum provision for integration, and description of 'what is happening' (Brennan, 1981;

Hegarty and Pocklington with Lucas, 1982). Brennan started from the assumption that 'the Warnock Report has identified the conditions associated with effective provision for children with special needs in ordinary schools' (Brennan, 1981, p. 19) and his work was mainly concerned with documenting attempts by particular schools and LEAs to integrate. Similarly special educational journals in Britain, notably *Special Education – Forward Trends*, now routinely include articles describing attempts at 'integration'. Hegarty and his colleagues at the National Foundation for Educational Research (NFER) have reported a study as to how integration is being interpreted and put into practice in 17 LEAs. In a useful discussion they noted that the concept is complex and dynamic, and that 'it has evolved from simple opposition to placement, to encompassing a variety of arrangements in ordinary schools'. However, they also point out that 'integration is not a self-evident goal and must be justified in a rational way' (Hegarty and Pocklington with Lucas, 1981, p. 14). Although the NFER studies are of very real value in documenting the varieties of 'integration' currently being developed, descriptive studies do not give much scope for discussion of conflicts that may be inherent in the processes, and of the vested social and professional interests that various forms of integration or segregation may be serving.

There is, in existing literature, very little discussion as to why integration has become a popular process; any notion that the concept may be problematic – may be serving other interests than that of the 'good of the children' – is conspicuously absent. Conflict, difference of opinion, vested interests, have been laundered out of much of the writing on integration.

There are, however, some signs of a critical literature developing (see Barton and Tomlinson, 1981). Booth (1981) has provided a critique of what he calls 'the authorised version of events' (p. 290). He ironically observed that, while central government has made noises for 20 years concerning integration, segregated provision has grown dramatically and certainly up to 1981 'indicated a general movement towards increasingly segregated forms of educational provision'. If the integration principle was really accepted 'we would anticipate teachers and policy makers trooping off to witness examples of good practice . . . We would find administrators eagerly reallocating money . . . We should be witnessing a careful costing of alternative schemes' (Booth, 1981, p. 300). Booth also examines some of the pressures which may work against the current enthusiasm for integration, notably the press for accountability: 'If teachers are to be held directly responsible for the progress of their pupils, then they may be increasingly willing to separate children they consider to have "real" intractable problems from those amenable to "ordinary" teaching' (Booth, 1982, pp. 309-10). Thus Booth begins to probe some of the contradictions inherent in the notion of integration, and point out that it is not an unproblematic concept. Dilemmas over the process of 'integration' are perhaps better recognised in other European countries, and in particular in the United States, where 'mainstreaming' has provided a focus for a large amount of critical literature (Sarason and Doris, 1979; Ysseldyke and Algozzine, 1982).

The 1981 OECD report on *The Education of the Handicapped Adolescent* maintains that, whilst there are many who agree in principle with the aims of integration, there are divisions of thought in terms of practical objections concerning its implementation, to the extent that:

> Some of them see the social objectives of integration as incompatible with providing high quality special education for children with disabilities and significant difficulties. Others see the degree of differentiation required of ordinary schools as impossible to achieve. Many see the social objectives as paramount and the achievement of educational standards of secondary importance (OECD, 1981, p. 139).

In the United States, Sarason and Doris (1979) contend that many schools are unprepared to deal with mainstreaming, some undertake the minimal requirements and those pupils labelled mentally retarded are benefiting least from such programmes. Strain and Kerr (1981) in a major examination of research findings in the United States, argue that a careful survey of the literature indicates that, as far as mainstreaming is concerned, 'no operational definition exists' and they ask 'what types of educational practices actually do qualify as mainstreaming' (p. 77). Ysseldyke and Algozzine have considered some of the factors that impede mainstreaming, notably teacher attitudes and public funding. In the American literature there is certainly more recognition that integration, at the levels of both conceptualisation and implementation, is characterised by ambiguity, contradiction and conflict.

A Misplaced Vision?

Any adequate understanding and explanation of the issues relating to special education must look beyond the individuals who are considered as having 'special needs', to the types of institutional and political arrangements that fundamentally influence the ways in which such minority groups are treated. By critically examining some of the presuppositions that characterise a great deal of the approaches in this sphere of human experience, we can begin to identify limitations and hopefully seek for more appropriate and inevitably fundamental changes.

Supporters of integration use a variety of arguments to justify their position; these include: a belief in an integrated society, one in which the handicapped, by right, share in the privileges and opportunities available; a belief that the educational system is one of the means that society provides for individual fulfilment and thus education is good for individuals; and a belief that successful processes of integration need, not just sufficient resources but, more importantly, the right sorts of teachers in terms of skills and attitudes. The Warnock Report illustrates these beliefs, and in the chapter dealing with 'Special Education in Ordinary Schools' the grounds for such practices are depicted as being part of a 'widely held and still growing conviction that, so far as is humanly possible, handicapped people should share the opportunities for self-fulfilment enjoyed by other people' (p. 99) – in this instance, that which is allegedly enjoyed through participation in the normal educational system.

This claim may be part of a misplaced vision, the convictions of which demand closer inspection. It is a romanticism that ignores the inequalities and contradictions that are endemic, not only to special education, but importantly to both the educational system with which further association is being sought and the wider society in which it is located. Too much is being uncritically accepted.

Special education in England – its goals and development – cannot be analysed or understood in isolation from the ideologies and practices of comprehensive education. The abolition of the tripartite system of education which had developed out of the 1944 Education Act, came about through strong egalitarian support for social and educational reform. This movement was based upon a number of important beliefs. First, education was seen in terms of an investment that would yield national and personal benefits, because a close relationship was envisaged between the products of the education system and the needs of industry (Dale, 1979). Second, in contrast to the tripartite system, comprehensive education would be involved in a greater development of talent which importantly would lead to greater wealth (Reynolds, 1981). Third, it was believed that the introduction of the comprehensive system of education would lead to the amelioration of inequalities of opportunity and thus reduce the social-class divisions within society

(*Unpopular Education*, 1981). Even though for many pupils within the state system of education certain forms of early selection were removed with the introduction of the comprehensive school, competition and differentiation remained endemic to schooling. 'Ability' was still very narrowly conceived in terms of the cognitive with success via competitive, formal examinations legitimating such attitudes and ideology. The social and personal implications of such practices are powerfully brought out by Hargreaves in a discussion of the comprehensive school system:

> This very narrow definition of ability, grounded in the curricular evaluation of the cognitive-intellectual, has its effects on pupils. Ability labels are not seen by pupils as mere *descriptions* of part of their total set of attributes as human beings; they are seen rather as generalized *judgements* upon them. Because the mastery of the cognitive-intellectual domain is so essential to success in school, ability labels carry rich connotations of pupils' moral worth (1982, p. 62).

Examinations influence the nature of the curriculum and an essential part of the public accountability of teachers is viewed by many in terms of exam results, while the emphasis upon formal assessment is being strengthened via 'overt government and local authority initiatives . . . there is increasing pressure on schools from community and management alike for standards, for qualifications — for visible, quantifiable testimony of pupil achievement' (Broadfoot, 1981, p. 200). In the English school system success and failure are perceived in individualistic terms, with credentialism remaining a central feature of the school system. Some aspects of the curriculum are more highly valued than others, with high status subjects being studied by the 'brightest', 'ablest' pupils, supported by the best staff and resources.

Social-class influences upon the quality and quantity of the education that pupils experience are still a potent force, and the vast majority of working-class children are amongst the failures or rejects of the school system. Discussing the way in which secondary schools fail abysmally to enrich the lives of these pupils, Hargreaves maintains that:

> To have dignity means to have a sense of being worthy, of possessing creative, inventive and critical capacities, of having the power to achieve personal and social change. When dignity is damaged, one's deepest experience is of being inferior, unable, and powerless. My

argument is that our secondary schools inflict such damage, in varying degrees, on many of their pupils (1982, p. 17).

Thus discrimination and stigmatisation have become established within
the formal school system. However, this should not be understood as
a licence to blame teachers. They are under severe constraints themselves, particularly as schools (and thus their tasks) are constantly being
expected to fulfil a very wide range of expectations (Grace, 1978). In
addition, in a period of recession we are experiencing an increasing intervention on the part of the state and this is not only at the ideological
level in terms of a redefinition of educational goals (Salter and Tapper,
1981), but also in the sphere of cuts in public expenditure. Indeed a
recent survey of schools by Her Majesty's Inspectorate demonstrates
clearly that the reductions in Local Authority spending are having their
effect on teacher-pupil ratios, resources and general morale amongst
staff and the Report contends that:

> To put it in a nutshell, many L.E.A's and schools are surviving finan-
> cially by doing less; but they are often obliged to take the less in
> the form that comes easily to hand rather than shaping it to match
> educational priorities (*Times Educational Supplement*, 9 April 1982,
> p. 7).

This type of decision-making cannot be explained merely in terms of
pragmatism and, even though there are inequalities in the actual allocation of cuts within and across Local Authorities and schools, a lesson
to be drawn from such events is that educational values have little or
no influence in such a process. The grounds for such decisions are to
be found elsewhere, and the results of a cost-efficiency model in the
reduction of teachers, the removal of certain subjects from the curriculum as well as the lack of equipment and resources, has to be understood
as part of the general encroachment and increased centralised control in
the sphere of education. The state of the economy and the political will
to support state schools are crucial determinants of needs, opportunities
and resources.

Before attempting to draw out some applications to the issues of
integration, this brief survey of some of the important aspects of 'ordinary' schooling needs to be viewed as supporting a major proposition with
reference to the role of schools. In this analysis the educational system is
seen as inevitably involved in a process of social engineering, and special
education is crucially a part of this process. Teachers do contribute,

consciously or unconsciously, to the reproduction of a particular form
of society and the development of specific types of 'educated' people
to meet the needs of such a society (Salter and Tapper, 1981). So, as
Hargreaves (1982) notes, they must increasingly appreciate the social
functions of schooling and be actively concerned with the sort of society
they want to create or maintain.

The Politics of Integration

A great deal of the literature fails to offer any serious attempt to discuss
the politics of integration. It is our contention that this must be given
paramount attention because integration is inevitably concerned with
social engineering via the education system.

Government policies for those with 'special needs', like other minority groups, are based upon contradictory ideologies. First, there is the
need to control such groups by not allowing them to have any damaging
effects in the spheres of culture and the economy. What constitutes the
'needs' of the 'special' is influenced by these intentions. At the same time
there is the desire to protect the more severely 'handicapped' and this is
expressed in policies of community care and equal opportunities − the
handicapped supposedly experiencing the same rights and privileges as
other members of the community or society. Policies are supposedly
based on two principles, those of assimilation − the merging of a previously alien, rejected group into the wider society − and equality of
opportunity − including the benefits that this affords. However, the
policies are constrained by competition over priorities and competition
over scarce resources. In the official documents on issues relating to
integration, the question of financial constraints is very evident, as can
be seen from some of the concluding remarks in the Government White
Paper entitled 'Special Needs in Education': 'Only when the economic
situation improves sufficiently will it be possible to bring to fruition all
the committed efforts of those engaged in meeting special educational
needs' (1980, p. 23). What is not acknowledged in this statement is that,
given the arrival of economic recovery, special education will be but one
group amongst a number competing for further financial support. It is
also alarming to appreciate that, given the lack of financial resources,
those that are available are distributed at the discretion of the local
authorities, because, as Lukes points out, the 1981 Special Education
Bill 'gives discretion to L.E.A.'s to provide *as much or as little as they
want*, because the definitions of special educational needs and special

educational provision are up to them' (1981, p. 319, our emphasis). There is now official legislative support to decide what is significant (and thus what is not) and back that judgement with all the resources available that they feel are necessary. This will lead to inequalities of allocation within and across local authorities and thus the quality of the services available. Educational values may have little influence on future decisions made about 'special' education.

However, our major criticism of the movement for integration is motivated by our belief that it is based on a totally unwarranted optimism. Despite the claims in the Warnock Report about the privileges and opportunities in our society in which the 'special' or the 'handicapped' should share, there is a vast amount of research evidence to show that our society, and in this instance the school system, are characterised by gross inequalities. Historically, equality of opportunity has not and does not exist for large numbers of the populace, who both within and after school experience the personal, social and economic effects of failure.

We are not arguing here that integration is of no value, nor that there ought not to be demands for such practices. What we are seriously suggesting is that, given the inequalities within society at large, and given those dominant assumptions and practices that are firmly established in our school system, particularly at the secondary levels, if integration is to have any major significance, then the struggle for its realisation must include a coherent, concentrated criticism of those unacceptable features of the education system and a demand for more fundamental social changes. To do less will mean that integration will lead to subordination in an already divisive system and be a further illustration of the way in which political rhetoric supercedes practice.

References

Barton, L. and Tomlinson, S. (eds.) (1981) *Special Education: Policies, Practices and Social Issues*, Harper and Row, London.

Booth, T. (1981) 'Demystifying Integration' in W. Swann (ed.), *The Practice of Special Education*, Basil Blackwell, Oxford.

—— and Potts, P. (1983) *Integrating Special Education*, Basil Blackwell, Oxford.

Brennan, W.K. (1981) *Special Education in Mainstream Schools – The Search for Quality*, National Council for Special Education (NCSE), London.

Broadfoot, T. (1981) 'Towards a Sociology of Assessment' in L. Barton and S. Walker (eds.), *Schools, Teachers and Teaching*, Falmer Press, Falmer.

Burt, C. (1937) *The Backward Child*, London University Press.

Dale, R. (1979) 'The politicisation of School Deviance: Reactions to William Tyndale' in L. Barton and R. Meighan (eds.), *Schools, Pupils and Deviance*, Nafferton Books, Driffield, England.

Department of Education and Science (DES) (1975) *The Discovery of Children Requiring Special Education and an Assessment of Their Needs*, Circular 2/75, HMSO, London.
—— (1980) *Special Needs in Education*, Cmnd 7996, HMSO, London.
E.241 (1981) *Special Needs in Education*, Open University, Milton Keynes.
Education Acts (1944) (1970) (1976) (1981), HMSO, London.
Egerton Commission (1889), Report of the Royal Commission on the Blind-Deaf-Dumb and others, HMSO, London.
Grace, G. (1978) *Teachers, Ideology and Control*, Routledge and Kegan Paul, London.
Hargreaves, D. (1982) *The Challenge for the Comprehensive School*, Routledge and Kegan Paul, London.
Hegarty, S. and Pocklington, K. with Lucas, D. (1981) *Educating Pupils with Special Needs in the Ordinary School*, National Foundation for Educational Research (NFER)-Nelson, Windsor.
—— and —— with —— (1982) *Integration in Action*, National Foundation for Educational Research (NFER)-Nelson, Windsor.
Kennedy, I. (1980) 'Unmasking Medicine', *The Listener*, 6 November 1980.
Lukes, J.R. (1981) 'Finance and Policy Making in Special Education' in W. Swann (ed.), *The Practice of Special Education*, Basil Blackwell, London.
National Union of Teachers (NUT) (1979) *Special Educational Needs: The NUT Response to Warnock*, London.
OECD (1981) *The Education of the Handicapped Adolescent — Integration in the School*, OECD, Paris.
Parfitt, J. (1975) *The Integration of Handicapped Children in Greater London*, Institute for Research into Mental and Multiple Handicap, London.
Pritchard, D. (1963) *Education of the Handicapped, 1760-1960*, Routledge and Kegan Paul, London.
Report of the Working Party on the Future of Special Education in Birmingham (1980) Education Committee, Birmingham.
Reynolds, D. (1981) 'The Comprehensive Experience' in L. Barton and S. Walker (eds.), *Schools, Teachers and Teaching*, Falmer Press, Falmer.
Sarason, S. and Doris, J. (1979) *Educational Handicap, Public Policy and Social History*, Free Press, New York.
Salter, B. and Tapper, T. (1981) *Education, Politics and the State*, Grant McIntyre, London.
Strain, P. and Kerr, M. (1981) *Mainstreaming of Children in Schools*, Academic Press, New York.
Swann, W. (ed.) (1981) *The Practice of Special Education*, Basil Blackwell, Oxford.
Times Educational Supplement, 9 April 1982.
Tomlinson, S. (1982) *A Sociology of Special Education*, Routledge and Kegan Paul, London.
Unpopular Education (1981) Written by Members of the Centre for Contemporary Cultural Studies at the University of Birmingham, Hutchinson, London.
Warnock Report (1978) *Special Educational Needs*, Report of the Committee of Enquiry into the Education of Handicapped Children and Young People, Cmnd 7212, HMSO, London.
Warnock, M. (1980) 'A Flexible Framework', *Times Educational Supplement*, 26 September 1980, p. 2.
—— (1982) 'Marxist Spectacles', *New Society*, 11 March 1982, p. 405.
Ysseldyke, J.E. and Algozzine, B. (1982) *Critical Issues in Special and Remedial Education*, Houghton Mifflin, Boston.

4 THE DIFFERENTIAL DIAGNOSIS OF SPECIAL EDUCATION: MANAGING SOCIAL PATHOLOGY AS INDIVIDUAL DISABILITY
Deborah S. Bart

In this chapter, I conceptualise and explain the role of special education as one sorting process for regular education and society. I analyse the effects of medical and psychological models and management practices stemming from such models in special education: particularly on the professionalisation and curricular content of the field, and on the relationship of these models and management practices to special education's role as a sorting agency for regular education and society. In this analysis I also take account of my own experiences as a teacher and diagnostician of children considered to have 'learning problems'.

The analysis suffers the flaws of any work analysing real practices and processes solely on the basis of limited observation and without a large and systematic empirical investigation. However, it is informed by theory and may have the potential to provoke debate. My aim is to present and make problematic field-related practices that are often taken for granted and not subject to systematic scrutiny. Of critical importance is the minimising or neglect of social factors in discussions concerning the identification and treatment of handicapped children. This, in itself, is an interesting social fact, and one that I suggest is purposeful, although not necessarily at the level of the individual practitioner. Rather, this neglect of social process by individuals is structurally produced and masks a perhaps unintended result on the part of individuals — the containment of behaviour conceptualised as social pathology; it ultimately functions to undermine the stated goals of professionals in the field. For example, the definition, diagnosis and treatment of special children — common professional practice as well as 'natural' components of the special child's education — are social processes serving societal containment functions, although they are typically conceived of as practices performed by and for individuals, especially for the benefit of those individuals served. By carefully delimiting deviant behaviour while participating in the planning of individualised educational programmes, diagnostic management practices crystallise the dual role played by special educational services.

This analysis of special educational practices should not be construed as cynical or disparaging of the well-intentioned efforts of individual practitioners and professionals in the field. Undoubtedly, the education of the special child has been and continues to be motivated by humanitarian, even idealistic concern. But well-meaning, individual intentions, constrained by organisational and structural demands, often reap unexpected consequences. As a result, advances in the treatment of special children — from their inhumane and brutal handling in the custodial institutions of the nineteenth century to their more enlightened care today — have always been informed by societal need.

The Role of the Social in Special Education

The social nature of special education and its role within regular education and society has been largely ignored by practitioners within the field as well as by fields that traditionally study society and its social institutions. In fact, until recently, the field has often received attention as a by-product of research concerning health and illness issues such as personal emotional disorders or deviancy (Sarason and Doris, 1979, p. 19), and, not surprisingly, has borrowed theoretical constructs from these fields to pursue its own research. Similar to the dominant research perspective in these areas, special education has evolved and developed within a pragmatic, scientific tradition. This research perspective, as well as the field's 'helping' orientation, has largely functioned to ascribe an individualised, objective character to handicapping conditions and to exclude discussions of possible social determinants. As a result, the handicaps of special children have been conceptualised primarily as defects or diseases of individuals rather than outcomes of social interactional processes.

The neglect of social factors concerning the etiology of 'familial' retardation is typical of analyses concerning the etiology of handicaps throughout the field of special education. Discussing the familial retardate, Sarason and Doris (1979) admonish special educators and other professionals involved in the field to be critical of diagnostic practices that separate physical and biological from social and cultural etiological factors (pp. 135-57). They point out that familial retardation is generally a school-related phenomenon — i.e. it is seldom diagnosed prior to a child's entering school and tends to disappear after schooling — and thus, implicate the school as a possible factor in the development of such retardation, despite more accepted genetic etiological explanations (pp. 152-5). Additionally, Sarason and Doris stress the importance of considering the interaction and bidirectional influence of all possible etiological factors (as opposed to their dichotemisation and unidirectionality) (chapters 2 and 3).

The Public School and the Special Child

The public school plays a central role in teaching functional skills to special children, as well as more generally preparing children to become adult citizens and workers, cognisant of their contributory value to the country's productivity. The nature and extent of the public school's participation in this socialising function is a current issue of debate, although there is general consensus that the school's role, in a broad sense, is one of 'cultural transmission' and the 'perpetuation of our social system' (Kauffman, 1981, p. 12). As part of the public education system, special education — in its education and training of special children — participates in this debate. It does so in two ways. First, the field through its provision of services to handicapped individuals, serves a societal function by enhancing the potential 'productivity' of special children. Second, special education, as a subsystem of regular education, affords some insight into the practices and trends of regular education as well as illuminating educational practices and processes within its own field. Thus, the interaction of the special child and public education provides a locus in which to examine the treatment of the special child as well as, more generally, to analyse the social function of schooling.

The role of special education within regular education is shaped by underlying assumptions concerning the individuals the field serves. Assumptions concerning normality and abnormality, giftedness and handicap, and the measurement and meaning of differences inform the overt purposes and goals of special education as well as their rationale. Thus they both underlie the pragmatic treatment of special children and shape conceptualisations of the social role of schooling. They affect questions concerning the purposes of education in a pluralistic society, and the proper role of public education for diverse individuals. For example, assumptions concerning individual differences affect the eventual treatment of such individuals: if a child's failure in school is attributed to some lack or flaw inherent within himself (notably, an insufficient mental quotient) rather than some insufficiency on the part of the school, the individual rather than the institution will be targeted for change.

Assumptions concerning the desirability of differences also affect notions of equality and the relationship of equality to schooling practices (e.g. that 'average' is normal; that average achievement denotes

equality of education). If educational policy dictates equality of outcome rather than equality of opportunity, efforts will be implemented
to bring special children up to the functioning level of 'normal' children;
if equality of opportunity predominates, emphasis will be placed on in-
suring special children equal 'access' to education, and the criteria established for the provision of an appropriate education for handicapped
children necessarily will be more limited. The process of interpreting
Public Law 94-142 (the Education for all Handicapped Children Act of
1975), thus, will reflect evolving educational ideology and assumptions
concerning special children. (To a certain degree, precedent cases will
also shape educational ideology and policy, since rulings from individual
cases handed down by the court will directly translate the concept of a
'free, appropriate education' into educational practice.)

To date, gains from legislation, particularly Public Law 94-142, out-
weigh growing backlash and current administration disapproval of special
policy. As a result, the 1980s still auger well for special education and
its clients — at least according to the perspective of professionals and
parent groups working to obtain equal education for special children.
Because the past two decades of legislation have significantly increased
educational opportunity for special children, many professionals and
parents now believe that *their* children will finally receive access not
merely to public schools, but to more meaningful education, the 'free,
appropriate education' legislated by the Education for all Handicapped
Children Act of 1975. Working together to establish this legislated
mandate as historical fact, special children's advocates are trying to
ensure some measure of programme quality by effecting interpretations
of pertinent legislation so that they encompass more than mere access
to education. Because the concept of a 'free, appropriate education' is
not clearly delineated and is open to interpretation, current debate
centres about what is meant by a free, appropriate education and how
this affects the achievement of meaningful educational programmes for
special populations.

The public school is curiously, or perhaps not so curiously, absent
from the centre-stage position held by many professional groups advancing the rights of the special child through lobbying efforts and consequent policy-making. Yet it is the public school that ultimately bears
responsibility for such children, either in actual teaching and/or training
or in monetary support for education provided privately. Waiting in the
wings, the public school finds its role in educating special children increasingly dictated by special interest groups and government legislation.
It is important, therefore, to understand the needs and motivations of

these groups and how their professional aspirations and goals inform the educational process of special children. That the special child's needs have become a kind of *cause célèbre* prompts many interesting questions as to why this is so and suggests the necessity of analysing educational practice and social processes in special education, especially as they relate to regular education.

The Role of Special Education in Regular Education

The belief that special children are somehow 'deviant' and that special classes are educational facilities necessary as 'holding places' or 'dumping grounds' for the atypical and asocial student is a predominant conceptualisation of special schooling, and one that has largely determined the field's role. These conceptualisations are supported by assumptions concerning normality and abnormality, and the relationship of these assumptions to beliefs concerning the proper treatment of individual differences. These terms are not without history; one is reminded of their legacy — the common nineteenth-century belief that moral degeneracy caused conditions ranging from mental retardation and physical disability to criminality, insanity and poverty. The notion of moral degeneracy as an explanatory concept for disability, and the equation of disability with criminality also informed educational and social programmes serving the handicapped and reinforced the segregated structure of such programmes. Additionally, the social–historical context in which special education evolved also fostered a climate in which social problems were seen as individuals' problems amenable to scientific treatment and control. The field's growth spanned decades witnessing increasing immigration and rapid urbanisation; the ascendancy of the mental testing and eugenics movements; and the growing importance of psychology and medical technology in the treatment of individual defect and disability. Further special education evolved at a time when compulsory education was beginning to be taken seriously at both state and national levels, and the school was increasingly conceived of as an important agent of social change. (Schooling could compensate for the negative and insidious habits families transmitted to their children while imparting the ideals and opportunities of democratic government and the virtues of good citizenship.)

The juncture of compulsory schooling and the rapid increase of special or 'ungraded' classes provides an historic example of this organisational solution to meeting social needs at the expense of individual development. When compulsory schooling mandated that all children attend schools and, as a consequence, schools were faced with the problem of educating diverse non-English speaking populations, an ancillary system — special or 'ungraded' classes — was created to deal with those students who failed to progress at normal rates. This was done at the behest of those experts (e.g. teachers, administrators and related medical personnel) who, having a personal stake in the perpetuation of the existing educational system, needed a rapid and non-socially disorganising solution to their newly acquired 'problems'. Ungraded classes for children who were mentally retarded, language retarded, physically handicapped and emotionally disturbed, as well as disciplinary problem and truant, provided such a solution. Classes for the latter existed previously and provided organisational models for the rapidly evolving special classes. These classes, despite efforts to classify children by specific handicap, were often heterogeneous accommodating variously designed 'problem' children. Criteria for inclusion in such classes varied enormously from physical diagnostic procedures, often as simplistic as viewing the child and concluding that he 'looks' mentally retarded, to mental quotient scores (especially after the wide acceptance of Binet's measures), to the inability to speak English, be attentive or well-disciplined.

Similar practices exist today. Classes encompass many individuals whose officially designated labels bear little resemblance to their described problem or behaviour. (Often the regular teacher is the only channel for special referral. As a result, the past failures of the regular classroom become the future students of the special classroom (Ysseldyke and Algozzine, 1983; Milofsky, 1976).) But they share a propensity for school failure and, often, membership in a low status social group. The disproportionate inclusion of low status minority children in special classes has characterised the field since its inception from the high numbers (proportionately) of immigrant children at the turn of the century to the current population of blacks and children of Spanish descent (Sarason and Doris, 1979, pp. 153-7 and 321-54). These children have been variously labelled morally degenerate, mentally retarded, situationally deprived and learning disabled. Whatever the label, it has functioned historically to maintain the institutional *status quo* by attributing failure to individual students and/or families. Additionally, this 'sorting' of low status minority children into special classes has virtually guaranteed their failure to be upwardly mobile. The hidden agenda in the categorising and labelling of weaker social groups has been referred to in many studies (Sarason and Doris, 1979; Mercer, 1973; Tomlinson, 1981). Tomlinson (1982) succinctly describes the exclusionary impact of such categorisation and subsequent entry into special education, writing that

It is important to stress at the onset that in modern industrial societies which increasingly demand qualifications and credentials acquired through the education system, to be categorized out of 'normal' education represents the ultimate in non-achievement in terms of ordinary educational goals. Occupational success, social mobility, privilege and advancement are currently legitimated by the education system; those who receive a 'special' rather than ordinary education are, by and large, excluded from these things (p. 6).

That the curriculum offered many special children functions to subvert their life chances is illustrated by the primacy given to manual and vocational training (with its eventual goal of employment in a sheltered workshop) in special education. Such training and employment in sheltered workshops — an end goal for many retarded children — ostensibly enables handicapped individuals to utilise their limited abilities in a way that most closely approximates 'normal' individuals; that is, such employment provides the handicapped individual with a measure of independence and the related satisfactions accruing from such independence. But it is this 'approximation' that henceforth rules their lives, and, often, it is to this approximation of normal life that handicapped children's earlier education is geared. Thus the special child is prepared for a career of approximation in a manner similar to that in which the professional's child is prepared for a career in the professions. In this sense, vocational training and sheltered workshops play a dual role. In addition to providing gainful employment to the handicapped, they also afford a means by which these individuals can return some measure of productivity to society, despite their recognised 'limitations'. Assessing such training from an immediate, pragmatic context masks its potentially limiting long-range effects.

This conservatism, perpetuated by special education, results from the field's competing roles — 'normalizing' special children through educational and vocational training while functioning as an agency of sorting and containment for regular education and society. For example, special programmes for the delayed and gifted may benefit individual students by increasing their skills, but they also call attention to individual differences and, as a result, create and perpetuate concepts of deviance and disability; at the same time, the existence of such programmes makes the student population in regular classes more homogeneous, and, thus, more manageable. This 'sorting' is necessary for the smooth operation of an educational system that structures academic success via progression through an age-related invariant framework and predicates future occupational success on a student's academic progress. Places for students failing to function in the regular classroom (i.e. progress through the grades at an appropriate rate), are a necessary component of this system, since these slots function as organisational 'safety valves', diminishing school responsibility for individual failure. Additionally, they provide a mechanism for preparing students for careers ostensibly differentiated by ability or merit, but, in actuality, differentiated by social or economic characteristics.

'Sorting': the Social Role of Special Education

The 'sorting' accomplished by special classes, whether achieved by teacher referral, psychological evaluation or IQ testing, is implicated in several major trends characterising current practices in special education, which can be generally described as 'behavioural' and 'medical' management of behaviour. Behavioural management, an application of the psychological principles of behaviourism and the philosophy of scientific management initially employed in industry to increase productivity, has enjoyed longstanding and continued popularity within special education, providing a basis for much of the field's curricular content and teaching methodology. An important principle of scientific management is the fragmentation of work tasks so that the 'conception' of the task is separated from its 'execution' — the former being the responsibility of management and the latter that of workers. This separation of design from execution functions to reduce workers' autonomy and maintain a hierarchical stratification within industry. It is promoted under the guise of improved efficiency and, thus, greater and more equitably distributed rewards. Behaviour modification, as a management strategy, is reminiscent of the social philosophy of scientific management, since it incorporates a similar fragmented approach to learning tasks. Stipulating that all learning is a process of negative and positive conditioning, it separates action from introspection. In doing so, it eliminates the notion that individuals are internally directed; as a result, it has the potential to promote strategies of management that negate individual responsibility or self-direction. As scientific management, it poses 'science' as the 'final arbitrator', eliminating the personal exercise of authority in management. Clinical management practices similarly negate their personal aspects of management by recourse to scientific authority. Medical management has pervaded the field since its inception, and there has been increasing use of the medical model for diagnosis and treatment problems. For example, early institutions serving the mentally retarded and/or physically handicapped were often founded and run by physicians; associations for the mentally retarded enjoyed a longstanding connection with those serving the mentally insane. Today, paediatricians, neurologists, psychiatrists and clinical psychologists continue to play an important role in defining, diagnosing and treating special children. The continuous and increasing 'medicalisation' of the field has had profound implications for special educators as well as special children and their families; these implications will be discussed more fully in subsequent sections of this chapter.

The scientific diagnosis and treatment of special children continues a tradition of educational reform begun by the common school reformers in the first half of the nineteenth century. Under the guise of liberating children from their 'naturally' unfit parents, the reformers masked their own self-serving interests and set the stage for future interventions of the state on behalf of children (Nasaw, 1981, chapter 5). This resulted in a progressive weakening of familial and local control of education and an uncritical acceptance of state intervention in family matters. Whether children were being 'saved' (Platt, 1969) from the pernicious influence of their families or the debilitating and damaging impact of their handicaps, parental input was little sought or valued. Today, by law, parents must be informed about a school's decision to test their child(ren) for possible handicapping conditions. Additionally, parents have the right to employ an outside examiner, if they disagree with the results of the school's testing or if they simply wish a second opinion, and must consent to final placement decisions. Obviously, the manner in which schools handle these matters (when and how they inform parents) will affect parental ability to participate in a fully informed manner. Despite the greater inclusion of some parents of handicapped children — especially middle-class ones — in their children's education and training, and this obvious difference from the exclusion of parents by the common school reformers, similar structural conditions support the treatment of these historically separate groups, and these conditions are manifest in the field's management practices. Both historically and currently, special children have been tacitly defined by dominant interests as 'socially disorganising' and have been systematically segregated through educational structures from their 'normal' peers; economically and socially dominant groups have implemented programmes of reform to shore up what they conceive to be an undermining of the social order by the 'deviance' of special children and handicapped adults. These groups have legitimated their behaviour by acting for the state within its *parens patrie* role (Kittrie, 1971, chapters 1 and 9).

This reading of special education as one sorting mechanism for regular education and society might be criticised as inimical to current beliefs about the special child and unwarranted by current practice in the field. Critics might argue that the notion of moral degeneracy as an explanatory concept for handicapping conditions has been scientifically put to rest, and the widely accepted notion that special children are different in degree, not kind, has supplanted notions of inherent differences and the segregative practices logically thought to follow from this perspective. Further, the custom of segregating the handicapped has been invalidated by the concept of 'normalisation' and precluded by mainstreaming practices. But why does a field pervaded by humanitarianism and moral fervour continue to be pejoratively characterised, and, more importantly, to debate issues and practices that were considered and rejected over a century ago (Sarason and Doris, 1979, pp. 355-92)? The tenacity of the characterisation of special education as a 'dumping ground' is a nagging reminder that neither attitudes nor behaviour have altered enough to produce a wider acceptance of the special child or handicapped adult, despite rhetoric to the contrary.

In the following section, I explain that beliefs and practices in special education have not changed significantly – demonstrating that nineteenth-century beliefs are still embedded in twentieth-century practices, particularly those practices that are employed in order to 'manage' the special child. I discuss these management trends and their putative shift from a punitive to beneficent nature in order to assess the impact of the field's therapeutic orientation on the special child, and to determine whether conceptualising special education as a 'dumping ground' is still warranted by current practice in the field.

Management Trends in Special Education

Special education and its management practices typify the contradictory nature of reform – self-serving and beneficent – which often masks underlying self-profit through moralising precepts and good works. Janus-like, caught between the tension of benefiting the majority or the special individual, special education – as many other reform-minded social institutions – has, wittingly or unwittingly, experimented with numerous mechanisms of social control in order to improve the lives of 'bad' or, as more recently conceptualised, 'sick' children (Conrad and Schneider, 1980a, pp. 17-27). From institutionalisation (e.g. of the mentally defective along with the mentally insane for their own good and protection) to 'normalisation' (e.g. placement of all handicapped children in their 'least restrictive environments'), professionals have been mandating the special child's fate in an arena where 'scientific expertise' has often functioned to legitimise essentially moral decisions of social and economic import. Like other 'child-saving' institutions that have received state legislated mandates to protect and improve the lives of dependants, the social institutions of special education have evolved from institutions characterised by a penal and retributive ethos to a therapeutic and clinical orientation (Conrad and Schneider, 1980a, pp. 145-71). As a result, the philosophy and pragmatic 'management' of special education — the definition, labelling and treatment of special children — has allegedly undergone a 'sea-change'.

The behavioural and medical management practices of special education reflect the field's therapeutic and clinical orientation, and also represent 'legitimating ideologies', functioning to bolster the social and educational structures from which they stem. They are comprised of both formal and informal beliefs about special children. I analyse these beliefs and assumptions, and their ideological transformations and relationship to social and educational structures, to determine whether the therapeutic orientation in special education denotes any significant structural change in the treatment and education of special children; for example, are current therapeutically-based programmes more beneficial than more narrow educationally-based programmes? Has the inclusion of medical professionals and paraprofessionals in the field of special education been of any appreciable benefit to the special child? Similarly, has the attempt to utilise medical models of diagnosis and treatment and scientific explanatory models of behaviour improved educational programming?

In order to assess the extent of change, one must look at, as well as beyond, the pragmatic everyday management of the special child by bringing a 'problematising' rather than a 'naturalising' analysis to the special child's treatment. By analysing how management trends interface with the interests of dominant social groups, one not only can assess the nature, extent and impact of treatment on the special child but also look beyond treatment *per se* to the underlying interests and conflicts shaping the field. For example, instead of accepting the notion that educational practice, i.e. educational management, benefits the special child, one might question how its exclusionary practice adversely affects him, and, if this is the case, determine whose interests are being served by the labelling and categorising — essentially processes of negative valuation — of special children. Further, how does this treatment serve

the interests of regular education, larger society and the varied professionals — especially medical, psychological and educational — who are
involved in the field? What are the needs of these respective professionals
and what are their interprofessional conflicts? What impact do these
needs and conflicts have on the care and training of the special child
(Tomlinson, 1982, pp. 5-25)? Answering such questions requires clear
conceptualisation of relevant issues as well as careful empirical study.
This chapter analyses such questions by presenting and problematising
relevant issues.

Management practices in special education have allegedly shifted
from a punitive to a therapeutic orientation. More medical, paramedical
and medically related professionals now work within the field of special
education; but their presence has merely changed the field's 'gatekeepers'
and gatekeeping style; social and educational structures representing
dominant social interests remain the same. This is not surprising since
underlying assumptions and beliefs about disabilities and their etiologies
— both lay and professional — have not altered in any significant manner.
Etiological explanations may have changed from morally to clinically
based interpretations of conduct, but both still ascribe a disvalued,
negative status to special children. Thus, despite a beneficent rather
than punitive social response, which exempts the special child from
bearing responsibility for his behavioural and cognitive shortcomings; a
'professionally' sanctioned philosophy of normalisation; and mandated
legislation for placing children in the 'least restrictive environment',
the educationally disabled are still conceptually individualised in both
societal reaction and treatment. That is, the source and treatment of
atypical behaviour are 'located' within the disabled child; it is the disabled child who must be managed, rehabilitated or trained.

A therapeutic context facilitates management because it includes
the notion of 'prevention'. In contrast to criminal sanctions, in which
punitive measures are implemented against a specific criminal act or
behaviour, therapeutic measures are extended to the person himself,
often independent of overt behaviour and symptoms. Since therapeutic
measures are also applied prophylactically, they may be implemented
prior to the manifestation of actual symptoms — for example, based on
family history, test results or behavioural and psychological interpretation — increasing the possibilities of unwarranted intervention. Thus
adherence to a philosophy of prevention can function as a legitimating
ideology for social control.

The Language of Management: Ideological and Naturalising

The scientific notions of 'prediction' and 'control' underlying medical and psychological explanatory models as well as accompanying scientific terminology, also contribute towards 'naturalising' a social context for early intervention. This is because prevention, prediction and control — the terms of therapeutic diagnosis and treatment — bear positive connotations, which pervade everyday awareness. Therapeutic terms common to special education and other rehabilitative fields project similarly positive connotations even though they are terms that focus on essentially negative, stigmatised conditions. For example, professionals discuss the special child's 'management', 'training' and 'rehabilitation', but at issue is the special child's disease, incompetence and disability. Seldom does one hear about special children's aspirations, contributions or potential, or how these qualities are developed or stymied by current educational practice. This is because the terms of the field are the language of management, not education, and they suggest that there is something awry, something to manage. The language of management confuses management with educational purpose.

This 'confusion' of education and management occurs because the language of management functions ideologically — it is pervasive, naturalising and objectifying, and it represents the interests of dominant groups (Persell, 1977, pp. 5-20). Additionally, it serves to mask less desirable feelings and their linguistic counterparts that are attributed to special children. As a result, underlying fears concerning the 'different' nature of handicapped children remain intact and become more insidious proportional to their repression. Instead of confronting their fears, individuals label the fear-producing phenomenon (i.e. special children) with neutral descriptors (e.g. those of the language of management) and are temporarily relieved of their psychological discomfort. Management itself (i.e. separated from the language of management, its ideological counterpart) is the logical and pragmatic outcome of a definitional system so commonly accepted that it 'saturates' commonsense awareness (Persell, 1977, pp. 10-11). Thus, although the linkages between ideology and services are not overtly perceived, ideological persuasion channels a demand for concrete services.

In special education these services — often a form of medical or behavioural management — are highly directive and controlled. The management trends supporting these services share several characteristics — both have a therapeutic rather than punitive orientation, utilise a medical model of diagnosis and treatment, and rationalise treatment via a labelling perspective. These organisational characteristics function to transform an essentially social process (i.e. management) into a 'scientific' one. The resultant conceptualisation of social problems as clinical problems focuses attention on the parameters of a problem and its possible courses of treatment; whether the behaviour or 'symptom' in question is, in actuality, a problem is by-passed in its definition and categorisation. The organisational features characterising management trends are mutually supportive – a therapeutic orientation provides a natural context for diagnosis, which, in turn, functions as a clinical form of labelling. As a result, diagnosis appears to be a natural and logical approach to the treatment of problems, and its resultant labelling, a needed and natural 'fact' rather than a social construction.

Medical diagnosis as a labelling process has both intra- and interpersonal consequences for the labelled individual as well as institutional and societal level ramifications. The physician as 'certifier' of illness often performs an institutional function, while dispensing an interpersonal service. The strain that may result from these opposing functions reflects the differing sources of his professional and technical authority – the former derived from societal and legal sanctions and the latter from the possession of 'expert' knowledge (Friedson, 1970a). Behavioural diagnosis functions similarly as a labelling process, although it focuses solely on overt behaviour – the etiology of the behaviour is not of interest. This contrasts with medical diagnosis, which utilises overt symptomology as well as clinical signs to get at and treat underlying pathology.

The physician's interaction with his client is affected by the differing sources of his authority – professional authority exacts compliance by its 'persuasiveness', and technical authority by its mystification (i.e. the unequal access to knowledge existing between physician and client). These sources of authority function to increase the power of the physician vis-à-vis the client, and contribute towards making individuals' access to medicine a source of social stratification. Both the 'professional' relationship between physician and patient and the role of the physician as 'diagnostor' contribute towards the labelling of the patient. Labelling is an integral part of medical and behavioural management, since, without the definitional act of diagnosis, further interaction or treatment would be impossible. The diagnostic process defines and categorises behavioural or physical conditions into scientific terms amenable to treatment. In doing so, diagnosis functions as a social as well as a scientific process, since the professional and technical authority of the diagnostor – and the consequent implications of this authority for the professional-client relationship — is an integral part of his diagnostic 'expertise' and, thus, of the diagnostic act itself. As a social construction, therefore, diagnosis symbolises and actualises the inequality existing between professional and client, an inequality resulting from differential knowledge and status. The special expertise of the physician provides a good example of this inequality, and its relationship to functional social processes. Parsons's (1951) conceptualisation of the 'sick role' is pertinent here (pp. 428-79). According to his model, which equates illness and deviance, it is the physician and the physician only who can confer 'conditionally legitimate' status on the sick individual and, thus, remove the negative implications of his deviant status.

Managing Disability as Illness

Although the Parsonian sick role has generated much criticism, it remains an important explanatory model — if not for sociologists of medicine whose critiques and countercritiques of it are numerous, then for many professionals engaged in the helping services, since its functionalist perspective accords well with their treatment aims and programmes. Because of its current acceptance by helping professionals and its continuing critique by sociologists, this model is central to the understanding of dominant conceptualisations of the social role of illness, particularly the notion of illness as deviance; additionally, it helps to explain how these conceptualisations interface with treatment responses, and how the notion of disability as illness benefits professionals and dominant societal interests.

Parsons's formulation of the sick role — in particular, the notion that illness constitutes a special category of deviance expressed in terms of role disturbance — continues to provide helping professions with a rationale for their treatment programmes. This accords nicely with medical and behavioural diagnoses, which have perpetuated two major conceptualisations of special children — that of deviant and disabled. Rationalising deviance as illness is not surprising given the increasing medicalisation of arenas of life formerly presided over by the criminal court system (e.g. the defence of criminal action via a plea of insanity); or by educational institutions (e.g. the definition and treatment of hyperkinesis); or just handled informally (e.g. the treatment of obesity). This equation of illness and health with deviance and its treatment functions to remove potentially disruptive behaviour (i.e. illness/deviance) from the social arena in the name of a universally ascribed-to value — health (Fox, 1977; Zola, 1972, 1975). The recognition of the desirability of health and the undesirability of illness is an important component of the Parsonian sick role, and it illustrates the manner in which moral valuation enters into the allegedly neutral process of diagnosis. According to Parsons's model, one is accorded the conditional status of 'being sick' if one recognises that being sick is an undesirable state, is motivated to get well by seeking appropriate professional help, and co-operates with mandated treatment (in the case of children, this responsibility devolves upon the child's parents). This 'conditional' exemption – dependent upon the proper attitude and behaviour of the patient and the nature and severity of his illness – confers a 'conditional legitimacy' on the individual's 'deviant' behaviour. In doing so, it removes a potential source of disorganising, socially-conflicting behaviour from society. Additionally, this conceptualisation of illness as non-threatening and non-challenging, not only preserves social norms, but strengthens them. Health and its counterpart – normal role functioning – is valued, and illness and its ensuing behaviour devalued.

Disability and the 'Sick Role'

Disability presents a special problem for the Parsonian sick role in that several of the role's assumptions concerning disease are not relevant; for example, the 'disease state' of the disabled individual is usually not temporary, and, as a result, he cannot be 'motivated' to 'get well' in the same sense as an ill individual, although he may be able to or wish to improve his condition (Freidson, 1965). 'Being sick' with its attendant legitimacy (granted under certain circumscribed conditions) is, therefore, not a viable option for the disabled individual, since, in general, his physical condition is irreversible, and accompanying stigma irremovable. For these reasons, Freidson suggests that the dimensions of personal responsibility and imputed prognosis – dimensions relevant to the imputation of deviance in sick individuals – are not adequate to ascribe deviance to disabled individuals. For example, when an individual is 'sick' and not responsible for his illness, he is, according to the Parsonian model, granted a conditionally legitimate status, especially if his prognosis for recovery is good and he fulfils other requirements of the model. But a disabled individual who, similarly, bears no responsibility for his condition is generally not considered 'legitimately' ill and is often stigmatised. Despite his attempts at normalcy or actual 'normal' behaviour, the disabled individual is treated as if 'sick'. When he fails to improve, he is personally blamed for his condition and/or stigmatised (relative to the disabling condition and societal attitude). These attitudes on the part of the lay and professional communities result because the disabled person's condition is incurable. At bottom, he remains disabled.

This imputation of deviance seems to occur, therefore, on the basis of knowledge of the handicapping condition alone, since the disabled individual often presents no deviant behaviour and supposedly is not considered responsible for his condition. According to Freidson (1965), the problem with the 'responsible-not responsible' dimension for assessing deviance within the disabled population and legitimising or not legitimising disability, is that it excludes the moral valuation often accompanying deviance. That is, the interpretation of a disabled individual as sick, and therefore as deviant, occurs more often as a result of moral valuation than empirical knowledge derived from social interaction; thus, his role 'may be constructed and maintained quite independently of the disabled person's motives' (Freidson, 1965, p. 81). For this reason, Freidson suggests the addition of two dimensions usually not included in assessing deviant behaviour within the sick role — the degree of stigma of the presenting condition and the prognostic category of 'improvable but not curable' (Freidson, 1965, pp. 76-81).

Perhaps even more than illness, disability is usually not motivated (Freidson, 1965, p. 88). Rather, an individual unfortuitously becomes the recipient of an illness or handicapping condition, which then becomes labelled and treated — not necessarily in that order. The need to label in order to treat exemplifies the ideal logic of the diagnostic-prescriptive model of treatment, but does not necessarily transfer into real practice; that is, diagnosing an illness or disability does not necessarily impose a stigmatising label on the individual. Negative labelling may also occur during or after treatment, since treatment often functions to organise informal beliefs (e.g. the 'naughty child') into formal, professional designations of deviance (e.g. the 'hyperkinetic child'). In the latter case, a linguistic label, which may even have been loosely applied to the child, gains credibility by virtue of accompanying therapeutic treatment and professional interaction.

The Professionalisation of Disability: Organising and Consolidating Deviant Careers

This relationship between treatment and labelling suggests the importance of helping service professions and their organisations in the shaping and production of individuals' deviant careers, especially when considered in conjunction with the notion that most handicapped individuals are not 'motivated' to be disabled and prefer to minimise their disabilities, assuming as normal a role as possible (Freidson, 1965, p. 88). If deviance occurs primarily as a result of treatment and institutional response, not individual 'motivation', then the relationship of a handicapped individual's motivation to the development of his deviant career is most usefully discussed in terms of how 'he performs in that role', not 'whether or not he has been placed in that role' (Freidson, 1965, p. 81). He elaborates:

> His motives may be involved in whether or not he rebels against the labelling, whether he falls into invalidism, or whether he becomes a showcase model of conformity to expectations, but the permanence and shape of the role he plays so badly or so well stand quite apart from his inclinations (p. 81).

This is not to suggest that deviance does not exist; that all deviance is a result of societal reaction; or that deviant individuals never label themselves as such or seek treatment voluntarily and willingly (Lemert, 1967; Erikson, 1962). Rather it is to underscore the notion that deviant behaviour occurs as a result of a complex *interaction* of societal response and individual disability and that, quite often, such response — whether lay or professional — increases, perpetuates, or produces deviance, especially through its role in organising deviance. Professional response (i.e. treatment) is particularly important because it often serves to organise lay response.

Deviant behaviour is 'stabilised' and 'consolidated' into a career when, because of societal response, an individual's perception of his self-identity no longer appears disparate with his social identity. This is accompanied by what Freidson terms a 'moral career' in which 'one's identity for others and one's image of self are deteriorating and being re-cast in another form' (Freidson, 1965, pp. 92-3). Within the diagnostic-prescriptive framework, this career consolidation often occurs when emphasis on diagnosis shifts to emphasis on treatment because treatment generally creates certain behavioural responses. (Labelling theorists describe this turning-point as irreversible (Erikson, 1962, p. 16), although the possibility of moving back and forth between deviant and non-deviant roles is not logically, or even possibly, precluded.) This movement between roles and, particularly, a permanent return to non-deviant status, is more difficult to effect within institutional structures and networks than, for example, social subgroups. Once referred, an individual largely loses the ability to be self-directive; instead, his fate is determined by professional and organisational characteristics. For example, a practitioner's expertise, ability and power to make decisions, and his therapeutic orientation — interventionist or non-interventionist — considerably influences the direction and quality of a disabled individual's course of treatment. Similarly, an institution's or agency's resources, relationships to other agencies (in terms of its clientele, resources and referral practices), and intra-organisational concerns will determine treatment practices and populations served.

Professional Concerns and Management Practices

The organisational and professional features of agencies intermesh with the presenting characteristics of a disabled person's handicap, requiring an accommodation between the organisation's resources (including its professionals' expertise and authority) and the complexity and severity of the person's handicap. This accommodation critically influences an individual's subsequent management and the implications of this course of management for deviance producing behaviour. In this context, issues of professionalisation and such related issues as professional status and professional overidentification become pertinent.

The professional(s) and professional service organisations within which a special child first interacts often determine his subsequent course of management. In addition to variables characterising individual practitioners (e.g. knowledge, decision-making power and therapeutic inclinations), an organisation's relationship to other organisations also affects management practices. Referrals made within and between organisations are critical to the definition of organisational relationships and extremely important to individuals' therapeutic courses. These referral practices and their characteristics – for example, whether referral networks occur within or extend across professions, and whether they are uni- or bidirectional – link an organisation's resources to its management practices. Differences exist between referral practices of various helping service organisations; for example, educational organisations generally have extensive referral networks and refer across professions (e.g. referrals are often made to medically, psychologically or legally related institutions), while medical organisations typically refer clients within their profession to subspecialities (Freidson, 1965, p. 90). As a result of these practices, an individual whose deviance is first suspected or identified within an educational organisation may be referred subsequently to any number of human service organisations – for example, to child-guidance clinics, or court affiliated or medical institutions. A reciprocal referral may or may not occur. When it does, these institutions may deem special educational services or supports as a necessary part of prescribed treatment. Thus, depending on the 'referral network', a disabled person's management may be abrogated after initial contact or indefinitely extended.

The extent of management depends on the 'accessibility' of the disabled person's handicap (i.e. how much is known about a particular handicap); the extent to which it is grounded in scientific fact; and the competence of professionals to diagnose and treat the alleged condition, so that a handicapping condition that most helping professionals feel competent to define and treat is managed by a wider spectrum of professionals than a handicap that professionals believe requires more specialised or technical knowledge.

These organisational variables, thus, combine to delineate a 'universe of deviance' (Freidson, 1965, p. 82) which, reflecting the contingent nature of these variables, is necessarily relative and not absolute. According to Freidson (1965), socially structured biases account for the identification of deviants and their accompanying assignment into deviant roles because 'the true universe or rate of deviance, whether defined by behavioral or biological criteria, is difficult if not impossible to define' (Freidson, 1965, p. 82). If organisations define and classify deviance according to relativistic, biased criteria and utilise referral practices characterised by organisational contingencies, then the differential treatment of special children, especially concerning deviance labelling, becomes less puzzling. The referral process plays a critical role in the labelling of deviance and the subsequent shaping of deviant careers because of its importance to organisational survival and professionalism. Referral networks work to the mutual advantage of organisations by creating and supporting a need for specialised services. Similarly, referrals with their attendant diagnostic and prescriptive processes enhance professionalism by increasing a clinician's status and by delineating professional boundaries. By defining such a deviant universe (i.e. individuals in need of treatment), these organisations rationalise the services they provide. One effect of this definitional activity is an artificial construction of the nature of deviance and the criteria necessary to identify it. The diagnostic requirement for precise classificatory criteria often results in an increase in the identification of disabled individuals and the number of 'conditions' needing professional attention. In fact, without a co-ordinating clinician or agency, an individual who is multiply-referred runs the risk of multiple treatment programmes — some duplicating, some contradictory. This professional 'overidentification' may even occur in treatment modalities — such as inter- and transdisciplinary health-care delivery teams — designed to minimise such overlap because issues of professional status continue to operate within these teams despite an espoused philosophy of egalitarianism. In fact, professional competition and issues of autonomy may increase rather than decrease, because of the co-operative team-work required by individuals who vary greatly in terms of their professional status and training as well as their intra-professional competence. Thus, on a pragmatic level, the inter-relatedness of interdisciplinary and transdisciplinary diagnosis treatment teams is often marred by interprofessional disagreements concerning client treatment. It is not unlikely that some tension occurs because of competing claims for client service and the differential status of fields participating in client management. While lower status professions may seek to enhance their status by adopting the paradigms and tools of higher status professions, and involving higher status professions in mutual client assessment. Higher status professions, on the other hand, may maintain their status by dominating diagnostic and remedial conferences and making their specialised knowledge inaccessible through training and licensing practices or through the use of technical intra-professional language. As a profession expands the scope of its responsibility and the need for more and more specialisation is created, dominant professions will delegate the less technical and more mundane practices of their professions to lower echelon professions or will grow horizontally, adding non-competitive specialities. Thus dominance is maintained by narrowing the top and increasing the base of the 'professional pyramid' or by horizontal growth within the profession.

A profession that first defines or labels a condition as deviant also maintains dominance; since the treatment and formulation of social problems are often predicated on their initial definition, the field that provides the dominant definition of disability or deviance simultaneously enhances its progressive sphere of activities. The delivery of services to deviant individuals is justified by these professional labelling practices, which serve to transform subjective, relativistic and abstract concepts into neutral, objective, 'real' and, therefore, unquestionable constructs. The objectification and standardisation of knowledge are crucial structural components of professionalisation and underlie the rationalised action of bureaucratic institutions. ('Helping' institutions are typically professional and heteronomous organisations.) Standardising knowledge is crucial to the maintenance of internal and external professional authority, since it contributes towards stabilising the internal hierarchical structure necessary for professional unification and provides a basis for the 'cognitive superiority' of the profession over lay, informal knowledge (Larson, 1977, pp. 40-52).

Professionalisation, Knowledge Production and the Service Market

Professionalisation brings together two processes that typically evolve separately: the accumulation of a body of abstract knowledge – which can be pragmatically applied – and the development of a market for professional services (Larson, 1977, p. 40). Standardisation or codification of professional knowledge contributes towards this convergence by making professional 'commodities' familiar to the lay public. According to Larson (1977), standardising a profession's knowledge base provides a 'transcendent, cognitive and normative framework', which functions to 'depersonaliz[e] ideas held about a profession's practice and products'. She contends that

> The more formalized the cognitive basis, the more the profession's language and knowledge appear to be connotation-free and 'object-ive'. Hence the superiority of a *scientific* basis for professional uni-fication: . . . it not only produces a more formalized language, but also links a profession to the dominant system of cognitive legitima-tion (pp. 40-1).

Thus standardisation of knowledge results in a value-free professional commodity, which appears independent of a profession's self-interest; it illustrates how ideology can transform what is essentially a market-orientated activity into a more ennobled ideal of service.

Both professionalisation and bureaucratisation perpetuate deviant roles and reify diagnostic categories by the way in which they assume responsibility for the monitoring and control of deviance (Freidson, 1965, p. 83). The reification of diagnostic categories functions to in-crease deviance because classification systems for disabilities and dis-orders make amorphous, abstract phenomena more accessible and, consequently, more 'real'. Both processes participate in mapping out and controlling a sphere of services. Professionalisation facilitates the development of a service market, while bureaucratisation expands the service delivery system through the fragmentation of the service process. Implicit in this assumption of responsibility is the notion that there are individuals to be responsible for or, in clinical terms, that there are conditions to treat. And treatment is facilitated by objectifying alleged illness conditions as well as diagnostic categories describing these con-ditions – the more objectified and reified the diagnostic categories, the less disputable their application. Without these naturalising processes, the value orientation inherent in the scientific treatment of deviance –

i.e. diagnosis and treatment – would become apparent and problematic.

As professional knowledge becomes more unified and standardised, it makes the separation between theoretical and practical knowledge more distinct (Larson, 1977, p. 44). As a result, organisations that produce knowledge – the university is prototypical – enhance this separation; this results in the subordination of practitioners to theoreticians and the replacement of apprenticeship by formal training (Larson, 1977, p. 44). Additionally, as standardisation of knowledge enhances the role of educators (and their organisations) as professional spokesmen and primary agents of professional training, it also functions to increase intra-professional specialisation. Larson comments that 'theoretical distinction tends to overshadow practical talent *at the same time* that it tends to become more esoteric, granted to specialists by specialists and fully meaningful only in their circles' (p. 45). This results in a profession's insularity, especially from lay review so that, according to Larson, 'at the level of theoretical production, colleague sanction of individual talents becomes more legitimate *at the same time* that it becomes narrower and less accessible to general review'. If, as Larson indicates in her analysis of the medical profession, the 'cognitive and technical basis' of professional training is the 'main support of a professional subculture', what occurs in professions unable to develop such clear bases of cognitive superiority? Larson suggests that such professions deliberately develop a mystifying presentation. She explains that these fields 'create and emphasize pure mannerisms (including cognitive ones, such as unnecessary jargon or unjustifiably esoteric techniques or 'pseudo-paradigmatic' changes' (Larson, 1977, p. 45).

Special Education: A Case of Incomplete Professionalisation

Special education represents an interesting locus in which to examine issues of professionalisation and their impact on the management of special children, since, in contrast to the field of medicine, it represents a fragmented, relatively powerless profession that has failed to achieve professional autonomy from lay influences and sits at the bottom of the educational hierarchy, subordinate to regular education. As a result, it represents an instance of 'incomplete' professionalisation – the 'cognitive base' of the field is unstandardised, and the profession has failed to secure a monopoly in the service market.

In her analysis of the medical and engineering professions, Larson has derived a set of conditions and structural elements favourable to securing a monopolistic service market. She describes seven structural elements characterising the process of professionalisation (i.e. the process of securing market control) and relates them to conditions favourable to this process. These structural elements include: the nature of the service marketed, the type of market and the type of clientele, the 'cognitive basis' of the profession, the profession's 'production of producers' (i.e. the training of a profession's members), the power relations of the profession (*vis-à-vis* other professions or the state), and a profession's affinity with other professions.

The Nature of the Service Marketed

Larson contends that the 'more salient, universal and less visible' the service market, the more 'favourable' the situation for professionalisation or monopolisation of a particular domain of professional services (Larson, 1977, p. 47). Consider the cases of health and educational services. The medical market very closely approaches these favourable conditions because the 'commodity' of good health is universally appreciated and strived for and medical services have low visibility — that is, they are provided within the privacy of a doctor's office and, generally, are subject neither to lay nor professional review. In contrast to medicine, special education serves a small percentage of individuals whose worth to society is generally calculated in debits rather than credits. The need for special educational services, therefore, is specific rather than universal and often not salient or understood. But special educational services are highly visible. They are provided within institutions open to public scrutiny and often are provided to more than one individual at a time (e.g. to small groups in resource rooms or to entire classes). These services are also subject to more lay review than, for example, medical services, for other reasons. Education has always been broadly conceptualised. As a result, the business of education is considered the responsibility of a wide spectrum of individuals other than educators. Thus, despite educators' efforts to restrict educational activity to their own domain, families and other professionals remain active in educating children. Additionally, local school boards' formulation and monitoring of educational policy and government's increasing role in determining educational policy also insure education's visibility. This lay monitoring and formulating of policy is unusual in medicine, and is probably related to the fact that the medical profession has standardised its cognitive basis; in doing so, it has effectively insulated itself from criticism. One might speculate, therefore, that the medicalisation of special education occurred not only as a result of the field's internal weaknesses and inability to control a market for its services, but also because medicalisation was viewed as a way to improve treatment for the special child, while improving the field's status through adherence to dominant research models and professional practices. That medicalisation resulted in the 'marketing' of more technical and 'mystifying commodities' – less visible and accessible to the lay public – was, most likely, an unintended result of efforts to improve the field's own research and status, not a conscious attempt to mystify.

The Type of Market and Clientele

Measured against Larson's second criterion for professionalisation, special education – in contrast to medicine – again fares poorly. Larson claims that the more universal the need for a particular professional service and the less organised the consumers of this service, the more favourable the conditions for the professionalisation of the service-providing field. The specific and limited need for special educational services has already been described in contrast to the universal need for medical service; what remains to be discussed is the level of consumer organisation within each service arena. In some ways, special children represent an unorganised population and, thus, as the prototypically disorganised patients of medicine do for that field, may facilitate the process of professionalisation. But, despite the fact that children represent a powerless, dependent group in our society, they are still more organised than patient populations, who, generally, are segregated from one another and typically come in contact with non-ill more than with ill individuals. Special children are more organised than patient populations for several reasons, including treatment and advocacy practices. In contrast to patients, special children comprise a more 'integrated' client group – they receive treatment and training together in a variety of agencies and institutions. Additionally, the efforts of advocates and their families, who have been actively challenging educational policy in the courts, contrast with patients, who typically have no advocates and generally are persuaded to conform to doctor's orders by their only potential advocates, their families. Currently, as a result of advocacy efforts, legislation dictates much special educational policy; and does so through the persistent relationship between funding and its stipulated criteria (Magliocca and Stephens, 1980, pp. 23-46; Goldstein, *et al.*, 1975, pp. 4-61). State and local funding for special programming requires schools' compliance with federal legislation, notably federal classificatory schemes developed for the purpose of identifying handicapped students in need of educational services: 'Funding is tied intimately to eligibility criteria, categories, and related labels; difference categories and labels warrant different state subsidies' (Goldstein, *et al.*,

1975, p. 18). In the recent past, federal aid for teacher education in special education was also tied to this classificatory schema, and the Bureau of Education for the Handicapped continues to be 'staffed and organized on the basis of the categories, and departments of special education which are recipients of the aid have mirrored the federal organization' (Goldstein *et al.*, 1975, p. 18). Unfortunately, these classificatory schemes have tended to stigmatise labelled children without necessarily identifying all children in need of service or necessarily leading to improvements in their education, since the schemes focus attention on the identification of handicaps rather than on appropriate educational planning (Magliocca and Stephens, 1980, pp. 23-46), which is left to building level personnel such as teachers and counsellors. Thus, as a result of an organised, politicised clientele (i.e. the efforts of parents and advocates working in conjunction with other professionals, notably lawyers) and federal legislative requirements, much educational decision-making has been placed in an economic rather than educational realm. This is especially the case because of the stringent requirements placed on programming by funding criteria; that is, programming becomes geared to the labels of children identified by federal classificatory schemes for the purpose of service delivery, instead of to their individual learning needs.

The 'Cognitive Basis' of Special Education; the Field's Relationship to Other Professions

Unlike medicine, which benefited from a 'powerful sponsoring elite' (i.e. the federal government), special education increasingly finds itself having to conform to state and federal regulations that constrain educational decision-making. Whereas government sponsorship helped medicine to maintain independence from other markets (as the state sought to protect the public from incompetent members of the professions), special education, through governmental regulation, has been placed in a dependent rather than independent position *vis-à-vis* other professional markets. That special education is currently controlled by regular education, other professions and the state, attests to its state of incomplete professionalisation – particularly its failure to achieve a unified cognitive basis with which to maximise a monopolistic delivery of services. Teacher education and credentialling practices as well as competing theories and paradigms have contributed to the field's lack of cognitive standardisation, and, in Larson's terms, the '[in]attainment of visibly "good results"' (Larson, 1977, p. 47). The field, for example, has relied heavily on psychological theories of behaviour, medical models of diagnosis and treatment, and normative models of teaching. This has resulted in the normative application of clinical teaching (Blatt, 1982, p. 53), an inherently contradictory process, since traditional psychological models of teaching focus on the individual, and normative teaching models employ standardised procedures to realise group goals. As a result, the special child's individual needs are by-passed, while the social context in which he learns is ignored.

The efforts of some special educators to turn special education into a respectable science of behaviour by, for example, embracing such reductionist models of behaviour analysis and treatment and largely ignoring social and educational models, is probably related to their awareness that scientific paradigms can function as legitimising ideologies for professional service. Adhering to the dominant paradigm might, therefore, unify the field and concomitantly improve the status of the profession. According to Larson (1977): 'A scientific basis stamps the professional himself with the legitimacy of a general body of knowledge as a mode of cognition, the epistemological superiority of which is taken for granted in our society' (p. 41).

Incomplete Professionalisation: the Therapeutic Antidote

Failing to standardise its cognitive base and, therefore, its training and credentialling processes, special education has achieved neither autonomy nor a monopoly of services; as a result, it has been regulated from without rather than from within. Instead of competitive divisiveness leading to unification — like the competition characterising the process of professionalisation in medicine — the field has been characterised by competitiveness leading to fragmentation and internal weakness. This has resulted in its domination by regular education, other professions and the state. For example, regular education generally determines the population of special classes by controlling the referral of special children from regular to special classes. Other professions (especially medicine and psychology) provide preventive and rehabilitative care to children by delegating responsibilities to the public schools, so that the schools, in effect, become accountable for the education of children diagnosed by the methods and concerns of other fields. This is particularly the case with children having severe handicaps since their handicaps are generally identified by medical practitioners before entering school and they are placed on treatment regimens often including educational prescriptions, e.g. programmes to improve developmental skills. School-age children who receive medical and psychological attention for handicapping conditions receive therapies that include educational considerations. And government increases the participation of other professions in the provision of special educational services through legislation based on classification systems utilising medical and psychological taxonomies, and through its requirement of multidisciplinary evaluations for the identification and programme placement of handicapped children. Whereas government helped the field of medicine maintain its dominance over other competing professional markets, special education, through government regulation, has been placed in a dependent rather than independent position. And its autonomy has been further weakened by the 'crises of legitimation' experienced by regular education, since, during such crises, special education is placed in the position of absorbing regular education's efforts to explain organisational failure.

I have suggested through a brief discussion using Larson's model that special education has failed to achieve professionalisation, and, as a result, suffers from a lack of autonomy and self-direction. This results from constraints placed on the field by the organisational requirements of regular education (e.g. to reduce the disruption of education for regular, non-handicapped students), by the competing claims of other professions concerning the health and training of special children, and increasingly by federally legislated requirements. The management trends of special education (i.e. behavioural and medical management) previously discussed in this chapter, reflect the influence of other professions on special education and re-emphasise the fact that special education lacks a truly educationally-based perspective in its theory, pragmatic work and professional training. But in defence of the profession, it should be noted that educating special children is considerably complex, and that their medical and psychological concerns are often important considerations in any educational planning. Special education, therefore, is not as easily reduced to a standardised body of knowledge as medicine, which generally focuses on the physical basis of disease. But the necessity of considering medical and psychological factors in the education of special children need not result in the indiscriminate application of other fields' epistemological models. Instead, special education should strive to attain educationally-based curricular and teaching practices. By doing so, the field would address, rather than avoid – through a therapeutic reductionist perspective – the complexity intrinsic to the teaching of special children. Current practices, however, indicate that clinically-based models are prevalent in the field. For this reason, I will briefly re-examine the effect of the therapeutic perspectives of medicine and psychology in special education in order to assess the impact of this therapeutic orientation on the teaching and curricular practices of the field, and the effect of these practices on special children and teachers.

The Medicalisation of Special Education: Treating Individual Disability or Managing Social Pathology?

While differing in diagnostic and treatment philosophies, the fields of medicine, psychology and education share a therapeutic – rather than punitive – orientation towards the management of deviance and disability. In special education this therapeutic orientation is reflected in the presence of medical practitioners within the field, especially paediatricians, neurologists and psychologists, as well as the field's curricular and professional practices – for example, the field's embracing of medical and psychological explanatory models and professional relationships typified by the patient–physician relationship (i.e. professional expert and dependent client). As previously discussed, these models and relationships are predicated on the definition of social problems as illness. The increasing 'medicalisation' of special education is, therefore, a product and reflection of the increasing reliance on therapeutic solutions to social problems conceptually individualised as illness. With the ascendancy of the therapeutic, social pathology is managed as individual disability. Special education, as medicine and psychology, participates in this process of deflection.

Therapeutic Management of the Individual

The field's movement away from segregation and incarceration of special children to integration and 'normalisation' reflects its propensity to categorise the social problems of children as illness. In doing so, it parallels attitudinal and pragmatic changes in other childcare areas, notably the juvenile justice system (Kittrie, 1971; Moran, 1980). This shift in institutional response from punitive to therapeutic has moderated assumptions about the handicapped; disabled individuals no longer are conceptualised as morally degenerate and sinful, but are now thought to be 'ill'. But this change in terminology has not altered the devaluation of the disabled by society. Illness, like degeneracy, implies that an individual has something wrong with him that needs changing. This social labelling of special children as 'ill' simply incorporates characteristics of former labelling of special children as 'bad', while providing a more palatable rendering of their socially disapproved status (Conrad and Schneider, 1980a, pp. 17-37). It provides an example of the increasing incorporation of social-behavioural problems under medical jurisdiction.

Because of their dependent status and continuing focus of professional interest, children comprise a population 'at risk' for medicalisation. This is particularly the case because society views the child as basically innocent and not (totally) responsible for his behaviour, and views the medical profession as essentially 'protective'. These notions of innocence and irresponsibility enhance the chances that childhood 'deviance' will be conceptualised as illness rather than wilful intransigence, since they imply that such children do not wilfully behave in a consciously negative manner. In this context, medical intervention in problems that are of educational consideration becomes more difficult to criticise, since the medicalisation of children's social-behavioural and educational problems locates itself within a general societal trend towards seeking therapeutic solutions to problems.

Management trends represent the pragmatic outcome of defining behavioural and educational problems therapeutically, and conceptualising special children as 'disabled' or 'deviant'. Often they perpetuate such conceptualisations. Along with functionalist social values, the organisational characteristics of management trends 'predict' the need for initial diagnosis and 'control' subsequent treatment, recommending that deviant children require behavioural management and disabled children medical treatment. And once behavioural and medical techniques are established or institutionalised in the social-educational structure, pupils to 'manage' or 'treat' become necessary.

The medical model of diagnosis and treatment and the relationship between physician and patient have been incorporated into special education's curricular practice and management philosophy. For example, extensive testing and retesting, diagnostic-prescriptive teaching and the quantification of data concerning handicapping conditions are common educational practices; furthermore, special children receive individual 'treatment' regimens and programming by expert professionals. Even though parents must agree to the individual education programmes (IEPs) that result from multidisciplinary assessments and conferences, they are often poorly informed or unable to assess critically the diagnostic and intervention procedures culminating in their child's IEP. As a result, they are like patients who are placed in a dependent position to physicians because they are unable to penetrate the technical presentation of information. That medical and behavioural diagnosis and treatment are social as well as scientific enterprises has been amply demonstrated by their respective literatures. A similar awareness of the social basis and import of special educational practices — especially the labelling of special children — is not broadly appreciated, and should be generated and pragmatically applied.

Labelling fosters deviance and disability by its potential to define problems where none may exist and initiate treatment that may not be needed. Deviant students are, often, treated by segregating them from their 'normal' peers. Rather than increasing conformity or normalcy, this practice increases deviant behaviour; through the development of deviant 'world views' and the acquisition of deviant knowledge and skills, students' 'deviant careers' are perpetuated and consolidated. Similarly, the aggregation of disabled children in treatment and educational facilities with concomitant emphasis on their disabilities rather than capabilities, and the differential treatment of special children in mainstream classes, increase their stigma and dependence (Erikson, 1962, p. 16). The propensity of medical specialists to seek out pathology also increases the chances that, once a child is labelled deviant or disabled, his behaviour will be subject to greater scrutiny, enlarging the possibility that additional pathology will be found. (Medical and behavioural intervention itself might cause further disabling behaviour, and result in clinical, social or structural problems (Illich, 1977).) In sum, both informal, everyday responses to deviant and disabled children as well as their more formal interaction with a network of bureaucratic helping organisations and their 'helping' interventions contribute towards the maintenance of special children's deviant status and resulting medical and behavioural management.

In sum, labelling is an integral part of medical and behavioural management, since, without the definitional act of 'diagnosis', further intervention or treatment would be impossible. Defining or treating a child as disabled or deviant directs attention away from the social and structural, since it takes the individual as its unit of concern. As a result, the source of deviant or disabled behaviour is always conceptualised as asocial and individual. By abstracting the individual from the social, social responsibility for producing or perpetuating deviance/disability is absolved. In the educational arena, the use of the medical model to diagnose and treat educational disabilities individualises failure — the disabled student's failure to learn is blamed on himself, his parents or, less frequently, his teacher maintaining the institutional *status quo*. This focus on individual etiology to the exclusion of social factors facilitates a definition of the normal or typical learner necessary for the referral of pupils to special programmes and maintenance of the system's equilibrium.

Institutional Management: Referral

Referral practices comprise another component of management functioning to perpetuate the *status quo*, since they serve to link initial diagnoses with subsequent treatment, with obvious consequences for referred individuals. Referral practices also define professional relationships, particularly relationships of status and power. The referral of special pupils from regular to special teachers is a case in point. These referrals — with their attendant labelling — serve the multifaceted needs of regular education; they organise special services for those needing and not receiving them in the regular classroom, participate in the process of securing federal funding for special programming and help to control the disruption of regular classes by so-called deviant children (Goldstein *et al.*, 1975). But these same labelling and referral procedures — resulting from multidisciplinary committee assessment — increase the marginality and relative lack of autonomy characterising special teachers, since they allow regular teachers to determine special student populations. In this respect they become important socialising factors in special teachers' professional careers, since these practices maintain the marginality of special education within the regular school system. Pupils — through referral and labelling — also lose autonomy because they become part of a process — largely inaccessible to them — that ultimately affects success in later life. That is, through referral and labelling, pupils are 'sorted' as deviant or disabled. This minimises individual differences within classes, fostering pupil 'exchangeability'. This exchangeability, accomplished most obviously through tracking programmes and more subtly through curricular management, facilitates more cost- and time-efficient management.

Curricular Management

In special education, curricular management occurs through individualised programming. The emphasis on individualised programming as an appropriate methodology to accommodate pupil differences and meet legislative requirements for IEPs, in actuality rationalises an isolated, fragmented and asocial approach to teaching. Both student-student and teacher-student relationships are affected by the impersonal and highly specified curricular form of individualised programming, which functions most obviously to minimise social interaction in classrooms. Less apparent is the fact that these curricular forms control and modify student and teacher roles. These programmes are supposedly geared to individual needs, emphasise basic and functional skills and provide a scientific approach to teaching. They replace teacher-designed curricula with carefully tested and standardised units of learning. A student progresses through hierarchically organised skill sequences based on programme pre-test scores. These tests determine which skill sequences he will learn. Post-test scores determine his rate of progress through the curricular programme. Apple (1980) describes the 'tightly controlled curricular form' of these programmes stating that: 'The goals, the process, the outcome and the evaluative criteria for assessing them are defined as precisely as possible by people external to the system' (p. 18). In sum, both teacher 'actions' and student 'responses' are prespecified by the curricular material.

Special — and regular — teachers increasingly receive curricular materials that are total instructional packages. These packages are replete with diagnostic testing for entry into — and exit from — the system and include related remediation materials. Depicted as the answer to the problem of irrelevant diagnostic assessments, these curricula currently enjoy much popularity in the field. To some extent this popularity is warranted, since these materials have attempted to provide educationally relevant testing and teaching materials. For example, these packages relate diagnostic testing to educational programming that focuses on the development of functional skills instead of sensory, intellectual or physical processes; 'promise' student programmes tailored to individual needs; and provide pragmatic instructional approaches that can be 'scientifically' controlled and monitored by teachers. But, despite these claims, care should be exercised before wholeheartedly embracing these seemingly 'can do no harm' diagnostic-prescriptive programmes, and their goals and educational relevance should be questioned. While such an individualised programme may be ideal in its abstract form, instructional methodology must be assessed within a pragmatic context, since it is within this context that the business of education occurs.

Despite the appearance of individualised programming — for example, there are multilevel skill sequences that are developmentally patterned — these curricular packages still ignore individual styles of learning because of their rigidly drawn diagnostic-prescriptive relationships. Additionally, these programmes are often utilised in such a manner that even their potential for individualising instruction is precluded. In classes where special children are still categorically labelled, placed in classes on the basis of these labels and then normatively taught, the same curricular material is used to achieve differing instructional goals.

In addition to not meeting stated goals for individualising instruction, these programmes' emphasis on basic and functional skills serves to track students and narrow their life options, since successive years of such curricular programming make entry into higher level curricular tracks nearly impossible. (After a number of years in a basic curricular track, a student no longer has the necessary curricular prerequisites for more academically-orientated tracks.) Such curricular tracking is rationalised by the 'science' of diagnostic testing. And remediation, which follows logically from this testing, becomes difficult to question, when the entire diagnostic-prescriptive process is insulated from criticism by its recourse to scientific authority. Besides 'sorting' students, these programmes isolate students from one another and fragment the learning process. By emphasising skill learning, they equate the acquisition of knowledge with the process of mastering small units of information. For example, in reading laboratories equipped with individualised programming units, students may come to associate reading with the mastery of skill sequences — reading for the main idea, for details or for inferences. In this context, reading becomes a process of acquiring pragmatic reading skills in order to become an efficient learner instead of being an integrated, meaningful process that is an end unto itself (Apple, 1980, p. 23).

Individualised programming, the logical accompaniment to pupil sorting, also works to the detriment of teachers. Because curricular management succeeds relative to its degree of standardisation, functioning best with homogeneous populations and the absence of teacher 'judgement', it 'deskills' teachers while it 'sorts' pupils (Apple, 1980, pp. 14-19). The teacher as expert is replaced by the teacher as technician, and a lower-echelon managerial role is substituted for previous curricular and developmental responsibilities. In this role, teacher judgement concerning pupil needs and instruction is precluded and former decision-making and knowledge are replaced by managerial functions that place priority on behavioural control and the smooth operation of the instructional system. Individualised programming facilitates behavioural control because group identity of students is difficult to achieve — students work independently of one another and interact, minimally, with teachers. In addition to student isolation, these programmes foster teacher isolation and alienation, since teachers' knowledge becomes irrelevant to meeting daily work demands, and professional communication (e.g. the discussion of curricular and behavioural concerns) is largely unnecessary after initial implementation of the programme. This isolation weakens professional development because it reduces and 'trivialises' teacher autonomy — the teacher may control his classroom but the control he exercises is largely predetermined by standardised curricular materials which, according to Apple (1980), 'encod[e] technical control into the very basis of the curricular form itself' (p. 20).

The process of stratifying students and teachers begins with professional diagnostic evaluations and finds its logical conclusion in the remediation of individualised programming. Diagnostic evaluations contribute towards stratifying students because the specialised knowledge of professionals necessarily results in the differentiation of individuals (Blatt, 1982, p. 52), and subsequent professional recommendations often specify educational considerations that become the school's responsibility to effect (see previous discussions of labelling and referral practices). These proposed treatments in the form of individualised programmes further stratify teachers because they are again placed in a subordinate position to others — the need for remediation is recommended by other professionals, and the remediation material designed by publishing houses. Thus special teachers have little autonomy to determine whom, what or how they will teach.

The labelling of students and de-skilling of teachers is partially rationalised by the acceptance of a clinical perspective within the field. This perspective has enabled the field to establish a high degree of pupil systematisation and teacher accountability — practices having more import for special administrators than teachers. The emphasis on individualised programming has been accepted because it has generally been thought to be the most effective and 'efficient' method to compensate for differences in handicapped children in order to bring them as close as possible to 'normality'. This preference for the most efficient method has occurred at the expense of clear conceptualisations of the field's role. By elevating the rehabilitative ideal and championing the 'right to treatment', special educators have, knowingly or unknowingly, elevated the role of the professional who provides and measures treatment at the expense of the special individual's freedom of choice. Additionally, the clinical orientation of the field has contributed to the stigmatisation of pupils, through labelling and tracking practices, and to the de-skilling of teachers, through application of the clinical diagnostic method to teaching. More significantly, this orientation has functioned to individualise failure by its focus on individual expressions of defect.

It is interesting, therefore, that individualised programming still continues to be described as 'pedagogically radical' in special educational literature (Chandler and Utz, 1982, p. 56). Even more interesting is regular education's incorporation of individualised programming with its emphasis on basic skills, a diagnostic-prescriptive format and behavioural management, since the practices and philosophy of special education have, generally, been anathema to regular education. During the early years of special classes, special educators suggested that their classes serve as 'testing laboratories' in which to develop new educational methods for teaching children. Their offer was not readily accepted, and both historically and currently, despite mainstreaming, communication between special and regular educators remains minimal (Sarason and Doris, 1979, p. 265).

It is ironic, therefore, that special education has come to illuminate educational and societal values concerning acceptable and non-acceptable pedagogical practice, and the typical and untypical learner. As a crystallisation of the unacceptable, special education defines the acceptable and demonstrates evolving educational ideology — the techniques and practices of the field are increasingly used in regular education. A need exists, therefore, to analyse the practices and trends of special education from a perspective other than the usual structural-functionalist one, moving beyond, for example, an uncritical acceptance of the field's clinical orientation. This is necessary for a more accurate sense of what is occuring in the field itself, as well as to broaden understanding of the processes of regular education, especially in relation to societal values.

References

Alonzo, A.A. (1979) 'Everyday illness behavior: a situational approach to health status deviations', *Social Science and Medicine, 13A*, 397-404.

Anspack, R.R. (1979) 'From stigma to identity politics: Political activism among the physically disabled and former mental patients', *Social Science and Medicine*, 765-73.

Apple, M. (1980) 'Curriculum form and the logic of technical control: Building the possessive individual' in L. Barton, R. Meighan and S. Walker (eds.), *Schooling, Ideology and the Curriculum*, The Falmer Press, Brighton, England, 11-27.

Becker, H. (1964) *The Other Side: Perspectives on Deviance*, The Free Press of Glencoe, London.

Bendix, R. (1956) *Work and Authority in Industry: Ideologies of Management in the Course of Industrialization*, Wiley, New York.

Berger, P.L. and Luckman, T. (1967) *The Social Construction of Reality: A Treatise in the Sociology of Knowledge*, Doubleday and Co., New York.

Blatt, B. (1982) 'On the heels of psychology', *Journal of Learning Disabilities, 15*, 1, 52-3.

Bledstein, B.J. (1978) *The Culture of Professionalism: The Middle Class and the Development of Higher Education in America*, W.W. Norton and Co., New York.

Bucher, R. and Strauss, A. (1976) 'Professions in Process' in M. Hammersley and P. Woods (eds.), *The Process of Schooling: A Sociological Reader*, Routledge and Kegan Paul, London, 19-26.

Burrello, L.C. and Sage, D.D. (1979) *Leadership and Change in Special Education*, Prentice-Hall, Englewood Cliffs, NJ.

Carlson, R. (1975) *The End of Medicine*, Wiley, New York.

Castel, R., Castel, F. and Lovell, A. (1982) *The Psychiatric Society* (trans) Goldhammer, A., Columbia University Press, New York.

Chandler, H.N. and Utz, V.R. (1982) 'Special education and the education administrator: An uneasy alliance', *Journal of Learning Disabilities, 15*, 1, 54-6.

Collins, R. (1974) *The Credential Society: An Historical Sociology of Education and Stratification*, Academic Press, New York.

Conrad, P. (1975) 'The discovery of hyperkinesis: Notes on the medicalization of deviant behavior', *Social Problems, 23*, 1, 12-21.

—— (1976) *Identifying Hyperactive Children: The Medicalization of Deviant Behavior*, D.C. Heath and Co., Lexington, Mass.

—— and Schneider, J.W. (1978) 'Medicine' in J.S. Roucek (ed.), *Social Control for the 1980s: A Handbook for Order in a Democratic Society*, Greenwood Press, Westport, Ct.

—— and —— (1980a) *Deviance and Medicalization: From Badness to Sickness*, C.V. Mosby Co., St Louis, Mo.

—— and —— (1980b) 'Looking at levels of medicalization: A comment on Strong's critique of the thesis of medical imperialism', *Social Science and Medicine, 14A*, 75-9.

Cousins, N. (1979) *Anatomy of an Illness: As Perceived by the Patient*, W.W. Norton and Co., New York.

Cromwell, R.L., Blashfield, R.K. and Strauss, J.S. (1975) 'Criteria for classification systems' in N. Hobbs (ed.), *Issues in the Classification of Children, 1*, 4-25.

Davis, N.J. (1975) *Sociological Constructions of Deviance: Perspectives and Issues in the Field*, Wm. C. Brown Company Publishers, Dubuque, Ia.

Donzelot, J. (1979) *The Policing of Families*, Pantheon Books, New York.

Edgerton, R.B. (1967) *The Cloak of Competence*, University of California Press, Berkeley, California.

Eisenberg, M.G., Griggins, C. and Duval, R.J. (eds.) (1982) *Disabled People as Second Class Citizens*, Springer Publishing Co., New York.

Erikson, K.T. (1962) 'Notes on the sociology of deviance', *Social Problems, 9*, 307-14.

Fabrega, Jr., H. (1979) 'The ethnography of illness', *Social Science and Medicine, 13A*, 565-76.

Fass, P.S. (1980) 'The IQ: A cultural and historical framework', *American Journal of Education*, August 1980, 431-58.

Figlio, K. (1978) 'Chlorosis and chronic disease in nineteenth century Britain and the social constitution of somatic illness in a capitalist society', *Social History, 3*, 167-97.

Fox, R.C. (1977) 'The medicalization and demedicalization of American society' in J.H. Knowles (ed.), *Doing Better and Feeling Worse: Health in the U.S.*, W.W. Norton and Co., New York.

Frampton, M.E. and Rowell, H.G. (1938) *Education of the Handicapped*, vol. I, World Book Company, New York.

Freidson, E. (1965) 'Disability as social deviance' in M.B. Sussman (ed.), *Sociology and Rehabilitation*, American Sociological Association in co-operation with the Vocational Rehabilitation Administration, Washington DC, 71-99.

—— (1970a) *Professional Dominance: the Social Structure of Medical Care*, Atherton, New York.

—— (1970b) *The Profession of Medicine*, Dodd Mead, New York.
—— and Lorber, J. (1972) *Medical Men and their Work*, Aldine/Atherton, New York.
Freire, P. (1968) *Pedagogy of the Oppressed*, The Seaburg Press, New York.
Gartner, A. and Riessman, F. (1977) *Self-help in the Human Services*, Jossey-Bass, San Francisco.
Gerson, E.M. (1976) 'The social character of illness: Deviance or politics', *Social Science and Medicine, 10*, 219-24.
Glassner, B. (1979) *Clinical Sociology*, Longman, New York.
Goffman, E. (1963) *Stigma: Notes on the Management of Spoiled Identity*, Prentice-Hall, Englewood Cliffs, NJ.
—— (1968) *Asylums: Essays on the Social Situation of Mental Patients and other Inmates*, Aldine Publishing Co., New York.
Goldstein, H., Arkell, C., Asheroft, S.C., Hurley, O.L. and Lilly, M.S. (1975) 'Schools' in N. Hobbs (ed.), *Issues in the Classification of Children*, vol. 2, Jossey-Bass, San Francisco.
Goldstein, M.S. (1979) 'The sociology of mental health and illness' in *The Annual Review of Sociology*, vol. V, 381-409.
Gove, W.R. (ed.) (1980) *The Labelling of Deviance: Evaluating a Perspective*, Sage Publications, Beverly Hills, California, 7-33, 111-75 and 381-408.
Gusfield, J.R. (1967) 'Moral passage: The symbolic process in public definitions of deviance', *Social Problems, 15*, 175-88.
Hargreaves, D., Hester, S. and Mellor, F. (1975) *Deviance in Classrooms*, Routledge and Kegan Paul, London.
Hobbs, N. (ed.) (1975) *Issues in the Classification of Children*, 2 vols., Jossey-Bass, San Francisco.
Hummel, R.P. (1982) *The Bureaucratic Experience*, St Martin's Press, New York.
Hurder, W.P. (1970) *Overview of Research and Education of Handicapped Children: The U.S.A. in the Sixties*, University of Illinois Press, Illinois.
Idler, E.L. (1979) 'Definitions of health and illness and medical sociology', *Social Science and Medicine, 13A*, 723-31.
Illich, I. (1971) *Deschooling Society*, Harper and Row, New York.
—— (1975) *Medical Nemesis: The Expropriation of Health*, Pantheon Press, New York.
——, Zola, Irving K., McKnight, J., Capias, J. and Spiaiken, H. (1977) *Disabling Professions*, Marion Boyars, London.
Ingleby, D. (ed.) (1980) *Critical Psychiatry: The Politics of Mental Health*, Pantheon Books, New York.
Jaco, E.G. (ed.) (1958) *Patients, Physicians, and Illness: Sourcebook in Behavioural Science and Medicine*, The Free Press, New York.
Kass, L.R. (1975) 'Regarding the end of medicine and the pursuit of health', *The Public Interest, 40*, 11-42.
Katz, M.B. (1968) *The Irony of Early School Reform: Educational Innovation in Mid-nineteenth Century Massachusetts*, Beacon Press, Boston, Mass.
Kauffman, J.M. (1981) 'Introduction: historical trends and contemporary issues in special education in the U.S.' in J.M. Kauffman and D.P. Hallahan (eds.), *Handbook of Special Education*, Prentice-Hall, Englewood Cliffs, NJ, 3-23.
—— and Hallahan, D.P. (1981) *Handbook of Special Education*, Prentice-Hall, Englewood Cliffs, NJ.
Kazdin, A.E. (1978) *History of Behavior Modification: Experimental Foundations of Contemporary Research*, University Park Press, Baltimore, Md.
Kirp, D.L., Kuriloff, P.J. and Buss, W.G. (1975) 'Legal mandates and organizational change' in N. Hobbs (ed.), *Issues in the Classification of Children*, vol. 2, 386-431.

Kittrie, N. (1971) *The Right to be Different*, Johns Hopkins Press, Baltimore, Md.

Knowles, J.H. (ed.) (1977) *Doing Better and Feeling Worse: Health in the United States*, W.W. Norton and Co., New York.

Larson, M.S. (1977) *The Rise of Professionalism: A Sociological Analysis*, University of California Press, Berkeley, California.

Lefton, M., Skipper, K.J. and McCaghy, D.H. (1968) *Approaches to Deviance: Theories, Concepts and Research Findings*, Appleton-Century Crofts, New York.

Lemert, E.M. (1967) *Human Deviance, Social Problems, and Social Control*, Prentice-Hall, Englewood Cliffs, NJ.

Levine, S. and Kozloff, M.A. (1978) 'The sick role: assessment and overview', *Annual Review of Sociology*, 4, 317-43.

Lorber, J. (1967) 'Deviance as Performance: The case of illness', *Social Problems*, *XIV*, 302-10.

Magliocca, L.A. and Stephens, T.M. (1980) 'Child identification or child inventory? A critique of the federal design of child-identification systems implemented under PL94-142', *Journal of Special Education*, *14*, 23-36.

Mercer, J.R. (1973) *Labeling the Mentally Retarded: Clinical and Social Systems Perspectives on Mental Retardation*, University of California Press, Berkeley, California.

—— (1975) 'Psychological assessment and the rights of children' in N. Hobbs (ed.), *Issues in the Classification of Children*, vol. 1.

—— (1978-9) 'Test, "validity", "bias", and "fairness": An analysis from the perspective of the sociology of knowledge', *Interchange*, 9, no. 1.

Merton, R.K. (1957) *Social Theory and Social Structure*, Free Press, New York.

Mills, C.W. (1943) 'The professional ideology of social pathologists', *The American Journal of Sociology*, University of Chicago Press, Berkeley, Chicago, Illinois.

—— (1959) *The Sociological Imagination*, Oxford University Press, Oxford.

Milofsky, C. (1976) *Special Education: A Sociological Study of California Programs*, Praeger Publications, New York.

Moran, R. (1980) 'The search for the born criminal and the medical control of criminality' in P. Conrad and J. Schneider (eds.), *Deviance and Medicalization: From Badness to Sickness*, C.V. Mosby Co., St Louis, Mo.

Nasaw, D. (1981) *Schooled to Order: A Social History of Public Schooling in the U.S.* Oxford University Press, Oxford.

Navarro, V. (1975a) 'The industrialization of fetishism or the fetishism of industrialization: A critique of Ivan Illich', *Social Science and Medicine*, 9, 351-63.

—— (1975b) 'The political economy of medical care: an explanation of the composition, nature and function of the present health sector of the U.S.', *International Journal of Health Services*, 5, 1, 65-94.

—— (1976) *Medicine under Capitalism*, Neale Watson Academic Publisher, New York.

Olneck, M.R. (1979) 'The IQ meritocracy reconsidered: Cognitive skill and adult success in the United States', *American Journal of Education*, *88*, 1.

Parsons, T. (1951) *The Social System*, The Free Press, New York.

—— (1975) 'The sick role and the role of the physician reconsidered', *Health and Society*, Summer, 257-77.

Persell, C.H. (1977) *Education and Inequality*, The Free Press, New York.

Pflanz, M. and Rhode, J.I. (1970) 'Illness: Deviant behavior or conformity', *Social Science and Medicine*, 4, 453-65.

Phillips, L., Draguns, G. and Bartlett, D.P. (1975) 'Classification of behavior disorders' in N. Hobbs (ed.), *Issues in the Classification of Children*, vol. 1, Jossey-Bass, San Francisco, 26-55.

Platt, A. (1969) *Child Savers: The Invention of Delinquency*, University of Chicago Press, Chicago, Illinois.

Rains, P.M., Kitsuse, J.J., Duster, T. and Freidson, E. (1975) 'The labeling approach to deviance' in N. Hobbs (ed.), *Issues in the Classification of Children*, vol. 1, Jossey-Bass, San Francisco, 88-100.

Reiff, P. (1966) *The Triumph of the Therapeutic*, Harper and Row, New York.

Reisman, J.M. (1976) *A History of Clinical Psychology*, Irvington Publishers, New York.

Robinson, D. (1971) *The Process of Becoming Ill*, Routledge and Kegan Paul, London.

Rosen, M., Clark, G.R. and Kivitz, S. (eds.) (1976) *The History of Mental Retardation: Collected papers*, vols. 1 and 2, University Park Press, Baltimore, Md.

Rosengren, W.P. (1980) *Sociology of Medicine: Diversity, Conflict and Change*, Harper and Row, New York.

Rothman, D.T. (1971) *The Discovery of the Asylum: Social Order and Disorder in the New Republic*, Little, Brown and Company, Boston, Mass.

Ryan, W. (1976) *Blaming the Victim*, Vintage Books, St Paul, Minn.

Sailor, W., Wilcox, B. and Brown, L. (1980) *Methods of Instruction for Severely Handicapped Students*, Paul H. Brookes Publishing Co., Bakersfield, CA.

Sarason, S.B. and Doris, J. (1979) *Educational Handicap, Public Policy and Social History*, MacMillan, New York.

Schur, E. (1971) *Labeling Deviant Behavior*, Harper and Row, New York.

Scott, R.A. (1969) *The Making of Blind Men: A Study of Adult Socialization*, Russell Sage Foundation, New York.

—— and Douglas, J.D. (eds.) (1972) *Theoretical Perspectives on Deviance*, Basic Books, New York.

Scroufe, A.J. and Stewart, M. (1973) 'Treating problem children with stimulant drugs', *New England Journal of Medicine*, *289*, 407-21.

Siegel, E. and Gold, R.F. (1982) *Educating the Learning Disabled*, Macmillan Publishing Co., New York.

Smith, M.L. (1982) *How Educators Decide who is Learning Disabled: Challenge to Psychology and Public Policy in the Schools*, Charles C. Thomas, Springfield, Illinois.

Sontag, S. (1977) *Illness as Metaphor*, Random House, New York.

Spector, M. and Kitsuse, J.I. (1977) *Constructing Social Problems*, Cummings Publishing Co., Mento Park, California.

Spring, J.H. (1972) *Education and the Rise of the Corporate State*, Beacon Press, Boston, Mass.

Strong, P.M. (1979) 'Sociological imperialism and the profession of medicine', *Social Science and Medicine*, *13A*, 199-215.

Sussman, M.B. (ed.) *Sociology and Rehabilitation*, American Sociological Association, Washington DC.

Szasz, T.S. (1970) *Ideology and Insanity: Essays on the Psychiatric Dehumanization of Man*, Doubleday and Company, New York.

Tomlinson, S. (1981) *Educational Subnormality: A Study in Decision-making*, Routledge and Kegan Paul, London.

—— (1982) *A Sociology of Special Education*, Routledge and Kegan Paul, London.

Tuckett, D. (1976) *An Introduction to Medical Sociology*, Tavistock Publications, London.

Vollmer, H.M. and Mills, D.L. (eds.) (1966) *Professionalization*, Prentice-Hall, Englewood Cliffs, NJ.

Waitzkin, H. and Waterman, B. (1977) *The Exploitation of Illness in Capitalist Society*, Bobbs-Merrill Educational Publishing, Indianapolis.

Weintraub, F.J., Abeson, A., Ballard, J. and LaVor, M.L. (eds.) (1977) *Public Policy and the Education of Exceptional Children*, The Council for Exceptional Children, Reston, Virginia.

Whitt, H.P., Meile, R.L. and Larson, L.M. (1979) 'Illness role theory, the labelling perspective and the social meanings of mental illness: An empirical test', *Social Science and Medicine, 13A*, 656-66.

Williams, J.I. (1971) 'Illness as deviance', *Social Science and Medicine, 13A*, 219-26.

Wolfensberger, W. (1972) *The Principle of Normalization in Human Services*, National Institute on Mental Retardation, Toronto, Canada.

Ysseldyke, J.E. and Algozzine, B. (1983) 'LD or Not LD: That's not the question', *Journal of Learning Disabilities, 16*, 1, 29-31.

Zola, I.K. (1972) 'Medicine as an institution of social control', *The Sociological Review, 20*, 487-504.

—— (1975) 'In the name of health and illness: On some socio-political consequences of medical influences', *Social Science and Medicine, 9*, 83-7.

5 THE ROLE OF THE EDUCATIONAL PSYCHOLOGIST IN THE POST-WARNOCK ERA
John Quicke

The main aim of this chapter is to make an assessment of the contribution of the educational psychologist (EP) to special educational practices. The enterprise arises from a consideration of the changing role of the EP from a rather narrowly conceived assessment/special treatment role to one where, in addition to this, more practical educational advice is required in relation to his/her recommendations in the ordinary school setting. This development in the role is in line with the spirit if not the actual recommendations of the Warnock Report, and the Education Act 1981, with their emphasis on the 'broader concept of special education' and normalisation, and is a direction which the profession itself has regarded as both positive and necessary.

My contention is that, despite the rhetoric of integration and normalisation, special educational needs are still largely defined in a way which involves relying on concepts from the traditional educational psychology paradigm, with the result that a genuinely alternative perspective on special needs has not emerged.

The Educational Psychologist and Special Education

The traditional role of the educational psychologist has been to provide an assessment of educational need to assist local authorities to allocate resources under the provisions of the various Education Acts in a way that was seen to be socially just. The knowledge and skills of the EP were exactly what was required by the architects of Fabian social policy. If, in the words of George and Wilding (1976, p. 132), 'The needs of the retarded child are greater than the needs of the normal child, just as those of the disabled are greater than those of the physically fit', then someone has to establish the criteria of need (when is a child retarded?) in a manner which could stand up to public scrutiny. This role of the EP was emphasised in the Warnock Report which recognised three kinds of contributions from this group in relation to the discovery of and assessment of special needs:

(a) their specialized knowledge of observation techniques and assessment procedures which would help teachers with school based assessments (b) involvement with assessment of children with special needs at a more advanced stage of the assessment process and (c) involvement with the monitoring of whole age groups of children at different stages during their school life (para. 14.7).

Although, at the time of writing, the role of the EP in special education selection procedures is not mandatory, there have been enough suggestions in Government circulars and recent legislation to indicate to local authorities the necessity of involving EPs in these procedures. Prior to Warnock, Circular 2/75 suggested procedures for the discovery, diagnosis and assessment of children with special needs which indicated that recommendations for special educational treatment should not be made by a medical officer but by an educationalist – in most cases an educational psychologist. EPs welcomed the new special educational forms because of the change of emphasis from 'handicap' to special educational needs and because the EP would be given more responsibility for assessment. Another circular, 3/74, issued by the Department of Education and Science (DES), the Department of Health and Social Security (DHSS) and the Welsh Office advocated a network of Child Guidance Services, which included official recognition of the School Psychological Service as an independent organisation with its own premises. Finally, the Education Act 1981 refers to 'psychological advice' in its Schedules: (2) Without prejudice to the generality of sub-paragraph (1) about regulations made under that sub-paragraph, shall require the local education authority to seek medical, psychological and educational advice and such other advice as may be prescribed' (Schedule 1, para. 1).

What was it about the knowledge and skills of EPs which appealed to policy-makers? Generally, it should be remembered that the two largest and 'newest' groups of children with special educational needs, namely those with 'learning difficulties' and 'emotional and behavioural disorders' were both, in the British educational system, mainly construed in educational/psychological rather than psychiatric/medical terms and it was educational psychology that provided the technology to enable these needs to be readily defined so that they could be 'objectively' identified. The allegedly 'neutral', 'objective' and value free concepts and measuring instruments of the EP have served a vital function for the system by bringing a semblance of order and rationality to a potentially chaotic and contentious area. It is no exaggeration that the development of special education, in the broadest sense of the term, was not only assisted by but in large part made possible by the EPs' technology.

It is thus probably no coincidence that the growth of the School Psychological Service was related to the gradual implementation of the 1944 Act with respect to special provision particularly for the educationally subnormal (ESN) and maladjusted. The rapid increase in the profession, for example, in the 1960s coincided with what Warnock (1978) describes as the 'revival of the idea of special education provision *in the ordinary school*' (p. 34), since this was where most children with learning difficulties and behavioural and emotional disorders were located. Educational psychologists were there to offer advice when

> the completion of the reorganization of all-age schools in the 1960's and the progressive ending of selection for secondary education which followed the issue of Circular 10/65 enabled ordinary primary and secondary schools to broaden their educational programmes and to take greater account of children's needs (Warnock, 1978, p. 34).

On a more contemporary note, there is some evidence of the expansion of some School Psychological Services in the wake of the 1981 Act, although at the time of writing the picture is not a clear one.

The Changing Context of Practice

Thus EPs have become established as an integral part of special educational structures. However, these structures and thus the role of the EP have been altering in subtle ways in recent years. The traditional assessment/special treatment role is still important, but 'good' practice in educational psychology is now perceived as more expansive than this. In special education there is clearly a new mood afoot. Although ideas like integration and normalisation have been around for some time, recent proposals have provided a much more explicit indication that, as far as possible, special educational needs should be met by modifying educational processes in the ordinary school. To most EPs this makes good sense. Merely slotting children into pigeon holes corresponding to the various handicaps, and packing them off to special schools, units or classes where they are 'dealt' with by allegedly specialist teachers has at best been regarded as but one (and by no means the most important) aspect of their role and at worst as a process which ultimately has negative consequences for the children concerned. For every child seen by an EP who requires a handicap label for administrative purposes, there are, in any case, probably five other referrals who certainly have unmet 'needs', and for whom the EP, if he/she is doing his/her job properly, should make practical suggestions as to how these might be met in the ordinary school.

An important corollary of this is that to be effective the EP must have direct access to the teachers in whose classes the pupils concerned will spend most of their time. Thus, the official view of the Association of Educational Psychologists (AEP) has been that the role of the EP involves an important advisory function, in addition to the traditional assessment and disposal role. Although there was much in Warnock of which the AEP approved, it was critical of the Committee's lack of appreciation of the functions of local authority psychological services. In particular the AEP rejected para. 4.62 which proposed that responsibility for special educational procedures should be delegated to the proposed Special Education Advisory and Support Services, on the grounds that this would provide additional and unnecessary 'link-personnel' between EPs and teacher colleagues (see AEP, 1978).

Such altered circumstances have produced something of a crisis in the practice of educational psychology. Clearly, a great deal of what went on under the traditional model was not appropriate, but what alternatives were available? At the risk of over-simplification, one might suggest that there were basically two different types of response by EPs: one of which involved a rejection of the paradigm on which the traditional model was based, and thus of an important source of legitimation for special education; and another which involved a less radical, more adaptive approach to change. The two responses are based on different sorts of critiques of this paradigm.

The Reconstructionist Critique

This takes several forms, but all have in common the criticism of educational psychology that as a discipline it is rooted in a positivist and individualist paradigm. This epistemological basis is most clearly demonstrated by the categories of ESN and Maladjusted which in traditional practice are premised on descriptions of disability which are already 'contaminated' by social factors, even though this is not acknowledged. The 'variables' of disability and social environment (including educational environment) are not, it is argued, analytically distinct as implied in many of the experimental and observational child development studies, and educational research studies carried out under the auspices of the traditional positivist/individualist paradigm (psychometrics is, of course, an important exemplar of this paradigm in action). Reconstructionists make the point that so-called 'within child' factors are not strictly speaking possessed by the child on his/her entrance to the social world but are always and already social, since they have been constructed from the beginning and indeed before the beginning of an individual's life by socio-cultural processes.

Of course, not all traditional EPs espouse every last premise of the philosophy on which their subject is founded, nor do they always use knowledge from this paradigm. But generally they would agree:

1. that it is possible to make theory-free observations and express these in a neutral scientific language, i.e. positivism;
2. that explanations of educational practices in the final analysis entail references to individuals as entities abstracted from society and possessing 'properties' or characteristics in which social phenomena are ultimately grounded.

The starting-point, therefore, of a reconstructed psychological practice is that the various categories of special educational need should be seen as socially constructed forms. There is some evidence in the recent literature (see DECP, 1976) that this is regarded by some EPs as a useful alternative perspective. The practice that has evolved from this lays great emphasis on the role of the EP in deviant labelling and the unintended consequences of psychological intervention. It is also a practice which challenges conventional definitions of 'handicap' and accepts the necessity for 'negotiating' definitions in the school context. Such negotiations are based on the notion that teachers and pupils are intentional social actors operating within a milieu of socially generated constraints, as indeed are EPs.

Such a perspective has, potentially at any rate, a certain appeal for EPs because it is obviously relevant to the concern to communicate directly with classroom teachers. It provides a rationale for handling 'problems', particularly in the area of prevention, and illuminates the social processes in which all participants are embedded. However, it would be wrong to claim that this has been a popular response. A more typical reaction has been that derived from the second type of criticism.

The Practitioner Critique

The main thrust of this is that the traditional paradigm represents knowledge which could be useful but which has never been properly applied to educational and psychological practice. Educational psychologists have been caught in a vicious circle which has been to no one's advantage — psychologist, teacher, child nor parent. Certain aspects of their knowledge, for example, psychometrics, have provided the 'tools' for the assessment and disposal role in relation to special education. They are now expected to give tests even when this is not appropriate, because this is 'what psychologists do'. The rest of their traditional knowledge is underused and therefore underdeveloped in its application to education (see several chapters in Gillham, 1978).

The pragmatic concerns, however, of practitioners (i.e. practising educational psychologists) have been changing, mainly as a result of developments in the way special education is being conceived. For various reasons, the current emphasis is on a role that involves developing intervention strategies more directly useful to the class teacher in the ordinary school. In pursuit of this, time spent giving an individual intelligence tests is at best of marginal use only and at worst time totally wasted. The EP now is much more concerned with developing that part of the traditional knowledge which can provide concepts, techniques and data which will enable him/her to put forward constructive and helpful proposals for changes in an ordinary classroom context. An example of this would be the resurrection of behaviourist learning theory as a rationale for remedial and behaviour modification programmes, and the use of humanistic psychology in dealings with teachers.

Both behavioural and humanistic psychology appeal because they can be seen as a legitimate part of the EP's traditional knowledge. They both claim to be 'scientific' (some doubts may be raised about humanistic psychology, but one of the leading gurus, Carl Rogers, places his psychology firmly in the positivist camp (see Rogers, 1961, p. 367)), and both are individualist in orientation. At the same time they offer more scope for exploration and investigation in the classroom context, even though neither operate against a sociologically adequate model of this context.

It is clear from this brief description that these two types of criticism are markedly different. The first is a fundamentalist critique of the dominant paradigm of practice, i.e. a critique of the very nature of the psychology which the EP is trying to deliver to schools, whilst the second is more to do with practical concerns, i.e. *how* to deliver this psychology in new circumstances rather than the question of whether it's worth delivering at all.

With the above considerations in mind an empirical study was carried out with the aim of illuminating the developing role of the EP in the present context. The question posed was did the way EPs construct their social practices represent a radical paradigm change or were they merely adapting to circumstances in a way which left the traditional paradigm intact?

An Interview Study

The empirical study involved in-depth interviews with a number of EPs (N = 10) who worked in a School Psychological Service in a mixed urban/ rural area in the north of England.

A probing interview technique was adopted, which, in style, would perhaps best be characterised as somewhere between the focused inter- view employed originally by R.K. Merton and more recently by the Newsons (1976), and the Kinsey model of the 'prosecuting lawyer rather than faceless and inoffensive social researcher' (see Ackroyd and Hughes, 1981). Such a technique is recommended for researchers who already 'know' the situation and have made some prior analysis of the social processes in which the subjects have been involved. The subjects were willing to participate and were extremely loquacious. Sometimes, when not being closely questioned, they spoke for several minutes with- out interruption. Most of them clearly enjoyed speaking about their work and, although their practitioner 'philosophies' were often some- what confused, the initial assumption that they would see themselves as responding to changing circumstances was borne out. The first strik- ing aspect of the interview responses was that most of these EPs were extremely cautious and uneasy about some of the more publicised aspects of their role and were clearly aware of many of the criticisms. This 'sensitivity' has also been noted by Tomlinson (1981):

> This uneasiness with the present system may stem from the kind of
> person who is selected to train as an educational psychologist. If, as
> the Summerfield Committee suggested, selection procedures look for
> 'sensitive' people, younger psychologists in particular are not likely
> to be dogmatic people readily accepting classificatory schemes and
> rigid procedures (p. 177).

These EPs were certainly young (under 40), critical of rigid proced- ures and possessed ideals to which they attempted to adhere. What most of them prized was what the AEP regarded as a crucial aspect of the 'broader' role of the EP, namely access to teachers which enabled them to influence the way children and 'problems' were defined in schools and classrooms, so that they could perhaps facilitate changes in attitudes, perceptions and behaviours of teachers.

One of the undoubted strengths shown by many of the EPs in this study was the ability to see through hypocrisy and rhetoric and to focus on the need for everyone concerned, including teachers, to 'face up to the situation'. Most were not particularly impressed with in-service training courses as traditionally defined, because they did not by and large help teachers tackle problems in the particular contexts in which they arose. Teachers required support and advice at the point of action, not in some remote academic or non-school setting. Similarly, if organisational changes did not result in 'real' changes in attitudes and behaviour, then they were worthless.

However, although some of these EPs referred to influences from labelling theory and sociology, it was doubtful if they were in fact working from a genuinely reconstructed knowledge base. The guiding influence of the traditional paradigm was not always obvious from their statements and observations, but was nevertheless still there as an important backdrop to practice. This will be demonstrated by an analysis of their responses to questions about the sorts of knowledge they used in practice. Most respondents drew a distinction between 'common sense' and 'knowledge from research and psychological theory'. Clearly the former was used frequently, but most emphasised that the latter did play a definite role in their practice. Some felt that it had helped to mould their personal conceptual frameworks. Their responses will be discussed under three headings relating to crucial issues and perspectives in modern psychological practice: the role of psychometrics, behaviouralism and non-directiveness.

Psychometrics

Although most of these EPs were critical of tests — particularly the traditional intelligence test — this did not imply that they did not use tests occasionally or that they were fundamentally opposed to the principles and practices of intelligence and abilities testing. Even if they were not used quantitatively, tests like the Wechsler or Stanford Binet or the British Ability Scales provided an interview structure which most of the EPs felt enabled them to 'get the feel' of a child or to establish rapport so that the rest of the examination would result in exchanges between psychologist and child that the former found useful. As one interviewee (psychologist H) put it:

I use the WISC because it's a useful opening to an interview . . . by the time you've finished the kid is usually fairly relaxed. They quite enjoy doing it, sitting down and doing something with an adult . . . and you're then in a much better position to talk about what you want to talk about.

As well as information about the child's attitude and emotional state, intelligence or abilities tests were also used to obtain information about cognitive functioning. Again, the aim of many of these EPs was not merely to obtain an IQ score, but to gain some impression of 'cognitive skills', the nature of the learning difficulty (e.g. general or specific) and how the child compared with other children of his/her own age group. Commercially produced intelligence tests were normally used, but the impression given by those who adopted a casual attitude towards tests was that this was only because there was no time to construct anything better. Psychologist C, for example, said:

> I suppose there are some advantages in having a box of bits that you have used with other kids, you can make comparisons. I actually believe that if you could ever get round to spending the time and thinking about it there are probably much better bits available in the classroom that you could use to design a test that had better bits than the Stanford Binet.

There is clearly no 'hard line' psychometric approach involved here, but the 'softness' of the approach should not deceive us into thinking that a new perspective is being demonstrated. Lurking in the background is what appears to be a positivist conception of what to expect of children at various ages and stages; that is, a conception that regards it as a relatively uncontroversial matter to assess a child's level, stage, need or skills with respect to emotional or cognitive functioning. Tomlinson's (1982) distinction between normative or non-normative is applicable here. She, of course, was referring to 'handicaps' but the same point can be made about any description of alleged needs. There are some about which there is a consensus (normative), and others which are more controversial where the nature and extent of need is disputed (non-normative). There is an assumption amongst most of these EPs — typified by the lack of fundamental critique of psychometrics — that there is a sense in which one can refer to features of child development as if these were generally agreed, as opposed to being the views of those employing a particular brand of psychological concepts.

Such a 'child development' model has always and continues to under-pin policy and practice in special education. It is directly responsible for the notion that special needs can be 'discovered' early, that it is possible to separate out children with such needs with a reasonable degree of ob-jectivity and that psychological profiles of strengths and weaknesses can be drawn up using 'natural' categories — cognitive, emotional, sensori-motor, etc.

Behaviouralism

In the words of one interviewee, the EP's role was essentially that of a 'behavioural change agent'. This is not to imply that most of the inter-viewees were 'behaviourists' in the narrow sense of the term — they were more eclectic than this — but they did in a general way consider that change is brought about by people altering their *behaviour* in relation to the problem situation, even if the rationale for the specific action taken was not always clear and the consequences somewhat unpredict-able.

There was a tendency in positivist and empiricist fashion to distin-guish between a realm of knowledge called 'theory' and a realm called 'fact'. This was typically expressed by referring to knowledge of 'what was actually happening' as opposed to what theoretically was supposed to happen. For example, psychologist C said that he did not focus on 'causes', i.e. explanations in terms of theories, but immediate questions like 'where do we go from here'. Although psychologist F used a number of theories, he was typically empiricist in his dislike of theory. 'I very much go along with Skinner in not having theories . . . don't bother with theories look at what's happening.' G often used a behavioural approach which to him meant making careful records and carrying out detailed observations of behaviour and looking at 'what is actually happening, not your opinion as to what you think is happening or what you feel is happening . . . but what is actually happening'. In short, un-like the reconstructionist, most of these EPs interpreted social practice at the level of behaviour rather than the level of action.

Non-directiveness

However, by far the most important feature of the role style and con-tent of these EPs was that which was derived from the practitioner 'philosophy' of non-directiveness. It was such a significant feature that I shall discuss it in more detail than I have the previous two orientations.

At first sight, the responses referring to this orientation appear to be consonant with a reconstructionist perspective. If 'expertism' is a feature of the positivism of the traditional role, then most of the respondents would qualify as anti- this role. Most of them rejected what they described as the 'expert role'. Psychologist E, for example, considered that he always attempted to approach teachers in a non-expert manner. If teachers did attempt to construe him as an expert with special skills and techniques from which could be derived ready-made solutions to problems, he tried to 'knock that idea down immediately'. Many other respondents made similar comments.

Similarly, non-directiveness was also linked with attempts to keep the burden of responsibility where it was seen to belong, i.e. with the teacher, or at least partly so. In so far as the traditional approach was associated with the notion of a helping profession that took away responsibility from the teacher and indeed the school, then this also perhaps reflected an alternative perspective.

Yet, there were several aspects of the way practice was constructed under the 'umbrella' of this orientation that raised doubts about its status as a reconstructed alternative. There can, of course, be no such thing as a purely non-directive role, and most of the respondents recognised this. Most of them perceived themselves as attempting to influence the course of social, educational and psychological development, albeit in a democratic manner and in a way which was less assertive than that of the positivist expert.

The following exchange with psychologist A demonstrates how the non-directive psychologist approaches a problem situation.

> A I usually found that most of the tests I used just gave an IQ score and I did not find it useful in relation to a problem situation, so now when there is a problem I ask myself where do we go from where we are at this moment? Quite often . . . well hopefully I get the teacher to decide for herself rather than me do a diagnosis of the problem.
>
> I So you adopt what might be called a reflective role?
>
> A Yes.
>
> I When you adopt this role are you conscious of attempting to influence the teacher in subtle ways?
>
> A Yes . . . but I would find it difficult to know always what influence I'm having. When a child is referred to me as a problem, I've got my own individual ideas about the problem situation and how to change that situation — yes, I may steer the teacher towards a perception of the problem which is mine, so that she may see the solution that I see . . . but she, of course, may see other solutions.

But the question is on what sorts of knowledge does the psychologist rely when formulating his/her 'own individual ideas about the problem situation and how to change it'? It is clear in many instances that these ideas are drawn from a knowledge base which is traditional in the sense defined above. In particular there is the emphasis on individualism. Throwing the ball back into the teacher's court implies a humanistic faith in the abilities of teachers to cope, but, if this is not accompanied by an appreciation of socially generated constraints, then it can lead, as with many of these respondents, to explanations of failure to cope couched in individualist terms.

Many of these EPs did in fact clearly favour such explanations. Psychologist F was one amongst several who relied heavily on the notion of 'competence' which he conceived as a continuum on which you could locate individual teachers.

> F They spread across a range, a continuum. One axis is the ability to get on with children who are upset. Another axis is those who are very good teachers who don't have very good relationships with children but they get by because the children feel they are being successful. Some teachers have a high score on both. You don't find many teachers at the bottom of both poles . . . people like that usually get out. Sometimes they're good teachers but they just don't understand the kid's point of view. Average teacher is somewhere in the middle. Sometimes they can be good on both axes but not successful as a teacher because they are bored and have lost their drive and that's where EPs and advisers come in.

Psychologist B said that he was keenly aware of the variability of skills and ability to cope between different teachers. The cause of the variability between teachers was a combination of personality and training and of these, in his view, the former was more significant. 'The ones who are coping are the middle-aged, kindly types who I wouldn't imagine had read much in the field of educational research for a fair time yet have a way with children which is second to none.' Another respondent, psychologist G, felt that the personality and competence of the headteacher was particularly important. 'Schools are different. They vary very much as a function of the behaviour of the head – the way in which he supports the teachers, his philosophy regarding children . . . the head will set the tone.'

Another individualist construct utilised a great deal by respondents was the notion of the 'caring' teacher. To some extent caring was a term applied to systems as well as individuals. Thus there was a tendency amongst some respondents to regard the primary sector as more caring than the secondary.

Psychologist B made several of these points which were typical of the sample.

B I feel that very little of secondary education is up to the level of primary education.

I Why?

B They're horrible, bare places compared to primary schools, sharply time-tabled divisions . . . poor contact between teachers and kids. For low ability kids I would much rather see an extension of primary type education continuing at secondary level.

I Roughly how many kids are you talking about?

B I'm thinking of children who are not going to obtain many OLs.

I The majority, therefore?

B Could be. My impression is that probably more than 50 per cent of kids are at any one time engaged in activities which are pointless and probably counterproductive and not what I consider to be education. The problem is that these schools are not caring establishments, like the primary school. They have pastoral care systems but these are not organised along caring lines. The teachers just regard problems as interference if you see what I mean.

However, even respondents with a more potentially sociologically orientated approach felt that in the final analysis it was a question of whether or not the teachers had 'caring' attitudes. Significantly the notion of 'caring' was closely linked to that of 'competence'. As psychologist F put it:

You know you can actually be cruel by being kind. People get confused between having a formal attitude towards children and . . . You can be a very formal teacher and very informal in your attitude towards kids. The pupils respond well to a teacher who is formal but who they feel cares about them as people. Other teachers are very nice to the kids but they're not competent teachers, they don't teach them effectively and the kids pick up the message quickly . . . she doesn't care, she's not bothered, you know.

The individualist approach to change emphasising teacher 'competence' and 'caring' is well within the confines of the traditional paradigm in psychological practice. It is also linked with broader aspects of the dominant ideology in special education. The competence/caring concept seems to represent a modern view (i.e. a view more in keeping with currently popular rationales of a mainly behavioural and humanistic kind) of what Tomlinson (1982) describes as 'benevolent humanitarianism' which has influenced practice in special education since its inception in the nineteenth century. This is individualist in the sense that changes are conceived as coming about largely through the development of individual charity and 'goodwill', allied, in the modern view, to ever improving teaching skills reflecting the alleged progressive and enlightened nature of the society we live in.

This is certainly an approach in tune with some of the major recommendations of the Warnock Committee. The Report refers to the quality of special education in all forms in all contexts depending 'as much on the skill and insights of teachers, supported by adequate resources, as on the institutional and organizational form that it takes' (para. 7.13). One of its three areas of first priority is teacher training (the other two being provision for under-fives and over-16s, see p. 336). The Committee recommend the establishment of a special educational element in initial training, short courses, full-time qualifying courses and other courses of varying length on different aspects of special education.

In summary, an impressionistic analysis of interviewee responses suggests that most of them were working within the parameters of the traditional approach. Their critique of psychometrics was not fundamental and most of them used tests even if only occasionally. Most of them accepted the positivist view that behaviour could be observed and recorded in a theory-free way, and their assumptions about change in the system were largely individualist. What was clearly involved here was not a radical paradigm change but an adaptation to changing circumstances involving intra-paradigmatic modifications. 'New' areas of psychology were brought into play, and the traditional repertoire, for example, psychometrics, was not so much cast aside as de-emphasised, and in some cases, placed almost permanently in cold storage.

Pragmatic and Paradigmatic Concerns

The data was further analysed utilising Hammersley's (1977) distinction between paradigmatic and pragmatic concerns. In relation to teaching, the notion of paradigm refers to 'how teaching ought to be, how it could be in ideal circumstances' (p. 38). This is a different meaning of the term paradigm from that used in the foregoing analysis, but the two can be linked without confusing the reader. The paradigm concern of the EPs in this study was to 'deliver' psychology to schools, and the kind of psychology most of them sought to deliver belonged to the traditional paradigm, i.e. positivist and individualist.

But these EPs made their deliveries to schools at the level of practice and their paradigmatic concerns were therefore mixed with pragmatic ones. The latter refer to concerns which relate to the circumstances of the immediate social context in which the EP is located, and the pressures which emanate from that context. For many EPs who aspire to a teacher- and school-orientated approach, the kinds of pressures with which they have to deal in order to 'survive' (see Woods, 1979) are largely to do with two important sets of factors — the first emanating from the material constraints (see Hargreaves, 1978) (e.g. the large number of 'problems', geographical location of schools, facilities, etc.) and the second from social and political pressures (i.e. the interests and expectations of others, particularly other professional groups, e.g. teachers and administrators). These constraints are well documented in the so-called 'reconstructing' literature (see Gillham, 1978; McPherson and Sutton, 1981).

In this study few EPs referred explicitly to the material constraints, but they were concerned about the expectations others had of their role. These expectations usually involve assumptions about the EP as someone who 'dealt' with the child, either by giving tests and recommending special placement (or not as the case may be) or by making recommendations about treatment based on an analysis of 'causes' within the child or the family. The EPs themselves, of course, were not against seeing individual children, but their aim, as indicated above, was to work with the teacher as well as or, in many cases, as an alternative to working with the child. This did not mean that they necessarily wanted to operate outside the traditional paradigm, but rather that they wanted to deliver their psychology in a more preventive rather than crisis-orientated way; that is, by changing teacher perception and behaviour so that the teachers would be likely to take responsibility for and resolve their own problems in relation to present and future situations.

To cope with these pressures these EPs had evolved a number of coping or survival strategies.

Playing the Psychometric Expert

Although, as indicated above, the EPs were not opposed to psychometrics in principle, there were many instances where they did not wish to employ this aspect of their knowledge but felt obliged to do so because of teacher expectations. The compromise they arrived at was to give tests in order to establish a foothold from which they could evolve a negotiating position. Once teachers saw that they were doing what psychologists were supposed to do, this gave the EPs more space to develop 'good' practice.

C I use a range of tests if I see it as in the child's interests for me to do so, as part of the negotiation. But at the same time I recognise this is going against my real beliefs about the best form of practice.

E I reach for a test if I'm copping out or decide I've got to be seen doing something . . . When I've sent my report in, that's when the work starts.

F Tests are a useful adjunct, a useful bit of information, though not necessarily for the purposes they were designed for but for administrative purposes or attitude change (laughs) it's very useful.

G . . . the other reason, possibly a little more manipulative, devious is that by using tests you establish some credibility. If you just went in . . . it's no good saying to the teacher, well, we're really talking about your responsibilities and how you are going to meet this child's needs . . . the defences will go up and that will be that. So you have to go some way towards meeting the expectation that you will use tests . . . and you gradually work your way from there.

Tests were also used as a response to time pressures: as psychologist G explained, 'I also use tests when there is only a limited time available.'

A third aspect of this coping strategy should also be considered. Although mentioned by only one EP in the sample, it provides evidence of a consideration which appears to be at the root of strategies adopted by other professional groups, particularly teachers (see Pollard, 1980; Woods, 1979). Some EPs used psychometrics to 'survive' in a mental health sense. Psychologist H stated:

It's a practice of psychology . . . it's undemanding and unstressful if you simply develop the test giving model . . . you would work out a very skilful way of doing it . . . but if you do reject that model like many psychologists who I come into contact with then you will have a lot of time taken up with a lot of worry . . . a lot of it gets recirculated; the problems, the worry, the anxiety, it doesn't seem to come out anywhere . . .

Although this particular respondent was referring to others rather
than to himself, it did seem to represent an option which was available
for the basically non-psychometrically-orientated EP who decided, for
one reason or another, that he/she wanted to 'cop out'. Another form
of 'copping out' involving psychometrics was to 'pass the buck'. Psychologist C explained:

> This school had a habit of picking out highly intelligent children and
> asking the psychologist to confirm this with intelligence tests. I found
> this very hard to cope with . . . I could not see the point of it. For-
> tunately, I don't have to do it. There's someone else in the team who
> doesn't have my hang ups and he goes along and makes a fairly re-
> stricted commitment of time and does what the head asks.

'Keeping Them Busy'

Another coping strategy was to throw the ball back immediately into
the teacher's court. This relied on the expectation that the EP always
required information about the school situation to complete his/her
diagnosis. In relation to special placements, for example, a fairly detailed
school report is usually required. By asking the teachers to provide detailed accounts of the 'troublesome' children they had referred, the EPs
were complying with the expectation of their role as assessment and
disposal officers, whilst at the same time creating the conditions for a
dialogue about specific behaviours and how these might be changed.
Psychologist E:

> When I saw the kid he seemed OK, so I said, right, let's get some
> data on this kid in all situations, OK? And I asked every teacher
> who came into contact with him to keep a diary on him; giving
> chapter and verse. You know . . . he threw three punches at his next
> door neighbour between such a time and such a time in my lesson on
> Thursday morning etc. As I suspected there were differences between
> lessons . . .

The same strategy was also used with children as well as teachers. Psychologist F:

> I suggested to the school and the child that they should make a pretty
> detailed record of what was happening and this was important for all
> concerned . . . There should be a lesson by lesson account of what
> the child was doing . . . the kid should have some responsibility for

ensuring its completion and that he should be given some opportunity for discussing it with a member of the pastoral staff.

If the strategy was successful, then eventually the teachers would begin to alter their expectations and start perceiving the role of the EP in a way that was more in keeping with his/her own perception of the role. This has clearly happened in the following example. Note that the psychology involved, however, is described in traditional terms.

J   I find experimental psychology the most useful area. You set up a problem or at least negotiate a situation as a problem.
I   You set the situation up.
J   Yes, but by using the experimental method it can dovetail with what the teacher's doing. You may not see the child yourself. Once you've got some idea of the problem, you can say 'Right let's get some data on the whole class' . . . It doesn't matter what that data is as long as it involves the teacher in activity, and maybe the class in activity as well, like a sociometric questionnaire for example. Once you've got this, even if it's largely irrelevant to the problem, it gives you something to talk to the teacher about. Teachers give positive reports of this approach. They know it's not always a case of doing something directly with the problem child. The data about the class enable you to set up an experiment. You can talk in terms of various things you're going to try, e.g. let's move him across to the other side of the class, and you set a time to evaluate it. Teachers like doing this because it doesn't take the responsibility away from them.

'Keeping them busy' was an acceptable strategy as far as most of these EPs were concerned because it was, after all, only a means to an end. It was a strategy that took account of existing teacher expectations. If these expectations were not modified then the EPs would have been compelled to operate a service which, in their terms, would have been below standard. It would also have been a service where the material constraints would have become more salient. For example, a reversion to an out and out casework model would have generated the typical pressures associated with a heavy caseload. At least one of these EPs, psychologist B, continued to operate in this way, even though he had accepted the necessity of more informal face to face contacts with teachers. His position is interesting because it highlights the dilemmas involved when a 'keeping them busy' strategy was *not* employed in the changed circumstances of modern practice.

> The way I tend to talk with staff at school means that the more visits I make to school the more names come out. Some people seem to be able to do the opposite whereby by going into school actually less names come out ... One of my biggest worries is just where do I stand with the names of children who have been referred. I'm a bit obsessive about this really. Sometimes I get to the point when I take some cases on whom I've given advice or made a recommendation back to the school, and ask to know what's been done. If one were to be more ruthless, yes, or aggressive perhaps with teachers, then perhaps one would not get many names. But I can't work like that. I feel that it's a trap I've got myself into. I leaf through a pile of files at the end of the year and I wonder whether I've got time to follow them up.

Playing the Bureaucrat

This was not a popular strategy amongst interviewees, but there was no doubt that occasionally it was useful to play the role of 'local authority officer'. Like the psychometric expert, this was used to gain entrance and establish credibility. The back up relied on, however, was not the mystique of special knowledge, so much as the power of the local administration to distribute resources according to need. It was assumed that teachers would accept the EP in the role of a 'means test' type bureaucrat. Psychologist F:

> When I go into school I am an officer of the local authority, and the school may overreact to you because they may be concerned with the interests of the individual child but in comparison with all the other children I know it's not feasible in terms of resources etc. and one has to act as a local government officer ... one has to say, 'one has to look at all the problems you know'.

From this point, of course, negotiations could proceed.

Discussion

The main aim of the strategic action outline above was to create a climate of negotiation which would enable the EP to deliver his/her psychology to schools more effectively. A successful outcome would be one

where the EP felt that he/she could apply the full range of psychological knowledge to 'problems' or in a preventive way, and had an opportunity to develop this knowledge by some form of action research. This enterprise might be described as reformist as opposed to traditional or radical. The changes involved are intraparadigmatic, i.e. they are based on delivering a psychology still rooted in positivist and individualist assumptions.

However, it is a commonplace that strategic action influenced by the pragmatic concerns of the immediate context can lead to a distortion of ideals. What were the prospects of these ideals being so distorted? At least two possibilities were noted — one involving the alteration of ends in a traditional direction, the other in a radical direction.

Scenario 1

The problem with temporarily accepting the assessment/treatment model for the sake of expediency is that such a model can be invoked frequently enough to indicate to others that it remains the most important identifying feature of the EP, whatever the claims or ultimate intentions of the latter. The reasons for it being so invoked (even in circumstances where ideally it should be playing a minor role) are mainly to do with the resonances that continue to permeate thought and practice amongst teachers in both special and ordinary schools. In a sense, changes in psychological practice are crucially dependent on the way these teachers resolve the dilemmas posed by their own concerns. If teachers in ordinary schools continue to have a vested interest in ejecting 'troublesome' children and special teachers in retaining segregationist policies, then what hope for EPs who want to break from the practices that partly reflected these interests? Similarly, whether integrationist policies are rhetoric or reality will also be a significant factor. Clearly, there is a constellation of forces involved here. Teachers' expectations are not homogenous — their attitudes towards integration vary from time to time and teacher to teacher. EPs have to make a decision about the forces with which they see themselves in alliance. By taking account of certain expectations, ones that constrain them into giving tests, they could well be legitimating the views of those whose position on current issues in special education is traditional. If these views, which arguably are still dominant in practice, prevail, then the traditional model of psychological practice will have a new lease of life.

There is plenty of evidence on the national scene that EPs continue to use psychometrics in association with an assessment/treatment and disposal model far more than some apologists for the profession would care to admit. In a survey carried out by the author, 94 per cent of the

291 respondents admitted to using an individual intelligence test regularly or occasionally, and 82 per cent on a regular basis. An analysis of the percentages for test use indicated the kind of diagnostic sequence that one might expect of an EP working in the traditional manner – an intelligence test followed by a reading test followed perhaps by a further assessment of language skills and/or perceptual motor skills. Within the traditional paradigm in the context of its application to special education, an important aspect of the assessment procedure has always been to provide information on current attainment in basic educational skills, particularly reading, and then to compare these with intelligence test scores (see Quicke, 1978).

In relation to the interviewees in this study, the question arises as to what extent might they have deceived themselves into thinking that they had shuffled off the traditional role? Although their intentions were reformist, the consequences of their actions, indeed their very presence as professionals who could, if necessary, provide 'objective' diagnoses, were possibly more traditional than they thought. This is always a possibility where 'casework ideology' (see Cohen, 1975) is not totally refused.

The foregoing refers mainly to strategic action involving psychometrics, but the same could be said of the other strategies – 'keeping them busy' and 'playing the bureaucrat'. Teachers gathering detailed information about school behaviour can be all part of the traditional diagnostic. The crossover from this to negotiation and attempts to alter perception and expectation is not always easy to make. It would be only too easy for the hard-pressed EP not to follow this strategy through to its paradigmatic end point, and use the strategy merely as a ploy to 'hold off' the referral in the context of a traditional model of practice. Similarly, putting on a bureaucratic public face to secure entry to schools has its danger. Like all strategic action involving compromises, the public face does not have to become internalised for the consequences to be out of line with desired ends.

Scenario 2

The prospects for a radical change of practice are bleak, if one contemplates the pervasiveness and tenacity of the traditional paradigm. None of these interviewees appears to have made radical category changes with respect to their views on, say, child development or change in the system. In pursuit of their pragmatic concerns, however, it is possible that certain alternative paths of a more radical nature are opened up. The 'keeping them busy' strategy can obviously be rationalised by references to positivist behavioural and individualist humanistic psychology, but there are other perspectives with which it is consonant. Thus psychologist E who asked the teachers to keep a diary on the troublesome child wanted a quantitative breakdown of behaviours, but he was also concerned with the differences of perspective amongst teachers and the conflict between the school's and his own assessment. Psychologist F was concerned with recording behaviour, but also with using this as a starting-point for discussion between the pupil and the pastoral staff. Psychologist J asserts his belief in the usefulness of experimental psychology, but is clearly more concerned with negotiation and group manipulation in the class context.

It is more difficult to see any radical potential in 'playing the psychometric expert'. Using tests is different from using experimental psychology or behaviourism in the way described above, because first teachers are not party to the test-giving procedure — it is something the EP 'does' to the child away from the class context, thus reinforcing the positivist expert image; and second, to put it simply, intelligence or abilities tests, however deviously employed, are still intelligence or abilities tests, whereas experimental psychology or behaviourism are loosely applied terms which often 'turn into' something else in practice, e.g. sociometry or interactionism. Using such tests in a 'soft' way or merely as a ploy to change teachers' attitudes does not alter the fact that such practices keep traditional notions of intelligence 'alive and well', and reinforce traditional beliefs about 'objective' assessments of need. If, as Cohen (1975) suggests, the radical should unmask 'pretensions and euphemisms', playing the psychometric expert does not appear to be an acceptable strategy.

Conclusion

It is clear from this analysis that neither the reformist nor the traditional approach to psychological practice contribute to a reconstruction of special education. The reformist model does not involve the complete rejection of the traditional paradigm, but rather is merely an intra-paradigmatic shift. This involves a change of emphasis from a 'within child' psychometric model to an individualist, teacher-orientated model. On the whole, this reform is likely to be buttressed and reinforced as EPs pursue their pragmatic concerns, but such reinforcement cannot be assumed. It is possible for the clock to be turned back when means distort ends, but distortion in a traditional direction is not inevitable.

Some of these psychologists are clearly moving towards a more explicitly sociologically-oriented perspective and away from the individualism of the traditional paradigm. In this sense, the pursuit of pragmatic concerns has given a potentially radical twist to their input to schools — from a radical viewpoint, a 'healthy' distortion of paradigmatic concerns. In some ways, this development is hardly surprising. Unlike their academic psychologist colleagues, these 'battle-worn' psychologists have had to survive in contexts where there was very little option other than to recognise and come to terms with the social and political climate of the schools within which they operated. It is important to remember that, although to an 'outsider' the EP may seem a powerful professional, EPs themselves often feel that they do not in fact have enough power *vis-à-vis* other professionals, or in relation to the local administration. It is not uncommon for them to establish alliances with certain groups against a 'common enemy'. Historically, for example, they have housed themselves under the educational umbrella, in alliance with educationalists against medics. One interviewee, psychologist D, was very explicit about the processes involved here and the importance of the power distribution as a determining factor. The alliance he described was one where the professionals established a united front against possible interference in the decision-making process by the administration.

> You may get a situation where the battlelines are drawn and given the power situation you don't feel very effective . . . It's usually when we're dealing with a special school placement . . . We're beyond the situation where the medics decide and I don't think we should swing it round the other way where we do things without working together . . . We suspect that, if we don't go to the selection meeting with an agreement, the person that represents the administration could well change the recommendation, so that means we have to arrive at a consensus amongst the professionals before we go to the meeting. If we haven't got it then we delay the meeting until we have.

This example, of course, illustrates the politicking to uphold a decision about a special school placement and therefore is scarcely radical in itself, but it is possible to imagine this political manoeuvring to be directed at different targets, for instance, in establishing alliances with 'integrationists' against 'segregationists'.

References

Ackroyd, S. and Hughes, J. (1981) *Data Collection in Context*, Longman, London.

Association of Educational Psychologists (AEP) (1978) 11 December, Special Educational Needs − Comments on the Consultative Document on the Report of the Committee of Enquiry into the Education of Handicapped Children and Young People, unpublished.

Cohen, S. (1975) 'It's All Right for You to Talk: Political and Sociological Manifestos for Social Work Action' in R. Bailey and M. Brake (eds.), *Radical Social Work*, Edward Arnold, London.

Department of Education and Science (DES), Circular 3/74.

Department of Education and Science (DES), Circular 2/75.

Division of Educational and Child Psychology (DECP) (1976) Northern Branch Meeting, 20 March, Account of Discussion of Hargreaves Paper − The Deviant Pupil in the Secondary School, Occasional Papers.

Education Act (1981), HMSO, London.

George, V. and Wilding, P. (1976) *Ideology and Social Welfare*, Routledge and Kegan Paul, London.

Gillham, B. (1978) *Reconstructing Educational Psychology*, Croom Helm, London.

Hammersley, M. (1977) *Teacher Perspectives*, The Open University, E202 Schooling and Society, Units 9 and 10.

Hargreaves, A. (1978) 'The Significance of Classroom Coping Strategies' in L. Barton and R. Meighan (eds.), *Sociological Interpretations of Schooling and Classrooms: A Reappraisal*, Nafferton Books, Driffield, England.

McPherson, I. and Sutton, A. (1981) *Reconstructing Psychological Practice*, Croom Helm, London.

Newson, J. and Newson, E. (1976) 'Parental Roles and Social Contexts' in M. Shipman (ed.), *The Organization and Impact of Social Research*, Routledge and Kegan Paul, London.

Pollard, A. (1980) 'Teacher Interests and Changing Situations of Survival Threat in Primary School Classroom' in P. Woods (ed.), *Teacher Strategies*, Croom Helm, London.

Quicke, J.C. (1978) 'The Professional Knowledge of Educational Psychologists', *AEP Journal*, 4, 9, 8-16.

Rogers, C.R. (1961) *On Becoming a Person*, Constable, London.

Tomlinson, S. (1981) *Educational Subnormality: A Study in Decision-making*, Routledge and Kegan Paul, London.

—— (1982) *A Sociology of Special Education*, Routledge and Kegan Paul, London.

Warnock Report (1978) *Special Educational Needs*, Report of the Committee of Enquiry into the Education of Handicapped Children and Young People, Cmnd 7212, HMSO, London.

Woods, P. (1979) *The Divided School*, Routledge and Kegan Paul, London.

PART TWO: THE NATURE AND USES
OF QUALITATIVE APPROACHES

6 THE LABELLING OF EDUCABLE MENTALLY-RETARDED CHILDREN
Louis Rowitz and Joan E. Gunn

A disproportionately large number of children assigned to classes for the 'educable mentally retarded' (EMR) in the United States are members of low socio-economic and minority racial/ethnic groups. Recognition of this fact has prompted much controversy among educators, psychologists, lawyers, researchers, parents, politicians and others.

The label educable mentally retarded is attached to children in an attempt to explain or delineate some observed problem connected with their performance. Since most problems related to human beings are socially defined, it is useful to examine the process through which certain conditions come to be defined as problems as well as the consequences of such definitions to any effort to understand the problem. A major research and policy question concerns the causes of the definition of educable mentally retarded and the problem that disproportionate numbers of minority and lower socio-economic groups appear to meet its criteria. The label educable mentally retarded is applied to individuals in educational institutions in an effort to explain or give meaning to observed behaviour. Labels are socially defined and will, therefore, usually reflect the value system of the majority society. It is important, too, that the point at which a condition is defined as a problem is also the point at which individuals are produced to occupy the deviant status within a given social milieu (Goffman, 1963).

This chapter will examine some of the historical events which have contributed to the designation of educable mentally retarded as a problem category. The relationship of past events and present ones in the labelling of educable mentally retarded will be discussed; available rationales as to why the problem existed will also be discussed.

This chapter also contains an epidemiologic study of differential rates of enrolment in classes for the educable mentally retarded as well as other special educational classes. The study was conducted in a mid-sized midwestern American city whose population is socially and economically heterogeneous.

In summary, this chapter will argue that (1) the status of educable mentally retarded can be viewed as part of a process of social control; (2) social and scientific advancements can rationalise the existence of a problem as well as legitimise special treatment; (3) historical factors can partially explain the generation of a deviant label; and (4) all these points can be demonstrated in the epidemiologic study of an American community.

This is not to imply that there is no such thing as 'mental retardation'. For many it is a very real and evident condition requiring special treatment and resources. We are concerned here with a large proportion of the retarded population, the educable mentally retarded, who often show no evidence of known organic deficit. These educable mentally retarded are generally identified via an IQ test. The socio-economic bias of the IQ test has been extensively discussed in the literature (Blanton, 1975). Yet the IQ measure, and more recently the adaptive behaviour measure which Mercer (1973) also found to be culturally biased, are used as the fundamental criteria for classification and placement in special educational classes.

It is obvious that tests which are biased in favour of mainstream cultural values and behaviour will classify children as deficient to the extent that their values and behaviour differ or are incompatible with the majority of society (Mercer, 1973). This is not mental retardation, but rather it is cultural differences evidenced in individuals and should not be confused with innate biological potential for intellectual and behavioural development.

Historical analysis demonstrates a general misperception and misgiving towards those initially labelled as educable mentally retarded. A corollary between past and present events suggests that this misperception and misgiving are still functioning in the labelling of children. The increased incidence of labelling minority group members as educable mentally retarded has been well-documented. The study of a mid-sized American city's special educational district included in this chapter further substantiates differential labelling of minorities.

Recent research in mental retardation and the consequent controversy relating to identification and classification has kindled interest in its historic roots in an effort to understand its place in society today. Hobbs (1975a, 1975b), Kanner (1964) and Rosen, Clark and Kivitz (1976) offered comprehensive historical accounts of the identification and treatment of the mentally retarded from about the beginning of the nineteenth century when interest in them began to develop.

Prior to 1910 and the development of an instrument to measure IQ, the retarded population was primarily composed of those whose defects were apparent: gross physical and mental defects (comparable with the most severely retarded). With the advent of the intelligence test in the early 1900s, individuals with learning difficulties were added to the mental-retardation group. Concern with the accurate identification of the 'defective' as well as the need to discriminate between those able to profit from the emerging compulsory educational system along with newly available statistical devices for comparisons and quantifications led to the IQ-testing movement. In the early 1900s (1905-11), Simon and Binet developed such an instrument. It was based upon tasks discriminating various age levels. It was assumed that the test would produce a dichotomy of those able to perform their age-graded tasks and those not able to: the mentally retarded (Kanner, 1964). However, it became evident that intellectual inadequacy was not an absolute all or none attribute. There were gradations from the slightest to the most profound.

The inclusion of these newly identified defectives under the medical classifications was assumed. By this time organic bases for much of 'mental deficiency' was well established and assumed for all cases. Therefore, as new cases of mental retardation were identified, their inclusion in the medical system seemed logical and self-evident.

Work on mental deficiency by Dugdale (1877), Goddard (1912, 1916) and others advanced the theory that society's ills were derived in large part from the genetic stock of the mentally deficient. With the aid of the newly developed IQ measure, testing of specific populations was made possible. Study after study showed the 'low intelligence' of wards of the state and other social deviants. For example, in Albany, New York it was found that 85 per cent of the prostitutes were 'feebleminded'. In a Kansas prison, 69 per cent of the white inmates and 90 per cent of the black inmates were found to be 'morons'. Another study showed 98 per cent of unwed mothers to be feebleminded. Still more interesting are the rates for feeblemindedness found among the various ethnics: 83 per cent for Jews; 80 per cent for Hungarians; 79 per cent for Italians and 87 per cent for Russians (US Immigration Bureau, 1912, taken from Bowles and Gintis, 1976). During the First World War and the administering of the Army Alpha (IQ) test in 1917, it was found that 45.3 per cent of all recruits were feebleminded, some fifty million individuals (Rosen *et al.*, 1976).

Concern with the general lack of observed intelligence of various racial and ethnic minorities continues to be a concern in the field of mental retardation in the United States. There have been many studies documenting the disproportionately higher numbers of racial and cultural minorities and disproportionately low numbers of white majority members in special educational classes.

Rivers (1973) found black children to be over-represented in special educational classes and 'educable mentally-handicapped' classes in San Francisco in 1973. Black students comprised 27.8 per cent of the total school population and 47.7 per cent of the educationally-handicapped population and 53.3 per cent of the educable mentally-handicapped population. A study of St Louis schools (1968-9) found blacks disproportionately over-represented and whites disproportionately under-represented. Blacks comprised 63.5 per cent of the total school population and 76 per cent of the special educational population, while whites comprised 36.4 per cent of the total school population and only 24 per cent of the special educational population (Hobbs, 1975a).

Simmons and Brinegar (1973) documented that recent changes in California laws have not equalised representation. They found that, while the total California school population was 8 per cent black and 15.2 per cent Spanish surname, blacks comprised 27.1 per cent in 1969 and 25 per cent in 1973 of the educable mentally-handicapped population and Spanish surname comprised 28.2 per cent in 1969 and 23 per cent in 1973 of the educable mentally-handicapped population. Jane Mercer (1973) in her clinical epidemiologic study in Riverside, California found rates for mental retardation based on lowest 3 per cent criterion on an IQ measure only to be 4.4/1000 for Anglos, 149.0/1000 for Mexican-Americans and 44.9/1000 for blacks. Hurley (1969) pointed out that 56 per cent of negroes failed the mental test administered by the Armed Services in 1962. Farber (1968) found a correlation (Spearman rank) to be .60 between the number of educable mentally retarded and socio-economic ranking.

In her Riverside, California study, Mercer (1973) was able substantially to reduce the rates for mental retardation for ethnic groups by adding adaptive behaviour measures and re-norming scores *within* racial/ ethnic groupings. According to the American Association on Mental Deficiency (AAMD): 'Mental retardation refers to significantly subaverage general intellectual functioning existing concurrently with deficits in adaptive behavior, and, manifested during the developmental period.' Significantly sub-average refers to two standard deviations below the mean, or the lowest 2.275 per cent (Grossman, 1973). Rates for Mexican-Americans were reduced from 149.0/1000 on an IQ measure to only 60.0/1000 with the addition of an adaptive behaviour scale, to 30.4/1000 using standard IQ scales and re-normed adaptive behaviour and to 15.3/1000 using re-normed IQ and adaptive behaviour. Rates for blacks were reduced from 44.9/1000 on an IQ measure to only 4.1/1000 when an adaptive scale was added. This rate remained the same when scales were re-normed.

Mercer (1973) also found that test scores for both adaptive behaviour and IQ were greatly affected by 'cultural modality'. Cultural modality referred to the degree to which an individual's cultural values and behaviour were congruent with the values and behaviour regarded as appropriate by the Anglo culture. The likelihood of being labelled retarded increased in relation to the degree of disparity between the individual's culture and the majority's culture. The effect of modality was substantial. Mercer found in re-norming the tests for blacks and Mexican-Americans that those individuals least like the modal culture scored one standard deviation below the norms for their own group. She recommended pluralistic multi-cultural assessment procedures (SOMPA) that considered both adaptive behaviour and socio-cultural background in interpreting the meaning of scores.

Since the curriculum and teaching style in the American public schools reflects the language, values and history of the Northern European Anglo culture, whose cultural values and behaviour have been established since colonial times, individuals not coming from this uniform cultural background will be seen as deviating from the Anglo norm. Schools themselves emerged in an effort to socialise immigrants into the uniform Anglo curriculum. All other values and cultures have traditionally been disvalued and/or ignored.

Therefore, those deviating from the monocultural model implicit in the uniform curriculum are likely to fail academically in school and deviate from presumed behavioural norms. These students were likely to be labelled retarded and subjected to placement in 'special' classes. The beneficial impact of these classes remains to be demonstrated. The negative expectations of the label mentally retarded have been well documented (Carling, 1962; Davidson and Lang, 1960; Haywood, 1971), as have the stigmatising effects of the label itself (Edgerton, 1967; Gallagher, 1972; Haywood, 1971; Jones, 1972). Most classes for the retarded gave the children little opportunity to be anything but dull (Hobbs, 1975a). Since special classes have not been demonstrably beneficial for those in them, perhaps placement is for the benefit of the 'regular' students, those exhibiting values and behaviour of, or consonant with, the culture of the majority. It would appear then that, especially for those 75 per cent of educable mentally retarded whom Mercer (1973) determined were incorrectly classified, whose only real deviation was low economic status in conjunction with incompatible cultural values and behaviour, the classification and placement of these poor children served to perpetuate the problems by the limiting and keeping separate of these children from majority children and thus perpetuating cultural and economic bias.

Bowles and Gintis (1976) argued with persuasive evidence that the educational system has been a reflection of the social order serving to preserve and justify it. Education has demonstrably never been a potent force for equality, but has been quite successful at allocating rewards and socialisation for employment of individuals in relation to their standing in society.

The failure of minority groups has been predetermined by the system's insistence upon a uniform curriculum based upon the majority culture. Students have failed to the extent that they have not been a part of or had values compatible with the mainstream. Their failure academically and on Anglocentric measures of behaviour and IQ was taken as evidence of inadequacies, and they have been labelled retarded and segregated.

Labelling as a Social Process*

There is much confusion when the term labelling is used. For the clinician, labelling is part of the diagnostic process. Diagnosis is often dependent on the proposed or actual disposition of the case. Diagnostic procedure becomes more accurate when treatment procedures are available and tested. As treatment procedures prove themselves, more individuals seem to be diagnosed in such a way as to allow the treatment procedure to be used. Moreover, diagnostic reliability is strongly related to the severity of disorder. As symptomatology becomes more evident and specified, diagnostic reliability increases. Moreover, it may be hypothesised that diagnosis of severely and profoundly retarded individuals is probably very accurate. As we move to moderate retardation, reliability of diagnosis begins to decline, and as we move to mild retardation, diagnostic reliability is very low. Mercer (1973) has shown that mild retardation labels are often inappropriately applied to many minority children of low income within schools in a manner similar to clinical diagnostic procedures but with the IQ test as the diagnostic tool. For mild mental retardation, diagnostic reliability seems directly related to socio-economic status.

Clinical diagnosis needs to be distinguished from research diagnosis. A research diagnosis is part of the process of collecting information

---

*This section of the chapter is based on an expanded version of Rowitz (1981).

on a sample of people. Classification is part of the research process. The researchers define the disorder to be studied and they diagnose the sample respondents on the basis of an objective series of criteria (Rowitz, 1974a). In actuality, researchers in mental retardation use clinical diagnosis in studies of treated prevalence or service use. Research diagnosis is used in many community surveys. Labelling occurs in both instances. The meaning of labelling, however, differs in each of the above examples.

Much discussion of mental-retardation labelling relates to the attachment of a deviant 'tag' or 'status' to an individual whose behaviour does not appear 'normal' to the identifier of the problem. Labelling does not occur in a vacuum. Labelling is a process which needs to be viewed in the larger perspective of a community social system. Those who are not normal tend to be seen as deviant along with others who do not fit into the mainstream of society. Glaser (1971) has referred to deviance as an attribute of an individual or some action by an individual which is regarded as objectionable in a particular social setting. There are many types of behaviour which do not fit the norm, but these forms of behaviour are not labelled deviant. Thus eccentricities of many types are tolerated, such as nose-picking by drivers during a freeway traffic jam. Yet some forms of behaviour are considered objectionable enough to label deviant. Deviance is thus often determined by the judgement of others. Erikson (1962) says deviance is not a property inherent in the action or attributes of a given individual. Deviance in the form of a label is conferred upon the acts or attributes of an individual by the audiences which view the act. Thus it seems that social groups create deviance by setting up and enforcing the rules whose infractions constitute deviance (Becker, 1963). If representatives of the community — the identifiers of deviance — are able successfully to apply a label to particular individuals, these individuals become deviant because of the attachment of the label. There is also an assumption that the individual will accept the deviant label.

MacMillan (1977) has correctly argued that the traditional sociological perspective on labelling discussed above is over-simplified. A number of factors may influence the labelling of an individual and the impact of the label on the individual. Some of these factors include the individual's prelabelling experiences emphasising family experience, peer group experience and school experience. Another variable relates to whether the individual carries more than one stigmatic label, whether the child has been informally called names by his peers and whether he is formally labelled mentally retarded in the school. Another series of variables relates to the reactions of the child's family to the mentally-retarded label. The actual label that is used may be important as well as several different labels for the same set of problems. Community and neighbourhood reactions may also be important. The interface between these variables needs to be examined in more detail. Later in this section, a conceptual scheme will be presented as one possible way to look at the overall problem of labelling.

There is often an assumption in the literature that labelling is always a negative event. Hobbs, in his works *The Futures of Children* (1975a) and *Issues in the Classification of Children* (1975b), has shown the various ramifications and complications of classification and labelling. In reviewing these books, MacMillan (1977) and Gallagher (1976) have independently looked at some of the 'sacred and profane uses of labeling'. Dealing first with the positive benefits of labelling, diagnosis and labelling have provided the basis for some form of differential treatment. When disorders are biological in orientation, the diagnostic-treatment orientation has been exceedingly useful. Also differentiation of problems such as emotional disturbance, mental retardation, perceptual handicaps, etc. have helped in more accurate treatment and treatment outcomes. For mild mental retardation, the diagnosis of mental retardation has been less beneficial.

Another benefit of labelling has been to determine the prevalence of the disorder which helped the clinician and researcher to gain more insight into the etiology, prevention and development of new treatment modalities for such disorders in the future. Gallagher has also pointed out that labelling may help us to sort out better the types of mental retardation that are genetic, congenital or socio-economic in origin.

Labelling has also served as a way to rally special interest groups. These various volunteer groups have worked to get improved services and more funding for their special groups (MacMillan, 1977). Labelling has also been beneficial to legislators, educators, researchers, parents and others in order to get additional financial support for research, training and the increased delivery of services. Gallagher (1976) has pointed out that in one recent year 800 bills were introduced in state legislatures supporting special provisions for handicapped children. Almost 250 of these bills have been enacted into law.

Relative to some of the profane uses of labelling, Mercer (1973) has strongly argued that labelling children mentally retarded harms more children than it helps. The harmful effects of labelling are seen in the over-representation of minority children in classes for the mentally retarded. MacMillan (1977) has clarified the issue by arguing that classification for purposes of treatment has been useful for physical problems and more severe mental retardation. Classification has been much less useful when we talk about cases of mild mental retardation similar to what Mercer is discussing. Sociologists argue that negative labels tend to stick and permeate the individual's whole life. Rowitz (1974b) has pointed out that mental retardation provides an interesting variation on this theme. Many mildly retarded children may be retarded only the six hours a day they are in school. The remaining eighteen hours a day, when they are home, they are considered normal in their home communities. Also for the mildly retarded individual, the label may be lost when the individual leaves school.

Labelling an individual mentally retarded often excluded the individual from certain educational opportunities (MacMillan, 1977). The longer a child was out of the mainstream of education, the harder it was for the individual to catch up.

Gallagher (1976) mentioned three other negative aspects of labelling. Labelling or diagnosing a client often tranquillised professionals. It allowed them to gain diagnostic closure on difficult cases. Once diagnosis had occurred, professionals could refer the case elsewhere for treatment, especially if they were unaware of any special treatments for the client. Labelling also focused the problem on the individual rather than the complex social and ecological conditions which might need social reform. This point is extremely important and is often forgotten in planning. Finally, Gallagher argued that labelling is a way to maintain the social hierarchy of the community by keeping minority children at the bottom of the social ladder. This is similar to the points mentioned earlier relating to Mercer's work.

In order to organise some of the previous discussion into a more coherent whole, a number of hypotheses will be presented which give some direction to the conceptual development of a theory of labelling in the mental retardation field. Much of the discussion to follow is a modification of the labelling theory posited by Thomas Scheff in the book *Being Mentally Ill* (1966). The labelling model is an alternative to the medical model. Scheff (1975) argued that the medical model and specific procedures in the diagnosis of mental illness are orientated towards the inner states of individuals. The labelling model is orientated to external events. Thus a concentration on the external reactions to behaviour does not mean to negate the reality of real internal stress or biomedical difficulties of an individual. Moreover, a labelling approach does not imply that a medicalisation of social problems is not occurring. In fact, this type of theory might possibly explain the consequences of medicalisation of problems such as mental retardation and child abuse.

In *Being Mentally Ill*, Scheff (1966) presented a labelling theory of deviance which was applied to mental illness. The theory involved a series of nine interlocking hypotheses. This presentation collapsed the theory into seven hypotheses which may lead towards a theory of labelling for the mentally retarded (see Table 6.1). Two Scheff hypotheses have been found to be not applicable to mental retardation. For the mentally ill, Scheff has hypothesised that the rate of unrecorded residual rule-breaking is extremely high. With regard to the rate of recorded mental retardation, we are often dealing with an inflated figure rather than a deflated figure which is the case with rates of reported mental disorder (Mercer, 1973). The second hypothesis which has been deleted relates to Scheff's argument that labelling is a single most important cause of deviant careers. This hypothesis is much too simplistic with regard to the labelled mental retardation population. For the profoundly retarded individual, labelling from a psychological perspective does not mean very much. For the individuals who are labelled mildly retarded, labelling may or may not affect them socially or psychologically. This reaction is often dependent on such factors as socio-economic status, race and ethnic background. The mental retardation label may not carry over into community relationships for some minority children. Also the school labelled individual may lose the label completely when he leaves school (Rowitz, 1974b).

Underlying all of the seven hypotheses in Table 6.1 is the concept of societal reaction or social control. A shift has occurred from a consideration of the etiology of mental retardation to a concern with how mentally retarded individuals are controlled. For the Hobbs report, Rains and her committee colleagues (1975) argued that development of the category of exceptional children was historically grounded in a perspective of help and service rather than punishment. The children who were considered exceptional were those who created social problems for institutions responsible for their welfare. Rains talked about the politicalisation of deviance. When agencies were studied that treated special populations, it was found that the organisation of those agencies and the determination of appropriate cases for the agency were often made quite independently of the acts, characteristics or qualities of persons coming to these agencies for service. In fact, the ideal type of agency case was often quite biased demographically and dependent on such variables as the professional's conception of those who were sick and needed help, the specific demographic characteristics of potential service users that an agency considered to be its clientele, and the

Table 6.1: A Comparison of Scheff's Labelling Theory of Mental Illness to Mental Retardation

Scheff's Labelling Theory for Mental Illness	Labelling Theory for Mental Retardation
1. Residual rule-breaking arises from fundamentally diverse sources (that is organic, psychological, situations of stress, volitional acts of innovation or defiance).	1. Residual rule-breaking arises from fundamentally diverse sources (that is organic, psychological, situations of stress, volitional acts of innovation or defiance and social incompetence).
2. Relative to the rate of treated mental illness, the rate of unrecorded residual rule-breaking is extremely high.	(Not relevant to mental retardation.)
3. Most residual rule-breaking is 'denied' and is of transitory significance.	2. Most residual rule-breaking is 'denied' and is of transitory significance.
4. Stereotyped imagery of mental disorders is learned in early childhood.	3. Stereotyped imagery of mental retardation is learned in early childhood.
5. The stereotypes of insanity are continually reaffirmed, inadvertently, in ordinary social interaction.	4. The stereotypes of mental retardation are continually reaffirmed, inadvertently, in ordinary social interaction.
6. Labelled deviants may be rewarded for playing the stereotyped deviant role.	5. Labelled mentally-retarded individuals may be rewarded for playing the stereotyped deviant role.
7. Labelled deviants are punished when they attempt to return to conventional roles.	6. Labelled mentally retarded individuals are punished when they attempt to return to conventional roles.
8. In the crisis occurring when a residual rule-breaker is publicly labelled, the deviant is highly suggestible and may accept the label.	7. When a rule-breaker is publicly labelled mentally retarded, the individual is highly suggestible and may accept the proffered role of the mentally-retarded person as the only alternative.
9. Among residual rule-breakers, labelling is the single most important cause of careers of residual deviance.	(Too simplistic a hypothesis for mental retardation.)

Source: L. Rowitz (1981).

pattern of inter-agency referrals that produced new clients. Moreover, the administrators and personnel of mental-retardation service agencies tended to want to select as clients those people who would most probably be labelled as a success in a treatment programme. Rowitz (1973) has shown in the study of a state operated clinic that the demographic changes in the characteristics of clinic users vary over time due to changes in such things as administrative decisions about geographic areas from which cases may come. Also the development and expansion of many alternative types of community services can affect the demography of service use and thus the labelling of individuals by various types of agencies (Rowitz, O'Conner and Boroskin, 1975).

It is almost impossible to write a chapter on the issues of labelling without giving some consideration to who does the labelling. The identifier of mental retardation in an individual may very well make a difference on whether the label sticks or not (MacMillan, 1977). It seems that labels given by physicians or by residential institutions may stick more than labels given by educational institutions. One factor which complicates all this according to Mercer (1973) is that the clinical approach to evaluation and diagnosis of a child is adopted by schools to classify children. An IQ test which is treated as a diagnostic tool is used to substantiate a need of a child for special treatment services. This appears to be an adoption of the medical model into the school evaluation process without the sophistication usually associated with medical diagnostic procedures. The IQ controversy is quite involved and is discussed in some detail by Filler and his colleagues in the Hobbs report (1975a).

The issue of the medicalisation of social problems is appearing a great deal in the sociological literature. Earlier, the difference between the medical model and the labelling model of deviance was discussed. Medicalisation is a political issue. The mental-retardation label can exist whether the identifiers of the problem are members of the medical profession or some other helping profession. The term medicalisation refers to defining behaviour as a medical problem or illness and mandating that the medical profession provides some kind of treatment for it (Conrad, 1975). Implied in the concept of medicalisation is the idea that sociologically or psychologically based problems can be defined as medical problems. Learning disabilities, child abuse, alcoholism and drug addiction are all undergoing medicalisation now.

Renee Fox (1977) has noted an increase in the number and types of behaviour that have come to be defined as illnesses. She has argued that historically many problems that are now seen as medical were earlier considered to be sinful. Religious leaders were the ones to determine the results of sin and the punishment for these sins. With the secularisation of society, many of these 'sins' became 'crimes' and were handled by the criminal justice system. Now we are moving into a period where aberrant behaviour of many kinds is seen as an illness to be treated by medical practitioners. Instead of 'child abuse', we now talk about the 'battered child syndrome'; instead of learning disabilities, we can now talk about 'hyperkinesis' or 'minimal brain syndrome'. Thus the medical profession has become very powerful in the United States. Fox believed the increase in medicalisation is due to such factors as the so-called medical mystique of physicians, the biotechnological capacities of modern medicine and the increasing costs of medical and health care.

When the mental-retardation field is viewed, the medicalisation waters become muddled. At times it appears that mental retardation should be viewed as a medical problem to be dealt with by medical expertise. On the other hand, we can also see the continuing 'educalisation' of mental retardation. United States Public Law 94-142 (1975) appeared to de-medicalise mental-retardation problems by making the school responsible for handicapped children between the ages of 3 and 21. The whole issue of social control is critical here and is yet to be resolved. It may be possible, as some believe, that a medical and educational interface will occur relative to the labelling of mentally-retarded children with an integrative 'help plan' for each child.

An important aspect of the behaviour of mentally-retarded individuals relates to the issue of competency. In fact, competency is an issue that can be viewed apart from labelling. Competency difficulties in the social and education areas can exist even without official labelling. Farber (1968) has argued that there is a distinction between deviancy and competency. A deviant is an individual who voluntarily commits an act or engages in behaviour which may lead to official labelling as a deviant. Other individuals may involuntarily commit acts or engage in behaviour which may lead to official labelling due to an inability to engage in socially acceptable behaviour. Farber has argued that mentally-retarded individuals fall into this latter group. This distinction may be too simplistic. Issues of competency may be due to organic deficits on the one hand or social dysfunction by middle-class standards on the other hand. Moderately, severely and profoundly retarded individuals more clearly engage in socially disapproved behaviour involuntarily. An important issue relates to whether individuals who are labelled mildly retarded commit socially disapproved acts voluntarily or involuntarily.

Labelling research needs to tackle the issue of competencies more vigorously. If we turn over the Mercer findings briefly, it is possible to raise the question of whether Anglo youngsters with competency problems may escape the mental-retardation label completely and be locked out of special educational programmes when they may be needed.

There are three loose ends in the discussion of a sociological approach to labelling. Mercer and her associates have developed a 'System of Multicultural Pluralistic Assessment — SOMPA'. SOMPA is an assessment of each child on many different aspects of his performance (Krasner, 1977). Mercer has been very critical of labelling that uses only one dimension such as clinical diagnosis or IQ score to determine mental retardation in children. Mercer believed that, if a number of measures were used from a number of different domains (intelligence testing on an individual basis, adaptive behaviour inventory measures, and so on), determination of mental retardation would be more reliable. SOMPA uses an Estimated Learning Potential (ELP) score. A child is evaluated according to the norms associated with children of similar social and ethnic background. Thus, a Mexican child with a score of 105 on the WISC-R might turn out to be 21 points above the norm for Mexican children rather than 5 points above the norm if all children were considered. Thus the ELP is in essence similar to a handicap score. What Mercer has created is a new system for labelling children which builds and accepts the cultural differences between groups. The SOMPA system would not help us much if the school system in which children are educated does not change. The SOMPA evaluation might label fewer children mentally retarded, but some of these children may still need special services. More than a new labelling system is needed to solve the problem of good education for all children.

A second loose end relates to the lack of much research data on the issue of self-labelling by mentally-retarded individuals. Rotenberg (1974) gave some possible direction to this type of study. He noted four levels at which self-labelling can occur. First was the level of auto-suggestive labelling in which the individual self-labels as a result of intrapsychic processes of distortion and misrepresentation of self. This labelling can be done by individuals with organic or functional forms of problems. The second level of self-labelling resulted from a social psychological transformation process of delabelling and relabelling. Mildly retarded individuals may do this when they leave school or an institutional setting. Transmutive self-labelling results from a belief in the magical power of the labelling procedures. Thus, an individual believes he is mentally retarded because others, more knowledgeable than he, have said he is. The fourth level is indicative labelling in which self-labelling results from the belief in one's *a priori* categoric ascription which the labelling process signifies. In other words, giving oneself a deviant label may bring about a self-fulfilling prophecy in which one becomes what one is labelled. This type of self-labelling may also be a relevant category for many mildly retarded individuals.

Finally, epidemiologic research is dependent on the identification of problems. Thus labelling may well be part of the epidemiologist's work. The interrelationship between elements of social control and labelling of behavioural disorders is often ignored by epidemiologists. It seems that a consideration of these interrelationships can benefit both the work of the epidemiologist and the social scientist studying the process of labelling. The study to be reported on next attempts to do this.

The Study

The special educational district of a mid-sized midwestern American city (population over 50,000) was chosen for study. The total public school population for this city was racially and ethnically as well as economically heterogeneous. Anglos constituted 62.3 per cent of the total school population; blacks, 23.0 per cent; Hispanics, 12.5 per cent; Asians, 2.7 per cent and American Indians, 0.2 per cent. The total public school population numbers 13,800 students and the special educational district's population was 1,612 (116.8/1000).

The special educational district offered several types of special educational programmes: trainable mentally handicapped (IQ < 49); educable mentally handicapped (IQ = 49-80); learning disabilities (LD); behaviour development (BD); educationally handicapped (EH); bi-lingual education, and hearing and visually impaired programmes. Each has varying criteria for placement and programme objectives.

A short one-page questionnaire was distributed to each of the 96 special educational teachers in the study city. All questionnaires were returned within a two-week period (March 1977). Special educational teachers were asked to indicate the total number of students by racial, ethnic and sex breakdown for each of their classes as well as the grade equivalent and type of special educational programme.

The ethnic/racial distribution in special educational classes was compared with expected distribution based upon total school population and rates were developed for each of the special educational programmes. These findings were compared with an earlier study completed in 1974 in the special educational district whose methods were identical to those in the present study. Comparisons were also made with earlier studies already presented in this chapter.

Although there were significant differences between the various special educational programmes, programme content and objectives, with the exception of behaviour development and hearing and visually impaired, the IQ measure was deemed an integral aspect for determining programme placement.

Relative to the 1977 distribution of racial/ethnic groups in the total school population compared to the special educational population, it was found that, while blacks made up 23.0 per cent of the total school population, they were 38.2 per cent of the special educational population. Hispanics were 12.5 per cent of the total school population and 11.7 per cent of the special educational population and Anglos, who comprised 63.2 per cent of the total school population, comprised 49.1 per cent of the special educational population.

In addition, it was found that 19.4 per cent of all blacks in this school district were enrolled in special educational classes. For Hispanics, 10.9 per cent of the total were enrolled in special educational classes, and for Anglos, 9.1 per cent of their total population were enrolled in special educational classes.

In computing rates per thousand of ethnic and religious groups enrolled in various special educational classes, the rates for enrolment in EMH classes was 62.3/1000 for blacks compared to 15.7/1000 for Hispanics and 9.7/1000 for Anglos.

It was also found that: (1) racial minorities (black) were over-represented in special educational classes; (2) Hispanics were *not* over-represented in special educational classes; (3) majority students (white) were under-represented in special educational classes; (4) racial minorities (black) were over-represented in classes for the educably mentally retarded; (5) ethnic minorities (Hispanic) were over-represented in classes for the educable mentally retarded; (6) majority students (white) were under-represented in classes for the educable mentally retarded; and (7) representation in classes for the trainable mentally retarded were approximately equal for all racial and ethnic groups.

The disproportionate representation for Anglos and blacks which was especially pronounced in educable mentally handicapped classes was directly attributable to the method employed for programme placement. According to the special educational district, in the study community the primary testing instruments to determine eligibility for educable mentally handicapped classes was an IQ measure (verbal and performance) and an achievement test. United States blacks have traditionally done poorly on both of these measures. The cultural and economic biases inherent in these instruments has been well established (Leacock, 1971).

While this disproportionate effect was quite apparent for Anglos and blacks, there appeared to be a somewhat less pronounced effect for

Hispanics in educable mentally-retarded classes and no disproportionate representation present in special educational classes. There was, however, a marked shift in Hispanic rates from 1974 to 1977 in both educable mentally-retarded classes and learning-disabled classes. Table 6.2 shows that the Hispanic rate for EMH in 1974 was 30.6/1000 compared to a black rate of 52.3/1000 and an Anglo rate of 7.1/1000. The 1977 Hispanic rate was 15.7/1000 which is a 50 per cent reduction. The rates for learning disabilities for Hispanics in 1974 was 15.3/1000 compared to a 1977 rate of 30.8/1000 which is a 50 per cent increase.

These changes were in part attributable to the special educational district's conscientious hiring of Hispanic psychologists to evaluate in terms of cultural background as well as academic and evaluations done in the student's primary language.

Also, the level of threat to cultural integrity, which was an important aspect for the process of social control, was not nearly as pronounced for Hispanics as it was for blacks. Hispanics comprised 12.5 per cent of the total school population. In 1970 the black population was only 12.8 per cent and Hispanic 7.2 per cent of the total. The black population had increased more than 20 per cent and the Hispanic by only about 5 per cent. The threat to cultural integrity was greatest from the greatest numbers. In fact, this midwestern city was fraught with large-scale urban problems. A large percentage of blacks were at poverty level, housing was of substandard quality and unemployment was high. The city was seen by many as being encroached by blacks. On its border was an almost entirely black city.

Reaction to this increased level of threat due to population growth was also evidenced in the increased rates for enrolment in EMH, EH and LD classes from 1974 to 1977 for blacks. In 1974 the rate for EMH was 52.3/1000 and in 1977 it had increased to 62.3/1000 (see Table 6.2).

Table 6.2: Comparison of Rates/1000 for 1977 with 1974 in Various Special Educational Classes for Ethnic/Racial Groups

	Anglo		Hispanic		Black	
	1977	1974	1977	1974	1977	1974
TMH	6.1	1.9	6.4	2.9	8.2	2.6
EMH	9.7	7.1	15.7	30.6	62.3	52.3
EH	34.4	44.8	51.2	58.3	76.4	66.1
LD	36.1	20.0	30.8	15.3	38.1	24.5
Other	4.5	2.7	5.2	4.4	8.8	10.5
Total	90.8	76.5	109.3	111.5	193.8	156.0

Mercer (1973), in her clinical study of rates for mental retardation in Riverside, California, found a similar effect. There, where Hispanics comprised the largest single minority group, rates were much higher (149.0/1000) than for blacks (44.9/1000) who were a much smaller minority.

Conclusion

The documenting of disproportionate representation of groups in special educational classes has been used in the past to lend further support to the theory that there are inherent differences between groups, whether biologically rooted or as a result of deprivation. A popular theory coined the 'culture of poverty' or 'cultural deprivation' conceptualises poverty as a socio-cultural pathology whereby its participants (chiefly minorities), although not responsible for its occurrence, are locked into a self-perpetuating cycle of poverty and pathology.

The usual types of conditions cited as causally related to all sorts of endemic pathological behaviour including mental retardation were such factors as: a high incidence of unwanted children to wed and unwed mothers; an absence of fathers in the home; a high rate of malnutrition both prenatally and after birth; a prematurity rate of double the average; increased exposure to health hazards; and deprivation due to un-interesting environment and lack of conversation (Hurley, 1969).

Many of these factors were a function of poverty itself, for example, malnutrition, prematurity, health hazards. It is unwarranted to assume that in the absence of poverty these traits would continue. The absence of a father in the home, the fracturing of families and/or the decreased participation of fathers in family life has been a fundamental aspect of industrialised society. Unwanted children were a universal phenomena, not a particular attribute of the poor.

Poverty theorists described it solely in terms of the grim and destructive results of poverty and discrimination and interpreted behavioural patterns among the lower class as isolated traits rather than in terms of the total context. Since the situations with which lower- and middle-class groups were dealing may differ widely, one could not assume that one form of behaviour was necessarily more effective than another (Leacock, 1971).

Moreover, the culture of poverty concept implied an untenable view of the process by which cultural traits are evolved and transmitted. First, it assumed that an individual's value orientations and attitudes were virtually set by the age of 6. The formulation of values was a life-long evolving process which was a process of adaptation and experience (see Table 6.1). Second, it assumed an unwarranted homogeneity of the lower class. It viewed culture as a mould for the personality. Within any culture there was a great diversity of behaviour styles and adaptation. The theory also assumed a circular relationship between the individual and the culture. Childhood experiences became encapsulated in the personality and were somehow projected into the structures that pattern adult attitudes and beliefs. Thus, it was assumed that culture perpetuates itself through the medium of the personality. Culture, however, was an outgrowth of adaptational behaviours which had been successful over time and therefore tended to take on values and tended to be institutionalised (Leacock, 1971).

It was commonly believed and supported by the culture of poverty theorists that the failures of the lower-class child in the educational system were causally related to lower-class social and family environment. There is, however, actually little real evidence to support these assumptions (Drucker, 1971). If a minority child appeared as 'culturally deprived', it was not because he was lacking in experience or in culture, but because the educational system was unwilling to recognise the alienness of his culture and the realities of his social world. It was not that the child was deprived of culture, it was that the culture which was associated with his parents was derogated because they were impoverished and powerless (Wax and Wax, 1971).

The observed failures of the lower class in the school system may not have been so much that these students were failing to learn due to their enormous deficits, but that the school system was failing to teach anyone adequately. The hidden curriculum of the middle-class home offered, for the children raised in it, a substantial compensatory programme to the school. The problem here was merely less visible among the middle class who have always motivated, prepared and tutored their children in the skills they themselves use in their daily jobs (John, 1971).

Teacher attitudes played an important role in who would and who would not achieve. Rosenthal and Jacobson (1968) documented substantial raising of IQ scores when teachers were led to believe that certain children were gifted. Becker (1969) found that middle-class teachers felt their lower-class children were 'morally unacceptable'. Leacock (1969) found that social class composition had the greatest effect upon academic achievement. The failure of minorities in the school system was not so much due either to 'inherent' or to 'cultural deficits' but rather to external attitudes and controls over which they were effectively powerless. The labelling and social control argument presented earlier is relevant here.

The distributions found for ethnic/racial groups seem to be fairly consistent with other reported studies (see Table 6.3). Each of them generally showed racial/ethnic minorities to be over-represented and Anglos to be under-represented in special educational classes and/or educable mentally-handicapped classes. Differences in rates may be accountable in terms of perceived level of threat, in conjunction with abilities to institute social control, through a label of a child as educable mentally retarded.

Table 6.3: Comparison of Other Distribution Studies for Mental Retardation

		Total school population	Special educational population	EMH population
San Francisco (1973)[b]	black	27.8	—	53.3
St Louis (1968-1969)[c]	black	63.5	76.0	—
	Anglo	36.4	24.0	—
California (1973)[d]	black	8.0	—	25.0
		—	—	27.1[a]
	Anglo	72.4	—	50.0
		—	—	43.1[a]
	Spanish surname	15.2	—	23.0
		—	—	28.2[a]
Midwestern city (1977)	black	23.0	38.2	63.9
	Anglo	63.2	49.1	27.4
	Hispanic	12.5	11.7	8.7

Note: a. 1969.
Sources: b. Rivers (1973).
      c. Hobbs (1975a).
      d. Simmons and Brinegar (1973).

This chapter initially began with the assumption that the values of a society function to determine to a large extent the meaning that will be ascribed to an observation of behaviour. It therefore seemed logical that, in an attempt to understand the perceived social problems of significant numbers of cultural and racial minorities qualifying as educable mentally retarded, the process through which or the conditions in which they were perceived as such, be examined.

The interface between material events and present-day circumstances of educable mentally retarded was drawn. Essentially it was found that there were similarities between past and present identification: (1) the

IQ test was the single most widely used instrument in the determination of status as represented by the label of mental retardation; (2) rates for educable mentally retarded were disproportionately high for low economic groups; (3) rates for educable mentally retarded were disproportionately high for minority groups; (4) the groups producing educable mentally retarded persons had a low standing in society in relation to the majority children; (5) failure to achieve in the uniform curriculum of the school system was explained as a failure in intelligence; (6) there was a general lack of organic involvement in the mildly mentally-retarded population which was distinctly different from the 'severely' and 'profoundly retarded'; and (7) the status of educable mentally-retarded was imbued with scientific objectivity.

The major research question, that the classification of educable mentally retarded can be viewed as a process of social control exercised over racially and culturally divergent groups and legitimated through the application of labels which is supported by federal legislation, generated several research issues: racial and cultural minorities will be over-represented in special educational classes and classes for the educable mentally retarded; majority students will be under-represented in special educational classes and classes for the educable mentally retarded; representation in classes for the trainable mentally handicapped (TMH) will be approximately equal. In this study these held true for black and white students and proved not as applicable for Hispanic students. It was reasoned, however, that, since social control was primarily a response to some perceived threat to the integrity of a group, that the groups over whom the greatest degree of social control would be exercised would be those who posed the greatest threat. Therefore, it may be that labelling will be higher for minorities with the greatest numbers. In fact, the proportion of black students in the total school population has increased 20 per cent in three years. And, for blacks, rates for enrolment in educable mentally-handicapped classes has also increased over a four-year period.

The rates for enrolment for Hispanics in educable mentally-handicapped classes were also affected by the school district's hiring of Hispanic psychologists to evaluate in the cultural context of the students.

Further research is necessary to validate the hypothesis of social control. One such area might be in the further validating of differential placement in special classes between groups with the same IQ score due to Public Law 94-142. Mercer (1973) found that Anglo students in educable mentally-handicapped classes were both more retarded and had greater numbers of handicapping conditions. Because there has always been a close relationship between minority group membership and economic status, it is difficult to assess which has the greatest impact, if at all. It may be helpful to compare placement both in terms of economic level and racial/ethnic identification. Of course, replication in other regions of the United States similar to the in-depth epidemiologic analysis that was done by Mercer (1973) would be invaluable. Further documenting of the deleterious effects of special placement would also be helpful and is probably potentially the most viable avenue of analysis to attempt change. When majority parents begin to believe that special placement is not beneficial for their children, then we may begin to see some changes in the structure. The restructuring of educational programmes may be beneficial to all its students.

In defining a condition as a health or health-related problem necessitating special treatment, treatment of those with the condition is legitimatised, i.e. for medical reasons. The school then becomes, by definition, a health-care provider. Incorrectly defining a condition as a health problem and thereby legitimating treatment, especially if the treatment has deleterious effects as the label of mental retardation and treatment seem to demonstrate, then the incorrect defining of the condition is all the more pernicious. If there genuinely is a problem and it has been incorrectly defined, then the net effects are: perpetuation of the problem, legitimation of social control and subjection to negative consequences inherent in the treatment and the label.

Finally the investigation of the process of labelling in schools from the study of the Scheff-Rowitz hypotheses presented in this chapter will also help us to understand better the underlying reasons for labelling and perhaps present some constructive strategies for lessening the effects of early socialisation towards ethnic stereotypes which permeate the American educational system and the American cultural framework as a whole.

References

Becker, H.S. (1963) *Outsiders*, The Free Press, New York.
—— (1969) 'Social class variation in the teacher–pupil relationship' in R.C. Sprinthall (ed.), *Educational Psychology*, Reinholt-Winston, New York.
Blanton, R.L. (1975) 'Historical perspectives on classification of MR' in N. Hobbs (ed.), *Issues in the Classification of Children*, Jossey-Bass, San Francisco.
Bowles, S. and Gintis, H. (1976) *Schooling in Capitalist America*, Basic Books, New York.
Carling, F. (1962) *And Yet We Are Human*, Chatto and Windus, London.
Conrad, P. (1975) 'The discovery of hyperkinesis: notes on the medicalization of

deviant behavior', *Social Problems, 23*, 1, 12-21.

Davidson, H.H. and Lang, G. (1960) 'Children's perceptions of their teachers' feelings toward them related to self-perception, school achievement and behavior', *Journal of Experimental Education, 29*, 231-40.

Drucker, E. (1971) 'Cognitive styles and class stereotypes' in E. Leacock (ed.), *Culture of Poverty: A Critique*, Simon and Schuster Touchstone, New York.

Dugdale, R. (1977) *The Jukes: A Study in Crime, Pauperism and Heredity*, Putnam, New York.

Edgerton, R. (1967) *The Cloak of Competence*, University of California Press, Berkeley, California.

Erikson, K.T. (1962) 'Notes on the sociology of deviance', *Social Problems, 9*, 307-14.

Farber, B. (1968) *Mental Retardation: Its Social Context and Social Consequences*, Houghton Mifflin, Boston.

Filler, J.W. *et al.* (1975) 'Mental Retardation' in N. Hobbs (ed.), *Issues in the Classification of Children*, vol. 1, Jossey-Bass, San Francisco.

Fox, R.C. (1977) 'The medicalization of American society', *Daedalus, 106*, 1, 9-22.

Gallagher, J.R. (1972) 'The special education contract for mildly handicapped children', *Exceptional Children, 38*, 527-35.

—— (1976) 'The sacred and the profane uses of labeling', *Mental Retardation, 14*, 6, 3-7.

Glaser, D. (1971) *Social Deviance*, Markham, Waco, Texas.

Goddard, H.H. (1912) *The Kallikak Family: A Study in the Heredity of Feeble-mindedness*, MacMillan, New York.

—— (1916) *Feeblemindedness*, MacMillan, New York.

Goffman, E. (1963) *Stigma: Notes on the Management of Spoiled Identity*, Prentice Hall, Englewood Cliffs, NJ.

Grossman, H.J. (1973) *Manual on Terminology and Classification in Mental Retardation*, American Association on Mental Deficiency (AAMD), Washington DC.

Haywood, H.C. (1971) 'Labeling: Efficacy, Evils and Caveats', Paper presented to Joseph P. Kennedy, Jr. Foundation International Symposium on Human Rights Retardation and Research, Washington DC.

Hobbs, N. (1975a) *The Futures of Children: Categories, Labels and their Consequences*, Jossey-Bass, San Francisco.

—— (1975b) *Issues in the Classification of Children*, Jossey-Bass, San Francisco.

Hurley, R. (1969) *Poverty and Mental Retardation: A Causal Relationship*, Vintage Books, St Paul, MN.

John, V. (1971) 'Language and educability' in E. Leacock (ed.), *Culture of Poverty: A Critique*, Simon and Schuster Touchstone, New York.

Jones, R.L. (1972) 'Labels and stigma in special education', *Exceptional Children, 38*, 104-10.

Kanner, L. (1964) *The History of the Care and Study of the Mentally Retarded*, Chas. C. Thomas, Springfield, Illinois.

Krasner, W. (1977) *Labelling the children: An interview with Jane R. Mercer*, National Institute of Mental Health, Washington DC.

Leacock, E. (1969) *Teaching and Learning in City Schools*, Basic Books, New York.

—— (1971) *The Culture of Poverty: A Critique*, Simon and Schuster Touchstone, New York.

MacMillan, D.L. (1977) *Mental Retardation in School and Society*, Little, Brown and Company, Boston.

Mercer, J.R. (1973) *Labeling the Mentally Retarded: Clinical and Social System*

Perspectives on Mental Retardation, University of California Press, Berkeley, California.

Rains, P.M., Kitsuse, J.I., Duster, T. and Freidson, E. (1975) 'The labeling approach to deviance' in N. Hobbs (ed.), *Issues in the Classification of Children*, vol. 1, Jossey-Bass, San Francisco.

Rivers, L.W. (1973) 'Mosaic of labels for black children' in N. Hobbs (ed.), *Issues in the Classification of Children*, Jossey-Bass, San Francisco.

Rosen, M., Clark, G. and Kivitz, M. (1976) *The History of Mental Retardation*, University Park Press, Baltimore, MD.

Rosenthal, R. and Jacobson, J. (1968) *Pygmalion in the Classroom: Teacher Expectations and Pupils' Intellectual Development*, Holt, New York.

Rotenberg, M. (1974) 'Self-labelling: A missing link in the "societal reaction theory of deviance"', *Sociological Review*, *22*, 3, 335-54.

Rowitz, L. (1973) 'Socioepidemiological analysis of admission to a state operated outpatient clinic for retarded children', *American Journal of Mental Deficiency*, *78*, 3, 300-7.

—— (1974a) 'Social factors in mental retardation', *Social Science and Medicine*, *8*, 7, 405-12.

—— (1974b) 'Sociological perspective on labeling (a reaction to MacMillan, Jones and Aloia)', *American Journal of Mental Deficiency*, *79*, 3, 265-7.

—— (1981) 'A sociological perspective on labeling in mental retardation', *Mental Retardation*, *19*, 2, 47-51.

——, O'Conner, G. and Boroskin, A. (1975) 'Pattern of service use by severely and profoundly retarded individuals: A preliminary analysis' in C.C. Cleland and L.W. Talkington (eds.), *Research with Profoundly Retarded: A Conference Proceeding*, Western Research Conference and Brown Schools, Austin, Texas.

Scheff, T.J. (1966) *Being Mentally Ill: A Sociological Theory*, Aldine Publishing Company, Chicago.

—— (1975) *Labeling Madness*, Spectrum Books, Englewood Cliffs, NJ.

Simmons, A. and Brinegar, L. (1973) *Ethnic Survey of EMR Classes 1973*, California Department of Education.

US 94th Congress, 6th session (1975) *Education for All Handicapped Children Act*, 20 USC 1401, Section 3, P.L. 94-142.

Wax, M. and Wax, R. (1971) 'Cultural deprivation as an education ideology' in E. Leacock (ed.), *Culture of Poverty: A Critique*, Simon and Schuster Touchstone, New York.

7 CASE STUDIES OF MAINSTREAMING: A SYMBOLIC INTERACTIONIST APPROACH TO SPECIAL SCHOOLING*
Robert Bogdan and Judy Kugelmass

With a few notable exceptions, research in special education has been atheoretical, or, more accurately, it has operated within the unconscious assumptions of the field's practitioners (Rist and Harrell, 1982; Tomlinson, 1982). These assumptions are: (1) disability is a condition that individuals have; (2) disabled/typical is a useful and objective distinction; (3) special education is a rationally conceived and co-ordinated system of services that help children labelled disabled; (4) progress in the field is made by improving diagnosis, intervention and technology.

While a number of people have critiqued particular assumptions (Braginsky and Braginsky, 1971; Conrad, 1976; Mercer, 1973; Schrag and Divorky, 1975; Scott, 1969; Szasz, 1970) and even the general approach (Sarason and Doris, 1979), there have not been systematic attempts to develop an alternative paradigm for special education. There have been explorations of the theoretical perspectives (bio-physical, psychodynamic, behavioural, ecological, sociological, counter-theoretical) which underlie both the identification and intervention strategies employed in the treatment of deviant children (Rhodes and Tracy, 1972). However, these investigations have not, for the most part, gone beyond being critical analyses in the abstract. The insight they offer is overlooked when research is conducted in special education. In short, most research has been *for* special education (serving the field as it conceived of itself), not *of* special education, that is looking at the field from an alternative vantage-point.

Fundamental questions regarding the children who are subjects of interventions are rarely posed in the research which attempts to explore the efficacy of special educational programming. Who are these children? Who has judged them to be 'special' and in what context has this judgement occurred? Without clear answers to these questions, how are we able to know if the programmes offered are 'successful'?

*The research reported in this chapter was supported by a grant from the United States National Institute of Education, Grant No. 353-2413-21304.

Research Project

With this perspective in mind, a three-year National Institute of Education (NIE) research project was undertaken. Entitled 'A qualitative-sociological study of mainstreaming' (Bogdan and Barnes, 1979), this investigation set out to discover what factors were responsible for the successful operation of special educational programming in 'least restrictive environments', that is integrating 'disabled' children with their 'typical' peers. The least restrictive environment is a practice stipulated under United States federal legislation, Public Law 94-142, which provides guide-lines for education for children defined as disabled. Twenty-five programmes were selected for study on the basis of their being nominated as examples of 'successful mainstreaming' by school district officials, teachers, parents, university professors and staff, and human service professionals in a typical North-eastern metropolitan area.

Following a qualitative research design (Bogdan and Biklen, 1982), investigators entered their settings as participant-observers. Our task was to gather data which would clarify what was going on in each school through systematic observations and to explore the perspectives of significant individuals regarding the school as a whole and special education's place within it. The methodology employed necessitated that the researchers attempted to free themselves of preconceived notions about disability, labels of exceptionality, and models of programming for both typical and exceptional children.

In most people's minds, 'disability' and 'mainstreaming' paint a clear picture: a child in a wheelchair, perhaps with cerebral palsy, or maybe mentally retarded, surrounded by non-disabled peers. As we entered the schools to start our observations, a clear concept of disability, mainstreaming and special education turned more and more into a mirage. For example, on an early visit to one of the high schools in our study, a girl in a wheelchair rode by us, coming the opposite way, as we walked down the hall with the school's principal. When the word disabled was used by one of us in talking about this girl, we were told by our guide that this teenager was not disabled. When questioned, the principal explained how, officially, students are designated as disabled only if they required special services, were reviewed by the Committee on the Handicapped and had an Individualized Educational Programme (IEP). The young lady lived close to school and did not need special transportation. She fully participated in the regular high school activities without special arrangements. Therefore, she was not perceived as a mainstreamed student because, in fact, administratively, she was not disabled.

In the same school, we met a young man named Louis. He was officially on the roster as being in a programme for 'learning disabled' students. The teacher in the programme seldom saw him. He participated fully in all regular high school academics and was planning to go to college. He had had academic problems in the past, but not any more serious than those experienced by a host of other students who had not been labelled learning disabled. The teacher explained his presence on the register by a story of how his influential parents thought he would benefit from the services provided in the learning disabled programme. Unlike the girl who passed us in the hall, he is officially considered handicapped and therefore is seen as a mainstreamed student.

The 25 case studies generated by our study consistently illustrated the variability used in defining children as handicapped. The teachers and students we spoke with across the many sites visited were sensitive to the administrative use of the disability designation. While they often used disability labels in discussions and to structure their relationship with labelled children, an irreverence to handicapped labels was also common. This was true not only for those designations recognised as representing the 'milder' handicapping conditions (i.e. educable mentally retarded (EMR), learning disabled (LD) and emotionally disturbed (ED)), but for more severely involved children as well. In one junior high school, for example, the teacher perceived her class of students who were labelled as 'trainable mentally retarded' (TMR) as being needlessly isolated from other students in their self-contained classroom, while her principal perceived these students as being mainstreamed. She perceived them as 'cream puffs', i.e. easy to work with students who were relatively well functioning. He saw them as extremely low functioning and clearly handicapped. The principal's perspective here, as was the case in other schools studied, was however a major factor in type of programming that went on.

These examples and hundreds of others in our study illustrate that the ways children are perceived, including whether they are thought of as handicapped and how they are educated, vary from school district to school district, from school to school, and from place to place within a given school. In addition, who was considered handicapped and what specific type of handicapping conditions a student has, varies from time to time. This finding is not unique to our study. Gajar (1979), Hallahan and Kauffman (1977) and Quay and Galvin (1970), for example, have shown that most children who are labelled as emotionally disturbed display significant deficits in academic achievement. These deficits are often equal to those exhibited by children labelled as either learning disabled or educable mentally retarded. The difference in which label is applied and in which programme is followed lies in the meaning attributed to the behaviour of the children in each group.

For the learning-disabled child, academic underachievement is perceived as a primary factor in their identification and so is focused upon in their educational programmes. They underachieve *because* they are learning disabled. Educable mentally-retarded children's underachievement for their chronological age is, however, expected because of their low 'measured' IQs. Underachievement in emotionally-disturbed children, on the other hand, is understood to be a consequence of their behaviour or affective disorder which has not allowed them to develop appropriate skills. These distinctions, however, ignore the reality we and others (Algozzine, 1977; Algozzine and Curran, 1979; Apter, 1982; Hallahan and Kauffman, 1977; Kauffman, 1981; Mercer, 1973; Rist and Harrell, 1982; Ross, 1980, Sarason and Doris, 1979) have found to be operating in the designation of a particular handicapping condition for any given child. That is, the assignment of a label of exceptionality has as much to do with the situation a child finds him/herself in as it does with the child him/herself.

The specific disability label attached to a child in our educational system is supposed to offer an explanation for the child's difficulty in school and suggest methods of facilitating his or her education. However, as our data suggest, a good deal more than the child's functioning is involved in decisions regarding special educational placement and programming. For example, one of the school districts that we looked at used the label of 'severely emotionally disturbed' for those children whose social behaviour was judged to be aggressive. The large majority (80 per cent) of these children were poor, black male children who had been attending schools which had predominantly white students and teachers. Forty of these students were placed in a special educational programme located in a predominantly black elementary school in a low income neighbourhood. Many were then able to be mainstreamed in their new school. For some, this meant being included in regular classrooms for all or part of their programme. For others, it meant having lunch in the cafeteria with the rest of the student body or participation in special activities (gym, music, art, field trips, assembly programmes, etc.).

Teachers at this school recognised that their ability to integrate these special educational students was, in part, related to the perspective they had developed towards their role. Dealing directly with children over concerns with social, emotional and behavioural issues was a part of their definition of themselves as teachers. In fact, they did not define the behaviour of most of the special educational students as disturbed or abnormal. One teacher put it this way:

> I've got a lot of kids that I think, if they were in another school, would be in a special education type situation. Carl's (the mainstreamed student) all right in this room. I think if you took him and put him in a very middle-class school, he'd freak them right out. I'm just a lot more used to that. In this class, I've got 22 kids and there are probably six or seven others that I'm constantly aware of: what they're thinking and what they're doing. And he would be one of those but no more so than six or seven others. I don't know that if Carl was at this school that he would have ended up in special education. He was at another school.

This woman's statement illustrates what we found to be true across settings and with children classified in all disability areas. That is, the identification of a child as handicapped has to do with how others define his or her behaviour. This definition is related to the setting in which the child finds him or herself and the expectations generated by the setting.

Certainly, the official definitions of various handicapped conditions, as set forth in Public Law 94-142 and states' regulations, have attempted to reduce the subjective nature of labelling. However, as our data clearly illustrate, the belief that it would be possible for any educational system to develop a method of classification of its children based solely on objective criteria, is misleading. Anthropological investigations (Calhoun and Ianni, eds., 1976; Wax, Diamond and Gearing, 1971; Weaver, ed., 1973) of education further substantiate this finding, i.e. educational policies and practices are reflections of the cultural systems in which they operate. The designation of a child as handicapped therefore represents a judgement by that system regarding a given child's ability to fit, based upon the meaning given to his or her behaviour.

The recognition that labels are attached to children in a subjective fashion and are often used to 'serve the purposes of the social agents who use them' (Kauffman, 1981, p. 15) is more than an academic exercise. First and foremost are the consequences of deviancy designations upon the children themselves. Labels of exceptionality have been shown to exert a powerful influence upon teachers' understanding of their students' behaviours (Foster, Ysseldyke and Reese, 1975; Gillung and Rucker, 1977; Rist and Harrell, 1982; Salvia and Meisels, 1980; Vacc and Keist, 1977; Ysseldyke and Foster, 1978). Some authors have argued that the expectations teachers hold towards their students, based on their definition of the child's handicapping condition, may in turn move the child towards conformity with this definition. Rist and Harrell (1982) described this process in the following way:

1. The teacher expects specific behavior and achievement from specific students.
2. Because of these different expectations, the teacher behaves differently towards the different students.
3. The teacher treatment tells each student what each teacher expects; it affects the student's self-concept, achievement motivation, and level of aspiration.
4. If this teacher treatment is consistent over time, and if the student does not actively resist or change it in some way, it will tend to shape the student's achievement and behavior . . .
5. With time, the student's achievement and behavior will conform more and more closely with the original expectation.

The data from our study indicated that, for some students, the above process indeed had the negative consequences it implies. For example, in the case of the children labelled as severely emotionally disturbed, who remained in special educational classes, the focus of their programme was turned away from academics and placed instead on their 'acting out' behaviour. Poor academic achievement was understood to be a consequence of 'inadequate socialisation'. A resource teacher expressed her understanding of their needs in the following way: 'Look, these kids are Emotionally Disturbed and not Mentally Retarded. In that case, they'd need special books.' The frustration the students experienced with academic tasks was not seen as responsible for their behaviour in class. Rather, because they were emotionally disturbed, the disruptive behaviour they exhibited was expected. No rational explanation was needed. The consequence of the lack of attention to academics was, for many of the children, that they fell further and further behind in their academic skills, making it even more difficult to integrate them back into regular classrooms. One of the special educational teachers expressed her frustration regarding the poor academic achievement of her emotionally disturbed students:

There is the element of Catch-22. They are sent to us for behavioral clean-up, and if we do our jobs right and everything works out right and we clean up their behavior, they have lost a year in the process. Or, if they come to us a year behind, we keep them a year behind and there is a problem with that . . . I have a nine year old. He'll be ten in July, and he's not reading on a second grade level yet.

The needs of these children have obviously been perceived in a narrow fashion. By defining programmes for emotionally disturbed children in a way which pays little attention to their cognitive needs, this school district can be seen to be using 'differential diagnosis' to the detriment of some of its students.

Conferring a label on a child does not, however, always result in negative consequences. Their identification as handicapped entitles students to services they may otherwise not receive. Labelling also serves to define some students to others in ways that make their behaviour understandable and therefore more acceptable. For example, a programme for high school students labelled 'learning disabled/neurologically impaired' was observed during its first year of operation. Prior to this programme, there were no others of its kind in this school district. Once the programme opened, it had to be filled, children had to be found, defined and sometimes relabelled. For example, one boy had been earlier labelled as emotionally disturbed, then educably mentally retarded, and finally as learning disabled. The labels he was given had more to do with what programmes were available than any hard and fast diagnosis.

This particular programme now offered an explanation to other students and teachers in the high school as to why this student and others couldn't read. Not only did the learning disabled label offer a less stigmatising explanation than other labels, it also served to define some students who had never before been identified as exceptional. The teacher's aide in the programme, a black inner city man in his late twenties and a graduate of the city's public schools, felt that the programme's positive effect had to do with how teachers interacted with students once they were labelled. He compared the treatment given to the learning-disabled student to that given to poor students when he attended the school:

When I was in school, the kids like the ones who are here felt humiliated. They would go into class and would be asked to read and the teacher would tell them, 'Come on now' and they couldn't read. Some of them would stop coming and some would get after the teacher and yell back.

The learning disabled/neurologically impaired designation and the class itself also helped to minimise some students' sense of humiliation, because it gave them a way of talking and thinking about themselves. Their high school was 'academic' for the most part, and those who could not read or write were made to feel out of place. Before the programme existed, students like these experienced the shame of being 'illiterate'. They now were handicapped and therefore not perceived as personally responsible for their reading deficits. Without the learning-disabled programme, these students had no chance of receiving a high school diploma.

The students took on the label of learning disabled and neurologically impaired and the teachers working with them were willing to use the designation to negotiate a place for the students in their school, a place that would be denied to them if their problems simply were defined as illiterate. The students could do special assignments in regular classes, have books read to them rather than read the required text. In fact, once a student was labelled as learning disabled, he could pass the basic reading competency test required for graduation even if he couldn't read. Learning-disabled students were able to have the reading comprehension paragraphs plus the multiple choice answers read to them.

The designation of special education/learning disabled and neurologically impaired was, however, something of which many of the class members were ashamed. Some of the students, when they were in class, sat against the wall that the door was on so that the people who were passing didn't see them. Others avoided being seen with some of the kids in the class, so they wouldn't get a bad reputation. For the most part, the students were willing to forego the stigma of being in the programme for a chance to, 'walk across the stage'. One wine drinking inner city teenager put the dilemma he experienced in the programme this way:

> Let me tell you that I am in this class but am not like most of them ... I'm slower than your average but in some ways I'm a lot faster ... See most of the kids that I hang out with in jr. high, they're in jail or kicked out of school ... Learning disabled is what they labeled me but I'm much more advanced ... Being in this class will help me graduate ... Only problem is that when they label you that, that's the way you're going to be known the rest of your life ... All I want to do is graduate, that's what I need. Now, if after being labeled and I don't graduate, then I really got it bad.

This quotation illustrates how students have their own ways of thinking about their placement and what it means in terms of their own lives. They are sensitive to the double binds of getting help under the designation of special education.

Recognising that disabilities are such flexible concepts presents quite a dilemma in trying to evaluate much of the research in special education. The literature is flooded with investigations of handicapped children, defined only in terms of their disability designation. Without further clarification regarding the specific characteristics of the children being studied, much of this research is invalid. The same is true for most efficacy studies. As our research has indicated, concepts such as self-contained classroom, resource room and mainstreaming are ambiguous and must be systematically observed and described in order to be understood. How can practitioners know that what they are doing is successful when they are doing different things with different children or, perhaps, doing some of the same things but talking about what we're doing in different ways?

Two Theoretical Approaches

The analysis of our data suggests that a useful approach towards addressing these concerns lies in the development of a theoretical approach towards special education which recognises its social, political and phenomenological nature. Borrowing from two theoretical perspectives, that of 'symbolic interactionism' and 'ecological theory', we have developed an approach that was useful in interpreting our findings. It is one which we believe can be applied by others engaged in similar research. This approach is also applicable to practitioners who are often caught in a web of terminology that may obscure rather than clarify the nature of their work.

Symbolic Interactionism

Symbolic interactionist theory stems from the writing of John Dewey, Charles Horton Cooley and George Herbert Mead (1934) and others, especially those associated with the Chicago School of Sociology (Blumer, 1969; Meltzer, Petras and Reynolds, 1975). (Other supporters of the approach include Howard S. Becker, 1970; Barney Glaser and Anselm Strauss, 1967.)

Compatible with the phenomenological perspective (Bruyn, 1966) and fundamental to the approach is the principal that human experiences are mediated by interpretation. Objects like wheelchairs, people like resource teachers and special educational students, situations such as mainstreaming and behaviour such as reading and writing do not produce their own meaning. Rather, meaning is bestowed upon them. While the educational specialist, for example, might define a language master or a tape recorder as a device to teach learning-disabled children to read, the teacher may define it as an object to entertain unruly students when she runs out of work for them. Or, place the speaking-machine with a non-western tribal group and it might be defined as a religious icon to be worshipped (Bogdan and Biklen, 1982). The meaning people give to their experience and the process of interpretation is essential, not accidental or secondary to what experience is. A person's world is their imagination of it. Humans, in a phenomenological sense, actively engage in the creation of their reality. To understand behaviour, we must understand ways of thinking and the process by which these ways of thinking are constructed. People act, not on the basis of predetermined responses to predefined objects but rather as interpreting, defining, symbolic animals whose behaviour can only be understood by entering into the defining process with them.

Ecological Theory

The 'ecological' approach towards understanding human behaviour focuses on the interactions which occur between individuals and the settings in which they operate. Settings are conceived as components of systems, each influencing and being influenced by the other. Schools, for example, can be conceived of as settings within the educational system which, in turn, interacts with the community. The immediate community is additionally influenced by the larger social systems of which it is an integral component. In fact, Bronfenbrenner (1977) conceives of the interrelationship between systems as a separate system, i.e. a 'meso-system'.

Ecological theory further clarifies the defining process discussed extensively by symbolic interactionists in its focus upon the interaction between individuals within the context of their environments. Wilson (1977) points out that not only do individuals influence reality by their definition of the situation (Blumer, 1969), but that the setting itself generates regularities in behaviour. Therefore, the behaviour of individuals must be examined in context. 'Human ecologists' stress the importance of 'fit' between an individual and his or her environment. There is a continual interaction between the two. In the case of organisations, such as schools, this interaction can be seen as a consistent pattern of interaction by its members, which allows for the continuation of the organisation and the perpetuation of its pattern of operation (Rhodes and Tracy, 1977, vol. I).

Following from this perspective, special education can be viewed as a component of the educational system whose function must therefore 'fit' into the operation of the larger systems. The ways that children are defined as exceptional must therefore be understood in these terms. In fact, there is a growing body of literature surrounding the education of children labelled as emotionally disturbed which employs an ecological perspective. This literature reflects this point of view both in its content and research methodology (Algozzine, 1976, 1977; Apter, 1982; Hobbs, 1975, 1980; Rhodes, 1970; Ross, 1980; Salzinger, Antrobus and Glick, eds., 1980; Swap, 1974, 1978).

Symbolic interactionists and ecological theorists recognise that individuals develop shared definitions as a means of communication which allows for the functional operation of systems. However, individuals employing these definitions on a day-to-day basis often mistake consensus for 'truth'. Shared definitions become reified. People come to believe that children actually read at 'levels', have IQs and are mentally retarded or emotionally disturbed (Gould, 1982). Such concepts must be bracketed, i.e. their common-sense use examined so that they can be taken from the realm of being taken for granted. In this way, they will not be mistaken for being 'objective', 'correct' or real in any larger sense of these terms.

Interpretation is essential and the meaning of interaction is paramount in order to understand what special education is all about. We would not deny that some students are more predisposed to read than others, or that a child who is blind cannot see. Rather, these phenomena need to be understood by looking at the interplay between how various people come to define these children in specific situations. Such things as internal drives, personality traits, reading levels and intelligence quotients take a backseat when special education is explored from this perspective. These theoretical constructs certainly might be useful to professional caregivers. However, they are relevant to our understanding of behaviour only to the degree to which they enter into and effect the defining process. These approaches are studied to understand the way professionals construct their world.

With this general introduction to symbolic interaction and ecological theory behind us, we turn to a list of assumptions which represent the application of these perspectives to special education and the situations we observed over two years.

There Are No Disabled Students in Any Absolute Sense.

Mental retardation, emotional disturbance, learning disability and even blindness and other specific disability categories are ways of thinking about others, attitudes we take towards them, ways of structuring relationships, and accepted processes and frames of mind. Whether we think of people in terms of disability (or any of the other sub-categories) and what criteria we use to determine whether someone is or is not, has to do with how the definers think about these things.

Following up on this point, there are no true counts of the number of people, for example, with mental retardation, or who are blind, or who have any other alleged disability, nor are there any 'correct' definitions of these things in any absolute sense (Bogdan and Kasander, 1980). Disability counts and definitions are reifications of customs and practice. Standardised psychological testing has made judgements appear to be truths. A child's performance on a *Wechsler* or *Stanford-Binet* has come to be defined, both in the professional and lay literature, as a real measure of 'potential'.

In spite of recent outcries, deploring the biases inherent in these tests, IQ remains synonymous with 'intelligence' in our culture. Although given less weight than in previous years, these scores are still used in the determination of who is and is not mentally retarded. Today, measures of 'adaptive behaviour' are combined with IQ scores, to give more sophisticated diagnoses. Really what has happened is that behaviours have been redefined. And, as a result, the number of retarded citizens has changed. As is the case with other constructions of disability and counts of the number of disabled people, the concept of mental retardation is temporal and represents larger political and social forces.

The Physical and Behavioural Characteristics of Children Designated as Disabled Enter Into the Process through which the Meaning of the Child Emerges but not in a Deterministic Way that is Commonly Believed.

Such things as not being able to read, or not being able to pass tests, or not being able to walk or having organic brain damage set parameters in which definitions develop, but they do not *determine* how people with these conditions will be defined. To say that disability is a social construction is not to deny physiological, behavioural and psychological differences among people; it is to point out the importance of the meaning (if they are perceived and how they are perceived) of these differences and to structure our actions towards those with specific designations.

Some people cannot see. Blindness tells us what not being able to see means (Scott, 1969). How blindness is manifested in the treatment of and reactions to people is what symbolic interaction dwells on. While not denying physical and behavioural realities, symbolic interaction emphasises that human beings have the capacity to change their world to be what they imagine it to be. Ecological theory recognises that this capacity is mediated by the interactions of individuals with each other and their environments. And so, for example, not being able to see does not need to mean that a child will be socially isolated and totally dependent upon others. The non-seeing child's functioning may instead be as dependent upon the definition given to his physical condition by those in a position to influence the circumstances of his life as is the physical reality of his blindness.

Disability Is Interactional.

Be it mental retardation, cerebral palsy, deafness, blindness, emotional disturbance or learning disability, disability is only in a particular and narrowest sense a condition that a person has. The word disability (and the many sub-categories under the heading) does not simply symbolise a condition that is already there in advance; it makes possible the existence or appearance of the condition, for it is part of the mechanism whereby the condition is created (Rose, 1962, p. 5). Disability is a designation and, therefore, embedded in social relations. As a concept, disability is a particular way of thinking and a way of acting and reacting. The creation of a disability concept and its application in specific settings, the effect it provokes, is derived from and sustained in interaction.

The implications of the failure to recognise the interactional nature of disability designations were clearly illustrated in the case of the students in our study who had been labelled as severely emotionally disturbed. This identification carried with it the implication that the difficulties these boys were experiencing had their origins within the children and their families. This definition failed to take into account that a good deal of the acting out seen in school was related to a mismatch between the expectations in the school setting and those the children experienced elsewhere. These expectations related both to social behaviour and academic performance. This resulted in the application of a stigmatising label and intervention strategies that were often inappropriate.

An 'ecological definition' of emotional disturbance, such as the following one offered by Apter (1982), would place the child's behaviour within its context and therefore suggest more appropriate interventions.

> From this outlook, emotional disturbance is not simply seen as the
> necessary result of intrapsychic conflict nor as the inevitable product
> of inappropriate social learning. Instead, according to the ecological
> model, disturbance resides in the interaction between the child and
> the critical aspects of the child's environment, that is, the child's
> system. More specifically, ecological theorists believe that what we
> know as emotional disturbance or behavior disorders actually result
> from a descrepancy between a given child's skills and abilities and
> the demands or expectations of that child's environment. (p. 2)

Following this perspective, interventions would include working with
regular classroom teachers towards developing an understanding of the
child's behaviour from the context of the other systems in which this
child operates. Likewise, families would become more involved in their
child's education. In this way, both systems' sets of expectations and
definitions could be moved in ways which would provide a more congruent environment for the child.

*When We Apply the Concept of Disability, or any Specific Designation
Falling under the Generic Term, We Represent a Situation in a Particular
Way.*

Disability can change the meaning of behaviour. The word disability, or
more specifically its many sub-categories such as mental retardation,
emotional disturbance and deafness, makes us selectively sensitive to
certain behaviours and actions. Things that might not have been noticed
before jump out and take on meaning within the framework of such
ideas. Behaviour and physical characteristics that were noted and interpreted in one way get interpreted in another way through the ideas
of special education. The case of the children labelled as severely emotionally disturbed in our study offers an excellent illustration of this
phenomenon. As handicapped children they were no longer perceived
as bad. Rather, they were seen as sick.

Disability categories give those who use them a sense of knowing
and therefore a way of relating and programming for those who fall
under their headings. Labelling a child suggests that he or she is understood as being like those in the category. A whole set of expectations
and assumptions are applied. Thus, the child is subject to a set of
behaviours, ways of thinking and settings that alter his or her circumstances. As our data suggest, these alterations may have negative as well

as positive consequences for the child.

How an Individual Defines Him or Herself in regard to an Alleged Disability Is a Function of and Is Constructed through Interaction.

People come to see themselves as blind, mentally retarded or by other epithets, or they reject such concepts. Whether they are ashamed or proud of their condition, or feel neutral about it, is mediated by significant others — parents, teachers, peers, attendants — who enter their lives through social interaction. People interpret others' gestures and actions in attempting to see themselves as others see them and thereby construct a self-concept. In fact, in rehabilitation, it has been found that an individual's prognosis for recovery may be strongly associated with this concept. People with particular disabilities do not have peculiar personalities or ways of thinking about themselves. For some, disability dominates how they see themselves. For others, it is an insignificant part of how they think.

How a person comes to think about his or her alleged physical behaviour or psychological difference in a particular way has to be understood in terms of the life history of the individual and how it intersects the institutions of which he or she is a part and the particular historical period in which he or she lives. People ought to be thought of as having a disability career, that is a series of stages and positions in which a perspective on disability and the relation to self is developed. Those who are judged disabled have a point of view about who they are, what they have been called and who has been doing the accusing (Bogdan, Taylor, DeGrandpre and Haynes, 1974). It is these thoughts that shape the way they react to the programmes they are in, not only the wishes and models of programme planners.

Disability, as Special Education Specialists Construct it, is a Particular Frame of Mind by which to Organise the World.

The salience of *their* way of seeing human differences in influencing how others see it, needs to be studied as an issue of the politics of competing perspectives. For example, whether a child is conceptualised as learning disabled or as illiterate is an issue that can only be understood in a political frame of mind. The study of development, the growth and the politics of special education and how they came to construct disability as they have, who they fought with in the process and what their common sense unnoticed assumptions are, is an important part of the study of special education. There are histories of special education written by people who are special educators but these should be the data of a symbolic interactionist history of special education, not the conclusion. A Catholic and an agnostic anthropologist can attend the same mass but experience it quite differently. In order to understand analytically the social history and the social dimensions of special education as a profession, it might have to be approached by non-believers.

Disability Is Situational.

Alleged differences, be they physical, behavioural or psychological, have particular meanings in particular settings. Not knowing how to read has a different meaning from one school to another. Its meaning in one class may differ from the meaning in another. The concept of the six-hour retarded student points out how a student may be defined as retarded in the context of the school but not be thought of in that way in his family or neighbourhood. Questions about the efficacy of various special educational programmes have to be approached in terms of the meaning of special education and various disability categories in the wide range of contexts.

The meaning of special education varies depending on where you sit in the school bureaucracy or in which system it is a part. Often rules are made at one level to be applied in another. It is the meaning of the rules of disability and not legislation that mediates how people behave. Often the images that people who formulate the rules have of how special education works and who is disabled are quite different from those of the people who deliver the services in the real life settings.

All Special Educational Programmes Exist in a Larger Context — They Are Part of Schools, School Systems, States and Nations.

Definitions, ways of thinking, do not get formed in a vacuum nor are they formed at random. They reflect the environments of which they are a part. They will reflect the values, the problems and the concerns of people who operate in those settings. They will also reflect economic conditions. Meaning does not occur in isolated bits. It is part of larger and complex clusters. To isolate education and the disabled from the context of the systems of which they are a part is to distort, leaving significant aspects unexamined. In order to understand the meaning of 'being behind at school' we have to go beyond the isolated pieces.

Disability Has Moral Meaning.

The way we think about people with alleged disabilities is filled with moral meaning (Bogdan and Biklen, 1977). One of the images that we have of the disabled is that they are dangerous. How is that image manifested in the media and in the lives of disabled and non-disabled people in our society? The meaning of disability in special education goes far beyond alleged physical behaviour and psychological differences. Disability has symbolic meaning that must be looked at in terms of what society honours — intelligence, confidence, beauty and success. Our society has traditionally been structured to bring shame to people with alleged disabilities. Some problems are technical — providing physical access to wheelchairs, building communication systems for non-verbal people — other problems are moral and social. They are located much deeper in the seams of our society than professionals in the field of special education touch.

References

Algozzine, B. (1976) 'The disturbing child: What you see is what you get?' *Alberta Journal of Education Research*, 22, 330-3.
—— (1977) 'The emotionally disturbed child: Disturbed or disturbing?' *Journal of Abnormal Child Psychology*, 5, 2, 205-11.
—— and Curran, T.J. (1979) 'Teachers' predictions of children's school success as a function of their behavior tolerances', *Journal of Educational Research*, July-August, 72, 6, 344-7.
Apter, S.J. (1982) *Troubled Children, Troubled Systems*, Pergamon Press, New York.
Becker, H.S. (1970) *Sociological Work*, Aldine, Chicago.
Blumer, H. (1969) *Symbolic Interactionism*, Prentice-Hall, Englewood Cliffs, NJ.
Bogdan, R. and Barnes, E. (1979) 'A qualitative-sociological study of mainstreaming. NIE proposal' (mimeographed), Center on Human Policy, Syracuse University.
—— and Biklen, D. (1977) 'Handicappism', *Social Policy*, April, 7, 5, 14-19.
—— and —— (1982) *Qualitative Research for Education*, Allyn and Bacon, Boston.
—— and Kasander, M. (1980) 'Policy data as a social process: A qualitative approach to quantitative data', *Human Organization*, 39, 4, 302-6.
——, Taylor, S., DeGrandpre, B. and Haynes, S. (1974) 'Let them eat programs: Attendants' perspectives and programming on wards in state schools', *Journal of Health and Social Behavior*, 15, June, 142-51.
Braginsky, D. and Braginsky, B. (1971) *Hansels and Gretels*, Holt, Rinehart and Winston, New York.
Bronfenbrenner, U. (1977) 'Toward an experimental ecology of human development', *American Psychologist*, 32, 513-31.
Bruyn, S. (1966) *The Human Perspective in Sociology*, Prentice-Hall, Englewood Cliffs, NJ.
Calhoun, C.J. and Ianni, F.A. (eds.) (1976) *The Anthropological Study of Education*, Mouton Publishers, Paris.
Conrad, P. (1976) *Identifying Hyperactive Children: The Medicalization of Deviant Behavior*, D.C. Heath and Co., Lexington, Mass.
Foster, G.G., Ysseldyke, J.E. and Reese, J.A. (1975) 'I wouldn't have seen it if I hadn't believed it', *Exceptional Children*, 41, 469-73.

Gajar, A. (1979) 'Educable mentally retarded, learning disabled, emotionally disturbed: Similarities and differences', *Exceptional Children*, March, *45*, 470-2.

Gillung, T.B. and Rucker, C.N. (1977) 'Labels and teacher expectations', *Exceptional Children*, April, *43*, 464-5.

Glaser, B. and Strauss, A. (1967) *The Discovery of Grounded Theory*, Aldine, Chicago.

Gould, S.J. (1982) *The Mismeasure of Man*, W.W. Norton and Co., New York.

Hallahan, D.P. and Kauffman, J.M. (1977) 'Labels, categories, behaviors: E.D., L.D., and E.M.R. reconsidered', *Journal of Special Education*, Summer, *11*, 2.

Hobbs, N. (1975) *The Futures of Children: Categories, Labels and their Consequences*, Jossey-Bass, San Francisco.

—— (1980) 'An ecologically oriented service based system for the classification of handicapped children' in S. Salzinger, J. Antrobus and J. Glick (eds.), *The Ecosystem of the "Sick" Child*, Academic Press, New York.

Kauffman, J. (1981) *Characteristics of Children's Behavior Disorders* (2nd edn.), Charles E. Merrill Publishing Co., Columbus, Ohio.

Mead, G.H. (1934) *Mind, self, and society*, University of Chicago Press, Chicago.

Meltzer, B., Petras, J. and Reynolds, L. (1975) *Symbolic Interactionism*, Routledge and Kegan Paul, London.

Mercer, J. (1973) *Labelling and Mentally Retarded: Clinical and Social System Perspectives on Mental Retardation*, University of California Press, Berkeley, California.

Quay, H.C. and Galvin, J.P. (1970) *The Education of Behaviorally Disordered Children in the Public School Setting*, Interim report, Philadelphia, PA: Temple University, Oct. (ERIC Document Reproduction Service no. ED053523).

Rhodes, W.C. (1970) 'A community participation analysis of emotional disturbance', *Exceptional Children*, Jan., *36*, 306-14.

—— and Tracy, M.L. (1972) *A Study of Child Variance* (vols. I and II), University of Michigan Press, Ann Arbor.

Rist, R. and Harrell, J. (1982) 'Labeling and the learning disabled child: the social ecology of educational practice', *American Journal of Orthopsychiatry*, *52*, 1, 146-60.

Rose, A. (1962) *Human Behavior and Social Processes: An Interactionist Approach*, Houghton, Mifflin and Co., Boston.

Ross, A.O. (1980) *Psychological Disorders of Children* (2nd edn.), McGraw Hill, New York.

Salvia, T.A. and Meisels, C.J. (1980) 'Observer bias in special education research', *Journal of Special Education*, *14*, 2, 261-70.

Salzinger, S., Antrobus, J. and Glick, J. (eds.) (1980) *The Ecosystem of the "Sick" Child*, Academic Press, New York.

Sarason, S.B. and Doris, J. (1979) *Educational Handicap, Public Policy and Social History*, The Free Press, New York.

Schrag, P. and Divoky, D. (1975) *The Myth of the Hyperactive Child*, Pantheon, New York.

Scott, R. (1969) *The Making of Blind Men*, Russell Sage Foundation, New York.

Swap, S. (1974) 'Disturbing classroom behavior: a developmental and ecological view', *Exceptional Children*, *41*, 162-71.

—— (1978) 'The ecological model of emotional disturbance in children: A status report and proposed synthesis', *Behavioral Disorders*, May, *3*, 3, 156-86.

Szasz, T. (1970) *Ideology and Insanity*, Anchor Books, Garden City, New York.

Tomlinson, S. (1982) *A Sociology of Special Education*, Routledge and Kegan Paul, London.

Vacc, N.A. and Keist, N. (1977) 'Emotionally disturbed children and regular classroom teachers', *Elementary School Journal*, 77, 4, 309-17.

Wax, M., Diamond, S. and Gearing, F. (1971) *Anthropological Perspectives on Education*, Basic Books, New York.
Weaver, T. (ed.) (1973) *To See Ourselves: Anthropology and Modern Social Issues*, Scott Foresman, Glenview, Illinois.
Wilson, S. (1977) 'The use of ethnographic techniques in educational research', *Review of Educational Research*, 47, 1, 245-65.
Wright, B. (1960) *Physical Disability: A Psychological Approach*, Harper and Row, New York.
Ysseldyke, J. and Foster, G. (1978) 'Bias in teachers' observations of emotionally disturbed-learning disabled children', *Exceptional Children*, 44, 8, 613-15.

8 ADOLESCENCE AND PHYSICAL IMPAIRMENT: AN INTERACTIONIST VIEW*
Alan Hurst

The International Year of Disabled Persons 1981, if nothing else, served to focus attention yet again on the problems faced by people with physical impairments. Some ten years earlier in Britain, the passing of the Chronically Sick and Disabled Persons Act had performed a similar function. Both events did acknowledge the needs of young people with impairments and, indeed, in the stages leading up to the passing of the act, its sponsor, Alf Morris MP, indicated that physically-impaired adolescents might have special problems in addition to those which might be termed the 'normal' difficulties of adolescence in Western advanced societies.

There is support for this view from a number of sources. Autobiographical accounts from physically-impaired people are one source; a typical comment is: 'One's teenage years are normally one's worst and with me it was no exception' (Sutton, 1972). Some research investigations have also drawn attention to problems and difficulties. One recent empirically-based study has attempted to compare a group of physically-impaired teenagers with some able-bodied peers in a range of educational, occupational and recreational contexts (Anderson and Clarke, 1982). The four major points in the final paragraph of that study constitute a valuable introduction to matters to be discussed in this chapter.

> First, the high incidence of dissatisfaction with their social lives both during school years and after . . . Secondly, how little control over their lives the young people felt that they had . . . Thirdly, the poverty of choice currently available to those unable to find open employment . . . Fourthly, how ill-prepared the teenager seemed to be for the realities of life as handicapped adults, and how inadequate was the help offered in the difficult transition period between school and adult life.

---

*I am indebted to my colleague, Ken Foster, for constructive comment on an earlier draft of this chapter.

A third source of support for the view that physically-impaired adolescents have additional problems lies in the work of those who have commented more generally on the nature of disability and handicap. One author has suggested that the very concept of 'adolescence' might usefully explain the social situation of physically-impaired people.

> Adolescents' status is marginal between the two (i.e. childhood and adulthood) — and the disabled are similarly marginal people. They occupy a position along the continuum from physically capable to physically helpless. The sense of marginality is intensified by the indefinite boundary between physical normality and physical disability ... There is, of course, a difference between the marginality... That of the adolescent is temporary, that of the disabled may well be life long (Thomas, 1978).

There is, then, a range of evidence to indicate the special nature of adolescence for those with a physical impairment. The aim of this chapter is to explore how far an interactionist perspective might contribute to an understanding of the situation. It will do so by drawing attention to several basic interactionist concepts and illustrating how they can add insight to an appreciation of the more general problems and difficulties. The chapter will then focus on three interactional contexts of great significance to young people and in which the concepts can be seen to be operating. Throughout the chapter extensive use will be made of previously published research, commentaries and biographical accounts; whilst many of these do not deal specifically with adolescence, they do raise issues which are applicable to that period in life. Their use in a chapter such as this is indicative of the lack of investigation undertaken in this area. Before proceeding further there are some essential preliminary remarks to be made.

Area of Concern

Because the variety of physical impairment is so great, it will be more useful to focus on one broad area. Thus, what follows concentrates only on young people of average or above average intelligence. Neither mental impairments nor multiple impairments of any sort will be covered, nor will sensory impairments. The area of concern will encompass four broad categories of orthopaedic and motor impairments. First, there are congenital conditions, including muscular dystrophy, spina bifida, cerebral palsy, osteogenesis imperfecta, etc. The second broad category covers skeletal deformities; included here are talipes, scoliosis, dislocation of the hip and achondroplasia. There are also those born limbless; here one must make special mention of those adolescents affected by their mothers' use of the drug thalidomide during pregnancy. Third, there are impairments resulting from diseases such as poliomyelitis, multiple sclerosis and rheumatoid arthritis. The final category covers those whose impairment is a result of accidents leading to amputations and paralysis. There are a number of other additional points to note. First, some physical impairments are amenable to medical treatment and surgery. Second, the age at which the impairment occurs is important; if it is congenital, a child can be taught from the start to make use of his abilities. Third, many physical impairments are obvious and visible in ways and to an extent not found with sensory or mental impairments. As will be seen, this raises problems in interaction, perhaps through an individual's own sensitivities, perhaps through the tendency of others to shun the company of a person with an impairment. Fourth, some conditions can lessen over time whilst others grow worse.

At this point it is appropriate to define impairment and to introduce the basic perspective of symbolic interactionism. Many approaches have tried to distinguish between defect, disability and handicap. Briefly, a defect refers to some imperfection; objectively viewed it could be trivial or serious, but there is no implication of adverse effect on the individual. (However 'defect' does have negative connotations; similarly 'handicap' implies a particular value position; thus throughout this chapter the more neutral term 'impairment' is used.) A disability is a physical condition which does produce malfunctioning but without necessarily interfering with an individual's normal life. A handicap is a disability which does have adverse effects on growth and development. It can also have adverse effects on adjustment to social life, partly because of environmental aspects (e.g. problems of access) but also because of social attitudes. These distinctions have been discussed more fully in other places, notably, and most recently, by Mark Philip and Derek Duckworth (1982). They draw attention to the schema suggested by the World Health Organisation and indicate its advantages. The key features are summarised and, as the following extract shows and despite the definition relating in particular to contexts of health and illness, it is moving towards an interactionist approach:

The state of being handicapped is relative to other people — hence the importance of existing societal values, which, in turn, are influenced by the institutional arrangements of society. Thus, the attitudes and responses of the non-handicapped play a central part in modelling the ego concept, and defining the possibilities of an individual who is potentially handicapped — the latter has a very limited freedom to determine or modify his own reality (WHO, 1980, and quoted in Philip and Duckworth, 1982).

The position becomes clearer if one sees having a physical impairment as a form of deviance, and then makes use of what has been described as 'labelling theory' (there is no specific theory; the term describes a set of interrelated concepts which are rooted in the symbolic interactionist tradition). A deviant is an individual who does not conform; it might be that norms of behaviour are not observed or rules broken. However, what is seen by some to be deviant is judged by others to be normal in other situations. Deviance involves normative judgements given from a particular viewpoint. (In relation to physical impairment many authors have speculated about the consequences for able-bodied people of a world in which the majority of people use wheelchairs.) This, then, is the starting-point for labelling theory; it emphasises the interactional processes in operation in defining something or someone as deviant. The key aspect is not the behaviour or the personal quality being judged; the reactions of other people are what matter. Summarised,

deviance may be conceived as a process by which members of a group, community, or society (1) interpret behaviour as deviant (2) define persons who so behave as a certain kind of deviant and (3) accord them the treatment considered appropriate to such deviants (Kitsuse, 1962).

An interactionist approach to physical impairment is one founded upon societal reactions. In discussing deviance in classrooms David Hargreaves and his associates suggested that several questions stem from such an approach (Hargreaves, Hestor and Mellor, 1975); modified and applied to physical impairment the questions become:

1. Who is labelled impaired, under what conditions, and with what purpose in mind?
2. Who is applying the label, in what terms, on what basis, and in what circumstances?
3. How does the application of the label affect or change the behaviour of the labellers to the labelled?

4. How does the recipient of the label react?
5. How is the label sustained, modified, or withdrawn?

These questions set the scene for the more detailed descriptions of the concept which follows, and in which some answers to these questions should begin to emerge.

A final preliminary involves a little further comment on the general characteristics of a symbolic interactionist approach. The theoretical basis of this can be found in the work of the American, George Herbert Mead. Symbolic interaction tries to explain how man comes to 'know' the world. Interactionists see this occurring in contexts involving other people. Man attempts to interpret the behaviour of other men. From the symbolic interactionist point of view, social interaction depends upon reflexive thought and the capacity for indication to oneself of the significance of the actions of others and the consequences of one's own actions. The emphasis is upon the dynamic aspects of human relationships and the way in which individuals can change and modify their behaviour in relation to perceptions of each other. Blumer (1962) has attempted to summarise the perspective in this way:

> The term 'symbolic interaction' refers, of course, to the peculiar and distinctive character of interaction as it takes place between human beings. The peculiarity consists in the fact that human beings interpret or 'define' each other's actions instead of merely reacting to each other's actions. Their 'response' is not made directly to the actions of one another but instead is based on the meaning which they attach to such actions. Thus, human interaction is mediated by the use of symbols, by interpretation, or by ascertaining the meaning of one another's actions. This mediation is equivalent to inserting a process of interpretation between stimulus and response in the case of human behaviour.

Interactionists emphasise that the meanings given to events and experiences are not fixed and immutable, but arise in the course of social interaction. Such interactions occur within an already existing world with an already agreed set of symbols (i.e. language); thus, existing definitions and meanings are available to be taken on by an individual. These meanings and definitions apply both to objects and experiences, and to individuals. An individual comes to 'know' what he is and how he is defined through interacting with others.

Essential Concepts

Within this theoretical framework, there are a number of key concepts. Each will now be examined in turn in relation to physically-impaired adolescents. The order of presentation adopted here is to begin by discussing those concepts more closely related to the individual before examining concepts which relate rather more to the context of social groups. It should be remembered that the concepts are being separated only for ease of analysis, and that in social interaction they are all operating and are mutually reinforcing. The concepts are: self, identity, role, status, social norms and cultural expectations, language and socialisation, and significant and generalised others.

Self

For Mead, the self consists of two interdependent parts, the 'I' and the 'me'. The former refers to the unrestrained driving force which initiates behaviour, whilst the latter exercises control on that behaviour as a result of previous social experiences. It originates in a three-stage process. In the first months and years of life a human infant gradually becomes aware of the social world through contact with a widening circle of other people. An infant can exercise no choice on who these people might be, but they are the ones who provide a conception of the social world. They introduce the gestures and symbols used to describe and interpret the social world. The second stage occurs when a young child begins to play at 'being other people'. This involves fragmented pieces of behaviour picked up in interaction with a range of other people, but especially those with whom there has been close and frequent contact. The final stage, the so-called 'game stage', is marked by the realisation that different behaviours are appropriate in different contexts. Different rules of good behaviour apply; these rules consist of the general expectations of others. Having reached this stage a number of characteristics of self will be formed. These are the ability to think about self and to reflect upon it as if it was another object or person. It is also clear that self is created as a result of social interaction, and that it is not fixed for all time. It changes and develops through interaction with others.

Self then is seen as a process formed in the same way as other objects, i.e. by 'definitions' from others. How we think of our 'self' depends on how others behave towards us. If, over time, their behaviour changes, our self concept might also change. If, in interaction with others, an individual becomes aware that he is different in some way, his self concept will be affected. In the case of those with physical impairments, there is ample evidence that this is what occurs (see the autobiographical accounts of the subjects in the study by Campling, 1981). Part of this can be explained in terms of physical appearance. There are many occasions in social life when individuals encounter each other for the first time; lacking any background information about each other, they use visual clues to help them define and interpret the situation. Many physically-impaired people are clearly aware of the impact of their appearance and its effect on the reactions of others. The self concept is largely influenced by the picture an individual believes others have of him.

> Many disabled women have poor self images, partly because of the attitudes of others towards them. One woman has described how, as an adolescent, her boyfriend would take her out in a wheelchair. Everyone assumed that she must be his relative, because they could not accept her as a typical girl able to attract a boyfriend . . . In a society where physical attractiveness in women is valued so highly, especially through the mass media, a negative value is placed on a physical defect and a damaged or distorted self image results (Campling, 1979).

Obviously, the reaction of others is crucial. An individual will react as others react to him. There are two aspects, then — how the group reacts and how an individual reacts. Taking the former, it is interesting to note that, as well as evidence from accounts of everyday experience written by physically-impaired individuals, there is also a good deal of evidence derived from experiments. Richardson and his associates were interested to investigate how similar the reactions of able-bodied children would be to other children with physical impairments. A group of ten- and eleven-year-olds, some with impairments, some able-bodied, were asked to give preference rankings to a standard set of drawings of children who differed only with respect to an obvious physical impairment. The pictures portrayed a child with no visible impairment, a child with crutches and a brace on one leg, a child in a wheelchair, a child with one hand missing, a child with a facial disfigurement and an obese child. The children's preferences occurred in that order, and the experimenters found the need to explain why their subjects, both impaired and able-bodied, reacted in the same way (Richardson, Goodman, Hastorf and Dornbush, 1961). Whilst such experiments in the artificial environment of a laboratory might be something of an anathema within an interactionist paradigm, the results do seem to indicate that the reactions to physical impairment are broadly similar, and that these reactions have socio-cultural origins.

Looking now at how an individual with a physical impairment reacts, the work of Goffman is a useful starting-point. He has indicated how, in face-to-face interactions, individuals can control the amount of information about their 'self' which is available to others (Goffman, 1971). Furthermore, in *Stigma* he highlights social situations where stigmatised and non-stigmatised encounter each other (Goffman, 1969). The term 'stigma' is used to refer to an attribute of a person that is discrediting in some way and leads others to treat him in a non-normal fashion. Goffman's use of the concept has been sharply criticised:

> He thus sees stigma, applied to physically impaired people, in non-oppressive terms. He takes as given . . . imposed segregation, passivity, and the inferior status of disabled people . . . It places all the problems on the shoulders of this group who are encouraged to believe that they should take their 'disability' as given (Finkelstein, 1980).

There is an important and valid point here, namely the oppressive nature of the imposition of a stigma. From here one could consider the situation of physically-impaired people in broader structuralist class conflict terms; however the point does relate closely to the earlier discussion of labelling theory. It is an instance of a label being applied upon unwilling recipients; moreover, as Finkelstein suggests, this application is at two levels — from society at large, and from the many groups of professionals whose functions bring them into close contact with physically-impaired people. He sees such groups as creating a paradox; on the one hand, they must try to do everything possible to ensure that physically-impaired people can participate in social life as much or as little as they themselves choose to; on the other hand, if the policies and actions are totally successful, the professional groups could well find themselves unemployed! Because of such constraints Finkelstein feels that the work of researchers and other involved professionals must be treated with some caution, and that, if the social situation of physically-impaired people is to change, one important aspect of that change must be an increased awareness amongst the researchers etc. of their own roles and positions. In terms of this change, he suggests that a three-phase process is underway. In the first phase, when society was less advanced and less industrial, physically-impaired people were an indistinct part of the lower social strata. In the second phase, with its increased industrialisation, specialisation and division of labour, they became a more distinct segregated group with specialist professionals and institutions provided by society supposedly for beneficial reasons. (A recent study has suggested that one should examine the covert intentions of some of the philanthropists who provided facilities in nineteenth- and twentieth-century Britain — see Ford, Morgan and Whelan, 1982.) The third phase is presently gathering momentum. Physically-impaired people are being seen no longer as dependent or deviant. Technology and material resources are available to make appropriate alterations to the physical environment, and there is a growing awareness of the origins, development and consequences of social attitudes. This final phase has not yet been completed. Many physically-impaired people still confront a range of social situations in which traditional norms and values are dominant.

At this point one can return to Goffman's analysis and in particular to his concept of 'passing' which he defines thus:

> By intention or in effect [a physically-impaired person] conceals information about his real social identity, receiving and accepting treatment based on false suppositions concerning himself. It is this second general issue, the management of undisclosed discrediting information about self, . . . in brief, 'passing' (Goffman, 1969).

Much depends on the visibility of the impairment but, even here, in certain situations, it might be possible to conceal information. For example, in a meeting where everyone is seated, it might not be obvious that one of those sitting is in a wheelchair. Because of the great rewards in being considered normal, many will try to 'pass'. Campling has suggested additional strategies for coping — 'normalisation', when individuals try to play down the consequences of their physical impairment; and 'withdrawal', where non-participation in social interaction means that any potential embarrassment is avoided (Campling, 1979). Although writing specifically about disabled women, these strategies can also be adopted by adolescents. Most significantly, she continues by pointing out that, whilst such strategies are used by able-bodied people occasionally, there is the possibility that they are always in use by physically-impaired people. There appear to be parallels here between the permanence of these strategies and the permanence of 'adolescence' as suggested by Thomas and referred to in the opening remarks of the chapter.

One author has used Goffman's ideas as a starting-point for an analysis of interaction between those with an obvious physical impairment and able-bodied people (Davis, 1961). Using information obtained from eleven subjects, six of whom had physical impairments which come within the scope of this chapter, the data are analysed in two ways.

First, there are the ways in which the impairment acts as a threat to social interaction. For example, there is a tendency for the impairment to become the focal point of the interaction. In normal encounters, participants direct attention to each other in a more general fashion. This does not appear to be the case when those with physical impairments meet able-bodied people. In talking of a job interview, Diana makes the following observation:

> Most of the talking was done by the younger personnel officer. He could see nothing but my chair, worse still he could not even say the word 'wheelchair', pointing at my chair and saying, 'How will you manage in that thing?' (Campling, 1981).

Second, there is the importance of physical appearance and the lack of control over this on the part of an impaired individual. Diana's remarks are also illustrative of another set of threats: in Davis's terminology, the impairment has 'inundating potential'. In everyday interaction, the extent of emotional display is kept within strict limits and yet, for some able-bodied people, contact with an individual with a physical impairment results in strong emotional feelings, thus making the encounter unusual. A physical impairment might also constitute a threat to normal social interaction because there is a contradiction of attributes. The remarks of Su illustrate this beautifully: 'I have been told by my friends that the notice I cause is due to the disparate images I present – "I'm young and attractive, I don't present the 'disabled' image expected!"' (Campling, 1981). A final threat results from ambiguity and uncertainty. Both physically-impaired and able-bodied people face dilemmas – is it better to invite an impaired person even though he cannot participate fully, or will not inviting him make him feel left out? From the viewpoint of an impaired individual, he might wonder whether he is invited because his company is really required or whether the invitation stems from politeness. Davis then goes on to suggest a number of stages through which social relationships between physically-impaired and able-bodied people pass in an attempt to make the situation normal. However, Thomas (1982) has suggested that Davis does not take into account the initiative taken by an impaired person in social interaction:

> The underlying theme is that the disabled person is essentially reactive to the behaviour of others . . . There is little room . . . for

acknowledging the skill of some disabled people in taking a positive lead in interactions, and almost no mention that disabled people are often extremely perceptive about others' feelings and reactions; they can be accomplished in making relationships work smoothly.

However, to return to Davis's analysis, at the end of the process as he describes it, the person's individuality and self become more important than the impairment. He has established an identity.

Identity

McCall and Simmons (1966) see this concept as crucial: 'Identification of persons and of other "things" is the key to symbolic interaction; once things are identified and their meanings for us established, we can proceed with our individual strivings'. Identification, then, relates to placement into categories. Having categorised a person, one knows how to behave towards that person. One knows the implications of persons in that category for a planned course of action, and so the plans can be modified accordingly. Putting this slightly differently, there are expectations about the behaviour and actions of persons for whom a category has been chosen. The degree of general agreement about the expectations relates to the concepts of role (see below) and of stereotype. The latter contains some truth and can be useful as an initial form of categorisation, but for an individual so categorised the stereotype is an incomplete fit. Stereotypes focus on generalities. Some qualities are exaggerated, others are omitted and ignored. Most people are aware of these aspects and do not make rigid judgements initially. Incoming information which arises in the course of social interaction is processed, and the initial categorisation modified, sustained or changed. On the basis of additional evidence, a more complete picture is built up and this will acknowledge what is unique about an individual. This leads on to making an important distinction between personal identity and social identity. The former relates to the individual and to how he would like to be categorised. Occasionally the desired personal identity and the assigned social identity coincide, but there are also many occasions when they do not. It is the incongruence between the two aspects of identity which emerge in a consideration of evidence relating to physically-impaired people. Mary Greaves's comment encapsulates this beautifully:

> I was just an ordinary little girl with fair curly hair wearing pretty dresses made by my mother until suddenly, one day in November when I was three and a half years old, I ceased being a little girl and

became a 'polio'. Just a few hours and I was 'neutered' — a sexless little creature (Preface to Campling, 1979).

Unsurprisingly, this is not an identity which the individual might wish to take on. Often this process is reinforced by 'official' identification, a clear illustration of this being the categorising system used by the Department of Education and Science (DES) from which the Warnock Report, by its notion of 'special educational needs', tries to escape.

A particular problem for those with a physical impairment is that their condition is frequently associated with a mental impairment by the general public. Lisa has this to say: 'Many people have supposed that because I am obviously disabled, I am mentally sub-normal and have, therefore, treated me as they would someone of low intelligence or as a child' (Campling, 1981). One consequence of this association is demonstrated in a recent study of Physically Handicapped and Able-bodied (PHAB) clubs in which many of the subjects questioned expressed unwillingness to accept mentally-impaired individuals as fellow members (Lam, 1982).

As the earlier discussion indicated, assigned social identity and desired personal identity can emerge and be negotiated in the course of social interaction. However, if physically-impaired people are prevented from participating fully in social life, the process of negotiation cannot occur and the perpetuation of stereotypes is assured. (The reference to PHAB clubs above is appropriate here in that these clubs are intended to bring together physically handicapped and able-bodied to participate in a range of social, cultural and educational activities.)

Role

Like the concept of identity, the concept of role is one which links society and the individual. It relates to the pattern of behaviour expected by others from a person in a particular social status. Thus, there are behavioural expectations associated with the role of husband, father, schoolmaster, etc. The cultural role for physically-impaired people in industrial society might best be described as the 'sick role'. 'It enables our societies to "get rid of" all the unease that people with disabilities carry for them. It offers an avoidance which is ideal because it is not only "humane" but a symbol of caring' (Shearer, 1981).

The origins of the concept's use in this fashion go back some 30 years to the work of Talcott Parsons, and it is now evident that, even within the area of medical sociology, the validity of the concept as applied to physical impairment is being questioned. For example, impairment is not a temporary state and, therefore, role expectations about illness behaviour, overcoming the condition and returning to normality are inappropriate (Kassebaum and Baumann, 1965). There has also been sociological debate about the concept's general use (for example, see Coulson, 1972). In particular, there is controversy as to whether roles are a part of an objective social structure — something which is there into which social actors must fit. The implication here is that this model of role theory assumes that all individuals will fulfil the same expectations in the same way. Although his analysis does tend towards this concept of role, Thomas's analysis does recognise that there are a number of roles apart from the sick role which are available to physically-impaired people (Thomas, 1966). For an interactionist, however, this does not go far enough. From this viewpoint, the alternative is to see roles arising through social interaction, and being created and fashioned by the individual. To use the terms proposed by Ralph Turner, it is the difference between 'role making' and 'role taking', the emphasis in the former being on 'process' and in the latter on 'conformity' (Turner, 1962). Many physically-impaired individuals do fight against role expectations; epitomising Turner's dichotomies, they refuse to 'conform' and to 'take' the role prescribed by society, preferring instead to 'make' a role on the basis of their abilities. It could be argued that it is during adolescence that this process begins.

Status

This concept is closely related to social role. It refers to the honour and prestige associated with an individual's position in society. In our society, the status of those with a physical impairment is seen as dependent. Often the condition does involve some dependency on others for assistance in some areas of social life. How this social constraint impinges on individuals varies. Whilst some might seek to minimise this and attempt to 'pass', others try to make use of their dependent position. The two modes of adaptation are clearly seen in a description of two physically-impaired graduates.

> Anita is well aware of the mechanisms used in the able-bodied world to deal with disabled people, and tends to use them in a way which some handicapped students regard as exploitative. 'I started sort of "giving up" and getting people to do things for me. I knew all along that I could cope, but I didn't let them know that I could.' She plays up her femininity to get help from men.

This contrasts with Anna 'who tries to make her handicap as inconspicuous as possible' (Statham, 1981).

The above examples both concern females. The possible differences in position of physically-impaired adolescents which might relate to sex and gender will be discussed later, but it is interesting to speculate how far Su's point is valid: 'I sometimes think that women in general find it easier to accept a disability, since it is still a widely accepted norm that women are dependent on men economically' (Campling, 1981). For both sexes, the dependent status is reinforced by social views and social attitudes to occupational possibilities for physically-impaired people. One way in which individuals achieve some independence is by obtaining full-time paid employment. For those with impairment, society erects a number of barriers — physical ones of access and social ones relating to views of the suitability of some jobs and the unsuitability of others. This leads to a consideration of social norms and cultural expectations.

Social Norms and Cultural Expectations

Norms refer to shared standards of behaviour; members of a group are expected to conform to these. These vary between societies and cultures (for some cross-cultural comparisons, see Hanks and Hanks, 1948). In society those with a physical impairment are perceived as not fitting in with social norms, and cultural expectations therefore differ. The kinds of expectations society has of physically-impaired people are partly rooted in the past, but many such expectations are still to be found. Wolfensberger (1974) suggested that expectations about people with physical impairments are influenced by the differing ways in which they are perceived. Kurtz (1977) adapted these in relation to mental impairment, but they are equally adaptable to, and applicable to, physical impairment.

First, our expectations are influenced by perceiving those with physical impairments as sub-human and lacking physical and emotional needs. This is clearly shown by society's lack of concern in the past for the personal relationships and sexual feelings of physically-impaired people. The situation is changing, but Angie has recently commented:

> I was about fourteen years old and had just finished preparing a salad in a cookery class. The teacher came over and said, 'What a good job you have made of that. You would have made someone a good wife.' 'What do you mean, I would have?' I asked. 'Well,' she replied, 'What I meant to say was if you marry a disabled man you would make him a good wife.' The school had really strange ideas on marriage and the

disabled. They believed if a disabled person got married, it should be to another disabled person as it would not be fair on the able-bodied person to burden them with a handicapped partner (Campling, 1981).

The above is quoted at length because it links closely to a second cultural perception, that is viewing those with impairments as some kind of threat. Because of this, society is very concerned to regulate and control their behaviour. In some cases, there is a possibility of a physical impairment being passed on to children, but, given developments in genetic counselling, the risk is minimised and certainly does not warrant the present extent of interference in the personal lives of individuals. The extent of this is shown particularly in studies of institutional care (see Miller and Gwynne, 1972).

A third way of viewing those with physical impairments is to see them as objects of pity, to be cared for and cosseted and kept happy. The low expectations frequently found in education reflect this. Again, Angie's comments are useful:

> From the age of six years old, I attended a residential school for disabled children. The school was very poor on education, so much so that, at the age of sixteen, I was only at the level of a nine year old (Campling, 1981).

Fourthly, expectations can be influenced by seeing physically-impaired people as eternal children. There are two points to note in this connection. Viewing individuals this way can be used to justify decisions being taken on their behalf; also the assistance needed by individuals is often of the sort normally associated with the care of children in our society (e.g. having to be lifted and carried, or the similarities between a child's pushchair and a wheelchair). One physically-impaired housewife comments: 'My husband often has to carry me. A friend said, "How good of you not to mind." Not mind! I hate it' (Shearer, 1981).

Fifthly, those with physical impairments are often perceived as having outstanding compensating qualities. They are seen as having tremendous burdens which they carry with great fortitude. Many individuals have experienced this:

> When they find out that I have been to university they often express admiration and wonderment — 'How marvellous!' they say — why is it marvellous? Just because I can't use my legs doesn't mean that I have performed some superhuman feat in managing to attend some

lectures and sitting a few exams — after all, I use my hands to write and my brain to answer the questions set in exams, not my legs (Su in Campling, 1981).

Finally, and hopefully increasingly less prevalent, are the expectations which follow from perceiving those with physical impairments as either objects of ridicule or of curiosity. There are still occasional references to the former. Sarah talks of her school days:

> When I was at junior school, I never had nasty comments made about my disability . . . The local integrated comprehensive was a different matter altogether . . . They used to ask questions like, 'Why can't you go to the disco?' I would say I didn't want to go and they would whisper and giggle (Campling, 1981).

One consequence of regarding individuals as curiosities was their appearance in side shows; this is documented more fully elsewhere (Drimmer, 1973). Curiosity has not disappeared and we can return again to Angie:

> One day whilst Tony was at work, the gas man came to read the meter . . . As he was leaving the flat he turned and asked if I was married. I told him I was and then a funny look came into his eyes and he asked if I had sex (Campling, 1981).

It should be pointed out that many of these perceptions are perpetuated in a number of ways. One study has presented a comprehensive survey of children's literature; the plots of a vast range of books are described in terms of their portrayal of particular physical impairments, together with an analysis of their implications (Baskin and Harris, 1977).

There are also examples from adult literature. Given its growth over the past three decades, one should also consider the influence of television and other forms of mass media. What are the images of physical impairment produced by those sources? How are those with impairments described and portrayed? There are two aspects to note here. First, there are the visual images of impairment and impaired people. Some of these originate with those whose responsibility it is to evoke sympathy and obtain donations to support the various charitable organisations. In carrying out this task, they will choose an appropriate image — an individual with an attractive physical appearance or someone who has 'triumphed over adversity'. From the viewpoint of the many others with similar impairments whose appearance might be less appealing or who have not experienced a similar degree of success, these images could be inappropriate, and indeed have harmful effects on self concepts. Second, one must consider the use of language.

Language and Socialisation

Language is of central importance in social behaviour. The 'objectivity' of society and what individuals consider to be 'real' experiences are closely associated with language use. Berger and Berger (1976) make this particularly clear:

> Language is very probably *the* fundamental institution of society as well as being the first institution encountered by the individual bio-graphically. It is fundamental because all other institutions, whatever their various purposes and characteristics, build upon the underlying regulatory pattern of language ... First of all, of course, it is the child's micro world itself that is structured by language. Language 'objectifies' reality — that is, the incessant flux of experience is firmed up, stabilised into discrete identifiable objects. Language also structures, by objectification and by establishing meaningful relations, the human environment of the child. It populates reality with distinct beings, ranging from Mummy ... to the bad little boy who throws tantrums next door.

Applying the above to physical impairment, Merry comments perceptively:

> I began to think about how much of the language used about us (who are disabled) is negative. Youngsters would look at me and ask, 'What's WRONG with that lady's leg?' and parents (if they didn't shut the child up and rush away guiltily) would reply, 'She's got a BAD leg.' ... People talk of us as invalids — in-valid! (Campling, 1981).

Given this central role of language it is appropriate to consider how language is acquired. As Berger and Berger indicate, experiences in the family are significant in the most formative years. Hence the need to consider socialisation and language together. It is at this point that attention focuses on the symbolic nature of social interaction.

Symbols are stimuli to which a meaning or a value has been assigned. People respond to symbols on the basis of the meanings or values. The symbols are learnt in interaction with other people; the meanings and values are shared; the symbols are 'significant symbols'. They can take the form of physical gestures, but, since human beings have both the physical capacity to produce a wide range of sounds, and the mental capacity to store a wide range of meanings and values, mostly symbols are in verbal form. Verbal utterances are given meanings and values which other people share — hence the development of language. Through interaction with other people using language, human beings are able to share in the stock of meanings and values which relate to other people, other 'things' and, importantly, their own selves. In the acquisition of language the early years of life are a crucial period. During the early months of life a human infant will learn by trial and error, and certain actions and behaviours will become habitual. An infant will also make a number of random physical and verbal gestures to which others attribute meanings and values. Gradually verbal gestures will increase in frequency and complexity and more meanings will be assigned and acquired. The process is quite rapid until a point is reached when a child possesses a vocabulary appropriate to and adequate for the particular social context of home and family. When this child enters new social worlds, there will be new meanings and values to be acquired quickly. In fact this is true for adults as well. Thus interactionists view socialisation as a process that continues throughout life as individuals encounter new social experiences in differing social worlds. The concept refers to the way in which the customs, traditions and rules of behaviour appropriate to a social setting are passed on to new members of the social group.

What happens in childhood is crucial and there are many research studies which document the disruption of normal family routines brought about by the presence of a physically-impaired individual (see Hewett, 1970; McMichael, 1971). However, there is a need for more interactionist-based work. One author has attempted an overview of the socialisation process which emphasises social encounters and makes use of much previously-published empirical work (Richardson, 1969), whilst another indicates some important considerations which can apply more generally than in his own analysis of adults whose impairment is adventitious (Oliver, 1981). The strengths of an interactionist approach as he sees it are, first, that it allows the individual some choice in deciding his own mode of adaptation to his physical condition. Thus, not all adolescents with similar degrees of paralysis of the lower limbs will relate to the world in the same way. This lends weight to the interactionist approach to role theory discussed earlier. Second, it acknowledges the importance of social interaction in giving meaning to the social situation of an individual with a physical impairment. The way in which other people act and react is a key determining factor. This leads one to note that interactionists make an important difference between those with whom individuals have contact. The difference relates to the amount of influence which they have over the individual.

Significant Others and Generalised Others

Significant others are those people whose views have the greatest influence on how the individual sees himself and the world. These change as time goes by and the individual enters new social contexts. At first, the strongest influence will be parents; later, the wider family, friends, teachers and those involved in aspects of social welfare can become 'significant'. This is true for both able-bodied and physically-impaired people. The concept might also be used more broadly to encompass the fact that it is not only from the point of view of the individual that those professionals involved in social welfare are 'significant others'. One might argue that society also sees them as 'significant', hence their power and influence on policy and provision. These are the people, then, upon whom much depends.

Mention was made earlier of Finkelstein's (1980) critique in relation to 'stigma' and to the role of professionals in applying and sustaining 'stigmatised' identities. Scott and others have also discussed the proliferation of the caring professions, the consequences of which might be that particular decisions are taken because of the need to maintain an appearance of professional competence, or because of professional jealousies and rivalries; decisions are not being taken for the well being of the person receiving the service. Referring to his own work with blind people, Scott (1970) comments:

> In the intensive face-to-face relationships between blindness workers and clients that make up the rehabilitation process, the blind person is rewarded for adopting a view of himself that is consistent with his rehabilitator's view of him, and punished for clinging to other self conceptions.

As well as those people with whom an individual has contact of a special kind, there are those generalised others whose opinions and attitudes will be conveyed during the course of everyday social interaction. An individual himself will possess attitudes, beliefs and expectations about these people. Both parties, then, have expectations, and usually these are broadly similar. Because of this shared nature it is possible to engage in and sustain social interaction. 'When Mead spoke of the generalised other, he was not referring to people but to a shared perspective' (Rose, 1962).

Turning to those with a physical impairment, the concern is with public reactions. The association of physical with mental impairment has already been noted. Another public reaction can be summarised in Su's words: 'Occasionally, people talk down to me' (Campling, 1981). This is related to the 'does he take sugar' syndrome, where remarks are directed to a third party and not to the physically-impaired individual. It also relates to labelling theory and to the concept of stereotypes, both of which have been discussed earlier. What is required now is to indicate how far a physically-impaired person might be able to reject an assigned social identity and how far it is possible to establish a unique personal identity. The ease of doing so relates partly to the groups to whom a person belongs or wishes to belong.

Reference Groups

From a methodological point of view it has been argued that the concept should refer only to 'that group whose perspectives constitute the frame of reference of the actor' (Shibutani, 1972). The reference group, then, consists of those persons whose views the individual takes on to give meaning to experiences of the social world. However, distinctions can be made between the group of which the individual is a member, the group whose norms and standards he takes on, and the group to which he would like to belong. For some individuals, all three might relate to one group, for others, these distinctions might be critical. In the case of physically-impaired people the impairment itself brings membership of a particular group. An individual is categorised thus for a number of social purposes. Where an individual is isolated and segregated in special schools, sheltered employment, long-stay institutions, etc., then the reference group might well come to consist only of those in the same social situation. On the other hand, a physically-impaired person takes on the norms and standards of able-bodied people, for instance in the desire for education and employment. Unjustly they have to fight to be treated as full participants in the social world with its independence, freedom of movement and access, etc. Thus, for an analysis of the concept in relation to physically-impaired adolescents, Shibutani's view does appear to be too simplistic.

Case Studies

Having discussed these important background contingencies, the chapter now turns to examine areas of social interaction in which these factors are operating and which appear to be of great importance for physically-impaired adolescents. These are the contexts of education and employment, recreation and social life, and family and home life.

Education and Employment

According to Clarke (1951) a child with an impairment needs education for three reasons:

> He must acquire sufficient personal status to make his way through the world as independently as possible in spite of his handicap; he will sometimes need the strength and consolation which comes from resources of the mind; he badly needs the self-confidence which educational ability engenders.

Against this, one must acknowledge the difficulties likely to have been encountered by an adolescent. As well as those aspects relating to self and identity discussed earlier, it could be that schooltime will have been lost because of time spent undergoing medical attention. Some educational skills might be lacking as a result of the loss of muscular co-ordination and manual skills, and of the lack of development which results from a limited range of social experiences. Parents will have been faced early on with the problem of whether to send a child to a special school or to a school for the able-bodied. This issue has been debated at length for many years and most recently in the report of the Warnock Committee. The advantages and disadvantages of each are well rehearsed and need not be detailed here. From an interactionist viewpoint, there are aspects favouring integration which relate to the earlier discussion.

First, in relation to the self-concept, there is evidence about thalidomide children which suggests that they might not have been receiving education most suitable to developing their assets to the fullest extent, thereby improving their views of self. In a survey of Scottish thalidomide children, all of whom were aged seven and over and were of average and above intelligence, 30 per cent were found to be backward in reading and 40 per cent in arithmetic when compared to their non-handicapped peers (Pringle and Fiddes, 1970). Similarly a study of spina bifida children has revealed that about one-third are considerably retarded in reading ability (and a large proportion in arithmetical skills), even though they have no mental defect (NFER, 1973). More recently the Report of the Warnock Committee (1978) commented:

> The evidence presented to us reflects a widespread belief that many special schools under-estimate their pupils' capabilities. This view was expressed in relation to all levels of ability and disability. Many people thought the curriculum was too narrow.

Yet educational success is crucial for all young people; for physically-impaired adolescents it could be of greater importance and might make up for a lack of opportunities open to them in other fields.

Second, from an interactionist viewpoint, education amongst able-bodied young people might contribute towards the elimination of some of the strangeness and uncertainty found in social interaction at the present time. This is not to equate educational success with integration. As with other aspects of the integration debate, there is also interactionist evidence which might favour the retention of segregated schooling, given the difficulty of and length of time needed to change public attitudes. Micheline found comfort in the company of other girls in a boarding school for the physically impaired:

> There were other people who had gone through that doubting too! . . . other young women who had had their self image as a woman so severely damaged that they too had wondered if they were entitled to anything life had to offer. My three years with nearly one hundred young women with disabilities began a slow healing process (Campling, 1981).

A recent study (Anderson and Clarke, 1982) contains comments from physically-impaired adolescents which also indicates problems relating to integration: 'One boy said, "I wasn't happy at first . . . I was the odd-ball . . . the target for aggression . . . to some extent I was bullied."' However, this study also suggests that such activities also occur in special schools. These comments serve to emphasise the need to approach integration with the individual in view, and that it involves a long process of interaction and negotiation. It cannot be rushed or enforced. Thus far, it has seemed an either/or question, but this is not the case. Both types of school might be needed. Just as there is a variety of provision for the able-bodied, there should be a variety of provision for physically-impaired children and adolescents.

One group of physically-impaired adolescents whose needs seem inadequately catered for are those who seek further and higher education. Numbers in both sectors have increased but, in terms of their proportion in the total population, they remain under-represented. It was only in 1971 that the first state-provided residential further education college opened. Its progress and other developments in that field have been well-documented recently, although the emphasis has been on curricular aspects, vocational preparation and general policy provision (see Dixon and Hutchinson, 1979; Panckhurst, 1980; Panckhurst and McAllister, 1980; Rowan, 1980). However, there are some data more relevant to an interactionist analysis contained in the recently published study of a group of physically-impaired young people on a vocational training course in one particular specialist institution (Jowett, 1982). Similar developments have also been reported for higher education, although the most recent survey available (National Innovations Centre, 1974) concludes somewhat pessimistically:

> The proportion of disabled students to the total comparable student population was so small compared with that of disabled people to the population as a whole, that the conclusion is inescapable that there are obstacles which many disabled young people who would like to go to a university or polytechnic cannot overcome.

A major problem has been the provision of finance to modify facilities to suit physically-impaired people. New building regulations, following the Chronically Sick and Disabled Persons Act, 1970, should ensure that all public buildings erected since that date are accessible to those with impairments. More physically-impaired adolescents might take up places, but the contrast with some other countries is most marked. In Sweden, students are provided with places in halls of residence, any necessary conversions being paid for by the state. The state will also pay for a personal assistant if one is necessary, and provide technical aids such as typewriters and tape recorders. Three-quarters of the student grant has to be repaid to the state, but this is spread over a long period after the student enters full-time employment.

Apart from brief autobiographical accounts (e.g. in Campling, 1981), there is a marked lack of interactionist research about physically-impaired students in education beyond school. It would be valuable to know more about selection procedures and the social interaction processes at work when physically-impaired young people seek places on higher education courses. Little is known about the impact of these processes, and of following courses in higher education, upon self concepts, status, etc.

Discussion of education leads on to a study of the employment situation. This has implications for self, social identity and reference groups which are well stated by Laura Brown: 'Who am I? Do I belong in the able-bodied or disabled society? . . . My prime reference group is the able-bodied, where I work, I have my friends, which is the way I think' (Shearer, 1981). Shearer goes on to comment that for able-bodied people it is possible to move between a number of social worlds, within each of which an individual can have a different social identity. This ought to be the case too for those with physical impairments.

From any person's point of view, being without work in a world where the norm is one of work can be harmful to the self concept. Ideally, for people with physical impairments, the work situation should be the same as that of able-bodied people. This would bring maximum income, a share in community life, and a positive view of self. For physically-impaired adolescents there are forces operating to prevent them from reaching this. First, there is some hostility and antipathy from certain employers who believe that physically-impaired people are unable to cope. Second, and related to this, there is also the view that physically-impaired people are only suited to perform certain tasks. Third, there are the broader social forces as represented by economic recession and widespread unemployment. In times of prosperity many physically-impaired young people have struggled to obtain appropriate employment. The large number of able-bodied young people seeking work in 1983 makes this struggle doubly difficult. Another source of work lies in sheltered employment. The implications of this for the self concept, identity, etc. can be seen as a little negative. Sheltered workshops accept the inability of physically-impaired people to attempt open employment. They also continue segregation and isolation with their unfortunate effects on social interaction. This last point is also a criticism which can be levelled against a third occupational possibility — working at home.

Having said all this, there is little interactionist research on how physically-impaired adolescents fare in their search for employment — *Handicapped Youth* surveyed young people with a wide range of physical impairments (Ferguson and Kerr, 1960); *Spastic School Leavers* was also a broad survey and many of its subjects would lie outside the concern of this chapter (Spastics Society, 1964); *Young Disabled People* (Jowett, 1982) focused on the occupational histories of a large sample of young people from one college established for the vocational training of the physically impaired; both *Disability in Adolescence* (Anderson and Clarke, 1982) and *What Sort of Life?* (Rowan, 1980) are concerned with the transition from education to employment. This last-mentioned study contains comment on 'significant living without work'. There is an expectation that some physically-impaired adolescents will not obtain full-time employment; the implication of this for the self concept and status should be evident. 'Significant others' and the 'reference group' of physically-impaired adolescents might well emphasise the norm of full-time paid employment. From an interactionist standpoint, Coe's (1979) remarks summarise the situation well: 'Only when the able-bodied cease to look for employment will I stop advocating the need for the handicapped to obtain satisfactory employment.'

As a final comment on employment and by the way of a link with the following section, one might note that a way of making profitable use of leisure time is to obtain a part-time job. In addition to the benefits of a degree of financial independence, such jobs could provide individuals with a more positive view of self, a new and different social identity, and some independent status. Yet, as Anderson and Clarke (1982) point out, in their own survey proportionately fewer physically-impaired teenagers had spare-time jobs compared to their able-bodied peers.

Recreation and Social Life

Discussion of the recreational and social life of physically-impaired adolescents can be introduced by the words of a physically-impaired girl:

> Young people want to experience life, to live fully. What happens to Mary and George when they go in search of pleasure? In a word — nothing. What would they be doing on a dance floor? Even if their infirmity is a slight one, who would want to dance with a girl with a limp? Here Mary is worse off than George as beauty and physical fitness are more prized in a girl that a boy. They both feel not wanted where young people enjoy themselves (Thunem, 1966).

All adolescents seek activities which will give them pleasure. It is perhaps possible to divide recreation into those activities involving physical effort and those which are passive. The former encompass an increasingly wide range of activities in which physically-impaired adolescents can participate on the same terms as able-bodied people. Both these and more passive pursuits provide useful contexts for social interaction between physically-impaired and able-bodied people thus ending the isolation of the former and the unfamiliarity with impairment on the part of the latter. They allow meetings on equal terms with no connotations of inferiority or dependency. However, the Spastics Society survey of school leavers mentioned above found that the young people had hobbies and interests similar to able-bodied young people, although many were of the sort that could be pursued alone — reading, listening to records, watching television.

A way of ending social isolation and meeting other people is to join a club or society. Ideally, this should be centred on common interests. Research in the London Borough of Tower Hamlets cites the Wingfield Trust Music Club, where young people, both physically impaired and able-bodied, met to listen to, play and discuss music. In contrast to this, there are the meetings and clubs run specially for people with impairments (for both, see Skinner, 1969). The members of the latter tended to be middle-aged; adolescents could feel out of place in that context (see Anderson and Clarke, 1982, for evidence to support this view). More significantly, a group composed only of physically-impaired people does nothing to break down the barriers to social interaction described earlier. This is not to deny the good work done by many associations for particular impairing conditions. Their regular meetings and activities have provided a most useful service in giving advice to their members, bringing public attention to the plight of physically-impaired people, financing research and providing facilities for those in need.

Nevertheless, from an interactionist perspective, there are basic issues relating to categorisation and social typing, and to social interaction well demonstrated in the following remarks made by Muriel:

> People tend to think they can put all the disabled together. Now you can put a group of doctors or a group of nurses, or any kind of people together, it doesn't mean to say that because they've got one profession they're all going to get on together, and it's the same with disabled people — we're people first and disabled second (Campling, 1981).

One organisation geared specifically to bringing together the physically impaired and able-bodied is PHAB (Physically Handicapped and Able-Bodied). There are clubs in all parts of the country where people can come together for leisure and social activities on equal terms. Whilst a recent study is not within the interactionist tradition, it does contain valuable material about interaction between physically-impaired and able-bodied young people (Lam, 1982). As well as physical barriers, the study illustrates many of the cultural expectations and stereotyping felt by both parties in the social encounter and described in this chapter.

One of the most under-researched problems and yet one of vital importance to a physically-impaired adolescent is the opportunity to meet people of the opposite sex. Personal relationships and the development of sexuality are a significant but neglected area. Younghusband *et al.* (1970) comment thus:

> Not only do recreational pursuits provide bridges to the world of the non-handicapped, they also provide opportunities to make relations with the opposite sex during adolescence, when most young people are looking for romance and eventually marriage. This is a particularly neglected aspect in living with a handicap, probably because it is so fraught with hurt, damaged self-esteem, and most important of all, because there are no easy and ready answers.

Moving from a general overview to an individual's feelings, Karen says: 'However, as an adolescent, I realised that boys do not react in the same way to a girl in a wheelchair as they do to other girls' (Campling, 1981).

Providing more information about sex and marriage only avoids the main issue. At a time when sexual attitudes are becoming liberalised, it seems that physically-impaired people might not be part of this. There has been a recent growth of literature in this field. These range from Stewart's (1975) report, *Sex and the Physically Handicapped*, which adopted an empirical approach, through prescriptive treatises like *Entitled to Love* (Greengross, 1976), to the more practical advisory books (e.g. *Sex and Spina Bifida*, Stewart, 1978). More interesting, from the interactionist standpoint, is Morgan's (1972) paper. She utilises Goffman's categories of the 'normals', the 'wise' and the 'own' to examine societal expectations relating to sex and physical impairment. (These three categories can be seen to parallel the Meadian concepts of generalised others, significant others and reference groups.) The 'normals', with their regard for physically-handicapped people as childlike, extend this to encompass the development of sexual feelings. Despite the increased knowledge about sex, the idea still persists that physically-impaired people do not feel the need for sexual fulfilment. The 'wise', those who have closest contact with physically-impaired individuals, are likely to be more aware of sexual development and sexual needs but perhaps are afraid of the consequences and so try to ignore the issue. The 'own', the impaired individuals themselves, are aware of the difficulties their physical condition can bring to a relationship. For example, Battye (1966), in a chapter entitled 'The Chatterley Syndrome', writes with great feeling about the problems of a physically-impaired husband; he takes as his model Sir Clifford Chatterley, who is deserted by his wife for another (able-bodied) man. Many of the women with physical impairments whose accounts form the book by Jo Campling describe the situation from the female side. In fact, they suggest that to be female and physically impaired is doubly difficult within our culture. One aspect of this, as indicated earlier, is the importance of physical appearance and physique in adolescence, particularly in relation to sex role and identity. There are many comments about physical appearance and its importance in initial social encounters. To take just one example, Julie writes:

> Encounters at parties or other social functions vary but tend to follow certain patterns. One is complete rejection, when even eye-contact is impossible, because people are embarrassed or indifferent and you are written off. Another is over-enthusiasm, when you may be treated as a novelty . . .

And later: 'No-one can convince you of your sexual prowess when half your body isn't really normal. You may also worry about your body shape.' And again: 'The inability of the disabled person to be purely physical showing body movement, posture, wearing attractive clothes, can be a great disadvantage within the "market place" of relationships' (Campling, 1981).

At this point, it is interesting to speculate on the significance of sex differences in relation to physical impairment. A paraplegic, Anita, continues the remarks made earlier (see under 'Status'): 'I'm always saying, "Right, I want a man . . ." Well, men can't say, "I want a lady to carry me down the stairs." There's a lot of sex in it, carrying and lifting me up and down stairs. I do feel very female' (Statham, 1981). Such views can be supported using evidence from other sources. One research project considered the self concept in relation to impact and obviousness of the physical impairment amongst adolescents, and found that the greatest problems were found amongst the females in their large sample, particularly those whose impairment was immediately obvious (Meissner, Thoreson and Butler, 1967). The thrust of these arguments is that, in fact, there are sex differences in relation to the social aspects of physical impairment. At one extreme it has been argued that in some Western societies to be female and disabled is to have a double impairment. This can be countered by suggesting that the social norms relating to physical appearance and physical fitness and their effects on concepts of self, identity and status bear equally upon both males and females, but that males also have a double impairment because of norms and expectations emphasising the male as the 'breadwinner' and providing for his dependents rather than being dependent himself. Perhaps in the near future there will be a collection of accounts written by physically-impaired men which might add further insight to the problem. Compared to some other countries, research in the broad area of social relationships has been lacking (see Lancaster-Gaye, 1972), but it is worth injecting a note of caution. Shearer (1981) puts it this way:

> It is perhaps just worth wondering in passing whether any other group of people would put up with such a public, publicised, enquiring going over of their private lives – whether, for instance, miners would relish public discussion about the effects of shift working and pit dust on their sexual relationships.

Family and Home Life

Parental attitudes are important in any consideration of adolescence. How an adolescent copes with feelings and emotions, self concept and a physical impairment depend a great deal on experiences within the family. All parents want a perfect child. A child with a physical impairment might experience some rejection, but the majority are accepted and loved by their parents. Trouble comes occasionally when parents encourage their children to utilise their abilities to 'pass' as normal. Davis (1963) quotes the experience of one parent who found that, when he allowed his daughter, who had polio and wore leg irons, to climb steps unaided, onlookers made offensive remarks. At best, people stare. This might cause some parents to be afraid to take their children out of their homes, thus leading to a child's lacking learning experiences. Also, since a child has to have some things done for him, an attitude of over-protectiveness sometimes develops and this can be more damaging than the physical impairment itself.

There have been many research studies in this area, and they have been summarised elsewhere recently (Philip and Duckworth, 1982). As in other areas, interactionist studies are few. Booth (1978) has examined the processes at work in the social creation of handicap with reference to mentally-handicapped children and some of his discussion is more generally applicable. He looks at how parents and professionals interact and how over a period of time a child loses the label 'normal' and is assigned the label 'mentally handicapped'. A mental impairment is not always obvious at birth, and parents, having assumed their baby to be normal, become anxious about aspects of development when the baby appears not to be making progress. They seek advice and help, often looking for a definite diagnosis which it might not always be possible to give. Following further tests and examinations eventually a conclusion is reached that a child has a mental impairment: 'Children are not born ready classified as sub-normal. They are assigned to the class of people called sub-normal as a result of a series of decisions spanning a period of time, involving parents, professionals and other people' (Booth, 1978). Voysey's (1975) concern is with the way in which parents try to maintain a picture of normality and their attempts at what Goffman termed 'impression management'. Because of threats to their own self concepts and social identities which can occur in interaction, she has shown how parents use a range of strategies both in interaction and everyday activities (with 'generalised others') and in meetings with professionals representing educational, medical and social welfare agencies ('significant others'). In some ways, this is the approach adopted in an American study of the upbringing of children with physical defects resulting from their mothers' use of thalidomide (Roskies, 1972).

Within the family a physically-impaired adolescent will have had a range of experiences, some happy, some less so. This is also true for able-bodied adolescents. Likewise, adolescents seek a degree of independence and some status. This might be more easily achieved by leaving their homes and their communities. For some physically-impaired young people this might prove difficult. For others, it might seem impossible and yet they still wish to leave home.

One solution is residential care. Some physically-impaired adolescents might not have had this choice, having been placed in residential care during childhood. Oswin (1971) has described the plight of these children. Having visited and compared three different types of institution, she concluded that, whilst some aspects of institutionalisation appear inevitable, more could be done for these children. If a physically-impaired adolescent chooses to enter residential care, he will find that he is entering a world already structured and over which he has little influence. The two worlds of staff and resident are described in Goffman's (1968) analysis of institutions for the mentally impaired. What Goffman described in relation to those individuals in the United States can be seen happening in institutions in this country (Miller and Gwynne, 1972). Whilst not specifically an interactionist study, it does provide valuable data. Having looked at a variety of institutions, Miller and Gwynne posit two models of residential care. The 'warehousing' model provides care and runs smoothly provided that the resident is willing to accept his low status and his dependency, and play the sick role. There is strong resistance to any attempts at individuality. The 'horticultural' model sees the residents as suffering deprivations which need to be overcome, thereby making for greater independence. Each has its own characteristic features and these are of great significance for the interactionist. In the former model there is a system of batch treatment with everyone doing the same thing at the same time; there is a great degree of depersonalisation which means everyone is treated alike, irrespective of personality. Opportunities for personal relationships are lacking. In contrast, the 'horticultural' model is characterised by great freedom and opportunities for residents to establish their own social identity and a unique self concept. Both models can be criticised on the basic level of perpetuating segregation and preventing that increased social interaction between physically-impaired and able-bodied people which is so necessary if existing social reactions are to be changed.

Conclusion

The purpose of this chapter has been to illustrate how the concepts and perspectives of symbolic interaction theory might usefully contribute to an understanding of aspects of the social situation of physically-impaired adolescents. Thus, it is appropriate to conclude by drawing attention to some of the overall strengths of such an analysis. This has been attempted elsewhere by David Hargreaves (1978) in response to a critique of interactionist theory offered by Sharp and Green. First, and perhaps most importantly, the perspective emphasises the viewpoint of the participants in social interaction. There is a heavy reliance on accounts given by the social actors themselves. The sources of evidence used in this chapter demonstrate this. Second, the perspective explores aspects of social life which, in the past, have been taken for granted, and, in doing this, it has provided concepts and theories which can be used in further description and discussion. Within the area of physical impairment, Goffman's concepts of 'stigma' and 'passing' are specific examples which have provoked controversy, although this chapter has shown how the more general concepts of self, identity, etc. might also be used as tools of analysis. Following from this, these concepts can be utilised not only by social scientists but also by the social actors themselves to analyse their social situation. Many of the accounts collected by Campling make reference to role, identity, status, etc.

Hargreaves describes two other advantages of the symbolic interactionist approach as the 'immunological' and the 'corrective' capacities.

The former refers to the ways in which suggestions for change often fail because they do not take into account the immediate context in which change is to occur. For example, policies and practices relating to the integration of physically-impaired adolescents into ordinary schools have not given adequate consideration to the full range of participants at the school and classroom level. Hargreaves's notion of the 'corrective' capacity points to ways in which broad general theories and principles might be proved to be too simple and inadequate by interactionist investigations. Again taking integration, this chapter has indicated that there are some teenagers who, having experienced education amongst able-bodied peers, express a preference for special schools.

Turning to criticisms of interactionist approaches, it has been suggested that such analyses have neglected to consider a crucial aspect of social life — the concept of power. However, it can be argued that this is not entirely accurate. Power can be analysed at a number of levels. At the level of social interaction between individuals, interactionists do acknowledge the concept, and there is reference in interactionist literature to negotiation. Within the context of this chapter, Thomas's critique of the Davis analysis of interaction between physically-impaired and able-bodied people refers to the power of the former to control the situation. At the level of social interaction between the individual and others who are representatives of the social structure, again the concept of power does not go unacknowledged. Finkelstein's contention that physically-impaired people have had to endure a period of oppression partly as a result of the creation of the caring professions was noted earlier; the use of such terminology implies an imbalance of power. At another level of social interaction, perhaps there is a problem in discussing power:

> Structural factors other than the merely symbolic may be features of interaction. It is crucial to consider the ways in which elements of the interactive situation may well not be acknowledged or understood by the actors involved, but that such factors nevertheless structure the opportunities for action in ways that are more complex than has sometimes been thought . . . (Sharp and Green, 1975).

The point at issue here is the extent to which interactionism might encompass the deeper structural barriers facing physically-impaired adolescents and which manifest themselves both as problems of physical access and resource provision, and social attitude. Sharp and Green also question how far participants are aware of such structural limitations.

It might well be that the perspective has its weakness here, but this is no different from other perspectives in that they too have their weaknesses. It is more advantageous to stress the complementarity of perspectives, particularly in attempts to link micro- and macro-levels of analysis. A structuralist neo-Marxist account could suggest an adequate explanation of the social situation of physically-impaired adolescents based on economic considerations and the distribution of resources in society.

It was indicated earlier, again following Finkelstein's analysis, that one might put forward a class conflict model on traditional Marxian lines. It is Marx too who is concerned with the development of class consciousness and the transition from a group being a 'class in itself' to a 'class for itself'. It could be argued that consciousness of self and social identity, status and social role, etc. is a necessary pre-condition for political involvement and social change. Symbolic interactionism provides a mode of analysis offering an explanation of how such consciousness develops. There is evidence to suggest that physically-impaired people are developing this consciousness; the growth of self advocacy movements in this country and in the United States suggests that impaired people are becoming a 'class for themselves' and are actively involved in the making of policy; no longer are they content to let others make decisions on their behalf. It might be that it is the educated intelligent young physically-impaired people, on whom this chapter has focused, who build on what has already been achieved, and who become the activists in the fight for further change.

References

Anderson, E.M. and Clarke, L. (1982) *Disability in Adolescence*, Methuen, London.
Baskin, B.H. and Harris, K.H. (1977) *Notes from a Different Drummer: A Guide to Juvenile Fiction Portraying the Handicapped*, Bowker, New York.
Battye, L. (1966) 'The Chatterley Syndrome' in P. Hunt (ed.), *Stigma: The Experience of Disability*, Chapman, Edinburgh.
Berger, P. and Berger, B. (1976) *Sociology: A Biographical Approach*, Penguin, Harmondsworth.
Blumer, H. (1962) 'Society as Symbolic Interaction' in A.M. Rose (ed.), *Human Behaviour and Social Processes*, Routledge and Kegan Paul, London, 179-92.
Booth, T.A. (1978) 'From normal baby to handicapped child: unravelling the idea of subnormality in the families of mentally handicapped children' in W. Swann (ed.) (1981), *The Practice of Special Education*, Basil Blackwell in association with Open University Press.
Campling, J. (1979) *Better Lives for Disabled Women*, Virago, London.
—— (1981) *Images of Ourselves: Women with Disabilities Talking*, Routledge and Kegan Paul, London.

Clarke, J.S. (1951) *Disabled Citizens*, Allen and Unwin, London.

Coe, D. (1979) 'Planning further education courses for handicapped students at national, regional, and local level' in K. Dixon and D. Hutchinson (eds.), *Further Education for Handicapped Students*, Bolton College of Education (Technical), Bolton.

Coulson, M. (1972) 'Role: a redundant concept in sociology? Some educational considerations' in J. Jackson (ed.), *Sociological Studies No. 4*, Cambridge University Press, Cambridge.

Davis, F. (1961) 'Deviance disavowal: the management of strained interaction by the visibly handicapped', *Social Problems, 9*, 120-32.

—— (1963) *Passage Through Crisis: Polio Victims and their Families*, Bobbs Merrill, Indianapolis.

Dixon, K. and Hutchinson, D. (eds.) (1979) *Further Education for Handicapped Students*, Bolton College of Education (Technical), Bolton.

Drimmer, F. (1973) *Very Special People*, Amjon, New York.

Ferguson, T. and Kerr, A. (1960) *Handicapped Youth*, Oxford University Press, Oxford.

Finkelstein, V. (1980) *Attitudes and Disabled People*, World Rehabilitation Fund, New York.

Ford, J., Morgan, D. and Whelan, M. (1982) *Special Education and Social Control: Invisible Disasters*, Routledge and Kegan Paul, London.

Goffman, E. (1968) *Asylums*, Penguin, Harmondsworth.

—— (1969) *Stigma*, Penguin, Harmondsworth.

—— (1971) *The Presentation of Self in Everyday Life*, Penguin, Harmondsworth.

Greengross, W. (1976) *Entitled to Love*, Malaby Press, London.

Hanks, J.R. and Hanks, L.M. (1948) 'The physically handicapped in non-occidental countries', *Journal of Social Issues, 4*, 11-20.

Hargreaves, D.H., Hestor, S.K. and Mellor, F.J. (1975) *Deviance in Classrooms*, Routledge and Kegan Paul, London.

Hargreaves, D. (1978) 'Whatever happened to symbolic interactionism?' in L. Barton and R. Meighan (eds.), *Sociological Interpretations of Schooling and Classrooms: A Reappraisal*, Nafferton Books, Driffield, England.

Hewett, S.J. (1970) *The Family and the Handicapped Child*, Allen and Unwin, London.

Hunt, P. (ed.) (1966) *Stigma: the Experience of Disability*, Chapman, Edinburgh.

Jowett, S. (1982) *Young Disabled People*, National Foundation for Educational Research (NFER)-Nelson, Windsor.

Kassebaum, G.G. and Baumann, B.O. (1965) 'Dimensions of the sick role in chronic illness', *Journal of Health and Human Behaviour, 6*, 16-27.

Kitsuse, J.I. (1962) 'Societal reaction to deviant behaviour' in E. Rubington and M.S. Weinberg (eds.) (1968) *Deviance: the Interactionist Perspective*, Macmillan, New York, 15-24.

Kurtz, R.A. (1977) 'The sociological approach to mental retardation' in A. Brechin, P. Liddiard and J. Swain (eds.) (1981) *Handicap in a Social World*, Hodder and Stoughton in association with Open University Press.

Lam, R. (1982) *Getting Together: A Study of Members of PHAB Clubs*, National Foundation for Educational Research (NFER)-Nelson, Windsor.

Lancaster-Gaye, D. (ed.) (1972) *Personal Relationships, the Handicapped and the Community: Some European Thoughts and Solutions*, Routledge and Kegan Paul, London.

McCall, G.J. and Simmons, J.L. (1966) *Identities and Interactions*, Free Press, New York.

McMichael, J.K. (1971) *Handicap: A Study of Physically Handicapped Children and their Families*, Staples Press, London.

Meissner, A.L., Thoreson, R.W. and Butler, A.J. (1967) 'The relation of self concept to impact and obviousness of disability among male and female adolescents', *Perceptual and Motor Skills*, 24, 1099-1105.

Miller, E.J. and Gwynne, G.V. (1972) *A Life Apart*, Tavistock, London.

Morgan, M.R. (1972) 'Attitudes of society towards sex and the handicapped' in D. Lancaster-Gaye (ed.) *Personal Relationships, the Handicapped and the Community: Some European Thoughts and Solutions*, Routledge and Kegan Paul, London.

National Foundation for Educational Research (NFER)/National Children's Bureau (1973) *The Child with Spina Bifida*, NFER-Nelson, Windsor.

National Innovations Centre (NIC) (1974) *Disabled Students in Higher Education*, NIC, London.

Oliver, M. (1981) 'Disability, adjustment, and family life — some theoretical considerations' in A. Brechin, P. Liddiard and J. Swain (eds.), *Handicap in a Social World*, Hodder and Stoughton in association with Open University Press, 50-7.

Oswin, M. (1971) *The Empty Hours*, Allen Lane, London.

Panckhurst, J. (1980) *Focus on Physical Handicap*, National Foundation for Educational Research (NFER)-Nelson, Windsor.

—— and McAllister, A.G. (1980) *An Approach to the Further Education of the Physically Handicapped*, National Foundation for Educational Research (NFER)-Nelson, Windsor.

Philip, M. and Duckworth, D. (1982) *Children with Disabilities and their Families: A Review of Research*, National Foundation for Educational Research (NFER)-Nelson, Windsor.

Pringle, M.L.K. and Fiddes, D.O. (1970) *The Challenge of Thalidomide*, National Bureau for Co-operation in Child Care, London.

Richardson, S.A. (1969) 'The effect of physical disability on the socialisation of a child' in D.A. Goslin (ed.), *Handbook of Socialisation Theory and Research*, Rand McNally, Chicago.

——, Goodman, N., Hastorf, A.H. and Dornbusch, S.M. (1961) 'Cultural uniformity in reaction to physical disabilities', *American Sociological Review*, 26, 241-7.

Rose, A.M. (ed.) (1962) *Human Behaviour and Social Processes*, Routledge and Kegan Paul, London.

—— (1962) 'A systematic summary of symbolic interaction theory' in A.M. Rose (ed.), *Human Behaviour and Social Processes*, Routledge and Kegan Paul, London, 3-19.

Roskies, E. (1972) *Abnormality and Normality: the Mothering of Thalidomide Children*, Cornell University Press, New York.

Rowan, P. (1980) *What Sort of Life?*, National Foundation for Educational Research, (NFER)-Nelson, Windsor.

Scott, R.A. (1970) 'The construction of conceptions of stigma by professional experts' in D.M. Boswell and J.M. Wingrove (eds.) (1974) *The Handicapped Person in the Community*, Tavistock, London, 108-21.

Sharp, R. and Green, A. (1975) *Education and Social Control*, Routledge and Kegan Paul, London.

Shearer, A. (1981) *Disability: Whose Handicap?*, Basil Blackwell, Oxford.

Shibutani, T. (1972) 'Reference groups as perspectives' in J.G. Manis and B.N. Meltzer (eds.), *Symbolic Interaction: A Reader in Social Psychology*, Allyn and Bacon, Boston.

Skinner, F.W. (1969) *Physical Disability and Community Care*, National Council of Social Service, London.

Spastics Society (1964) *Spastic School Leavers*, Spastics Society, London.

Statham, J. (1981) 'Four physically handicapped graduates' in T. Booth and J. Statham (eds.), *The Nature of Special Education*, Croom Helm in association with Open University Press, 186-91.

Stewart, W.F.R. (1975) *Sex and the Physically Handicapped*, National Fund for Research into Crippling Diseases, Sussex.

—— (1978) *Sex and Spina Bifida*, ASBAH/SPOD, London.

Sutton, A.H. (1972) 'Marriage and the handicapped' in D. Lancaster-Gaye (ed.), *Personal Relationships, the Handicapped and the Community: Some European Thoughts and Solutions*, Routledge and Kegan Paul, London.

Thomas, D. (1978) *The Social Psychology of Childhood Disability*, Methuen, London.

—— (1982) *The Experience of Disability*, Methuen, London.

Thomas, E.J. (1966) 'Problems of disability from the perspective of role theory', *Journal of Health and Human Behaviour*, 7, 2-13.

Thunem, J. (1966) 'The invalid mind' in P. Hunt (ed.), *Stigma: The Experience of Disability*, Chapman, Edinburgh.

Turner, R.H. (1962) 'Role-taking: process versus conformity' in A.M. Rose (ed.), *Human Behaviour and Social Processes*, Routledge and Kegan Paul, London, 20-40.

Voysey, M. (1975) *A Constant Burden*, Routledge and Kegan Paul, London.

Warnock Report (1978) *Special Educational Needs*, Report of the Committee of Enquiry into the Education of Handicapped Children and Young People, Cmnd 7212, HMSO, London.

Wolfensberger, W. (1974) *The Origins and Nature of our Institutional Models*, University of Syracuse.

World Health Organisation (1980) *International Classification of Impairments, Disabilities and Handicaps*, WHO, London.

Younghusband, E., Birchall, D., Davis, R. and Pringle, M.L.K. (1970) *Living with Handicap*, National Bureau for Co-operation in Child Care, London.

9 SOCIALLY PRODUCED IDENTITIES, INTIMACY AND THE PROBLEM OF COMPETENCE AMONG THE RETARDED*
David A. Goode

A substantial lack of observational studies on the social organisation of life with severely impaired persons has had profound, though as of yet unstated, effects on our understanding of these types of people. With the notable exception of Edgerton's ethnographic work (1967) and some few others (Bercovici, 1980; Blatt, 1970; Bogdan, 1976; Jacobs, 1969; Langness, 1982), the vast majority of papers in this field have been either clinical or experimental, relying almost exclusively upon 'scientific' procedures such as: hypothesis generation; sampling; measurement of variables; hypothesis testing; statistical analyses of data; theory building and the like. A quick turn through any major journal in the field, aside from polemical essays, will prove this characterisation true.

The results of naturalistic observation of the retarded in a variety of social contexts are beginning to become known to human services professionals. Some of these findings, such as those from three observational studies of retarded persons which I will describe in this chapter, are disturbing, even startling, by scientific and common-sense standards. As the reader will soon see, observational studies of the social organisation of life with severely damaged persons may consistently lead one to interesting, if not profound, contradictions and paradoxes about human relationships. At least this has been true for me, today as much as ten years ago when I entered the field. My own ethnographies of the retarded were conducted in the United States during the period from 1973 to 1978 when few observational studies had been published. As a matter of standard procedure I kept a cassette recorder on at all times during field visits. This provided me with an audio record of field observations and, in this case, allowed me to hear the content of the nurses' remarks.

* Research included in this chapter was supported under PSH Grant No. HD04612, No. HD-05540-02, The Mental Retardation Research Center, UCLA, and a grant from The Joseph P. Kennedy Junior Foundation. Miss Pamela Aregood provided prompt and precise secretarial support. A list of 26 persons currently interested in naturalistic observation of the retarded is available from: Keith T. Kernan, Ph.D., Socio-Behavioral Group, Mental Retardation Research Center, School of Medicine, University of California, Los Angeles, CA 90024.

I employed these tapes as mnemonic devices, later producing the 'field notes' which are presented in this chapter.

One contradiction, which is central to understanding the consensual bases for meanings we assign to behaviours of severely handicapped or retarded humans, concerns the regular production of antithetical testimony about the abilities or disabilities of particular clients. For example, parents, caretakers and physicians often produce antagonistic descriptions of such people. Through socially constructed agreements pertinent to their own social relationships with clients, they grant them, if you will, radically different identities – disagreeing in a fundamental way about details of behaviours and their underlying competences. It is this phenomenon, in this case literal contradiction, which I will explore below. In so doing I offer both a substantive investigation into the social lives of the retarded, as well as a sociological method for studying these. While it may not be possible to do explicit justice to both topics within the context of a single chapter, the reader will profit by having been alerted to these two 'levels' in the text.

Socially Produced Identities

When I was first hired to do ethnographic research with the developmentally disabled, Bob Edgerton, the principal researcher, suggested I begin by taking a tour of a local State Hospital for the retarded. Part of the tour included a visit to the 'Acute Unit' – that building wherein severely afflicted persons requiring regular medical assistance were housed. A section of the building was a 'tour ward' which served as a way for physicians and nurses in training to see a variety of syndromes of mental retardation – a sort of living atlas of retardation laid out so that, the further into the ward one went, the more severe the disease sequelae became. There was a central hall with semi-private rooms staggered on either side housing the patients and it was thus possible to turn back when one had seen 'enough'. Although not a common procedure, non-medical personnel, such as myself and a colleague who had accompanied me, were occasionally allowed to tour the ward. When the following incident occurred, we had already visited many of the rooms and, as my fellow researcher put it, had descended deeper into 'hell' than she had bargained for.

I went into one of the rooms near the end of the hall and saw a huge bed board at the head of the bed whose occupant was hidden from view. The room was empty, without objects on the walls or toys. It was brightly lit. I walked toward the bed and peeked over the edge and was as intensely horrified as I have ever been in my life at what I saw. A *huge* head, later I was told over forty pounds, attached to this stunted body. Horrible bedsores covered what appeared for a moment as an almost unreal monstrosity – like a Hollywood inspired nightmare, though *too* real, too much an actual sensory experience to ignore as fantasy. He, it turned out to be a he, was the most profane looking human being I had ever seen.

I immediately became nauseous and broke out in a cold sweat and light headedness. I grabbed the bed board for support, felt faint and tried to keep myself upright without 'letting go of the cookies'. A nurse must have seen me. She miraculously appeared, grabbed my arm and talked in a calm and reassuring manner. Although at the time, due to the degree of physical distress, I did not hear a word she said, without her reassuring tone and physical support I probably could not have collected myself and left that room as quickly or as inconsequentially as I did.

A few moments after this incident a young physician on the ward told me this man 'was hydrocephalic' and had been born before the invention of the shunt operation which prevents the accumulation of cerebral-spinal fluid and enlargement of the skull. In this case the head had grown so large that intracranial pressure rendered the person deaf, blind, completely paralysed and without a behavioural repertoire or measurable (or otherwise) signs of intelligence, a significant list of problems for someone to have. The clinical profile was hopeless – no possibility existed for remediation, therefore the case was essentially custodial, the person as low functioning as one could find.

It was not till I got back to UCLA (the University of California, Los Angeles) and listened to the audio tape of my ward tour that I was able to hear what the nurse had been saying to me. It went like this: 'Oh, I see you've found Johnny, my favourite. I've been here three and a half years and he's my special favourite. He's eighteen and I'm his mommy during the day. I wake him when I come on shift, wash him and dress him. We have our routines . . . He loves rock and roll, I usually open the window up so it's bright and put on the music loud. He loves when I take his hands and clap them to the beat. He has his likes and dislikes you know. He loves his red flashlight . . .' As I listened I could only ask myself, what happened to the person I had seen? This description did not 'jive' . . . a deaf-blind, completely paralysed, grotesquely hydrocephalic person with 'likes and dislikes', his own routines and who someone calls her 'favourite'?

The tape puzzled as well as impressed me. I listened to it a couple of times, became convinced of its importance and brought it to Edgerton. He was also impressed by the discrepancy in our respective descriptions of Johnny — although he did not know exactly what to make of it. Neither did I. I was, however, convinced that this nurse knew something which I did not about disabled persons.

Some nine years have passed since this event and I believe I have come to a theoretically satisfactory and clinically useful interpretation of the affair, one which is labelled above by the terms socially produced, or sociogenic, identity. The phrase refers to how a person's identity — who he or she is taken to be in terms of the significance or meaning attached to his or her body and behaviours — emerges out of a concrete and particular social situation and is a product of social interaction within that situation. For example, in the above case three kinds of social relationships with Johnny led to three distinct impressions of him. First, my own relationship to him, that of unknowledgeable stranger, led to a common sort of identity to be afforded him — that of profane object, monster or object of disgust. Second, we note the physician's description of Johnny which emerged out of non-intimate, clinical relationship. From 'the medical perspective', he was described primarily in negative diagnostic terms, as essentially, irremediably flawed and without positive prognoses. Both my own and the physician's efforts at identity-making resulted in deeply pejorative conceptions of this man, though employing substantially different vocabularies.

This was not the case when we examine the nurse's view of Johnny, a view which was the product of long-term and intimate interaction with him. Within the context of such a relationship, Johnny was not seen in an essentially negative fashion. In fact, her description was quite positive and emphasised his abilities and the quality of their shared lives. The nurse's account was about a person who was by and large hidden from the physician, me and other non-intimates. From within this long-term, intimate, routine life they shared, she had gained a unique vantage-point, probably afforded no other person, from which to appreciate Johnny.

To her, Johnny's identity rested upon the detailed knowledge which could only come from being his 'mommy' five days a week for three years. Such a relationship maximised the possibility for empathy, persistent identification and heightened sensitivity to 'Johnny's perspective'. It was *this social relationship* which allowed her to achieve a definition of the person inconsistent with either clinical or 'horror-object' identities. As we shall see below, lack of agreement between socially generated identities, reflections of real differences in the social organisation of interaction out of which identities emerge, will be a phenomenon of both theoretical and clinical import.

In human services for the developmentally disabled this phenomenon expresses itself ubiquitously: a parent and clinician argue about what a child can or cannot do; a custodian on a ward disagrees with a physician about what is best for a child; a client whom I initially found distasteful to look at becomes 'cuter' as I get to know him better; a parent says, 'I just start gettin' kinda cynical when that language therapist starts tellin' me about my Billy after a half hour with him'; and so forth. These incidents illustrate how different social identities afforded to developmentally disabled persons emerge as problematic issues in professional human services and in helping relationships generally. From the cumulative experience with a variety of clients in differing living standards, what appears most significant and consistent about differing identities granted to the retarded is how intimate relationships with even severely afflicted persons often lead to positive identities for the client — inconsistent in detail with negative faulted, non-intimate identities such as found in clinical description.

The fact that the retarded are open to identity-making which is not the product of intimate and detailed knowledge of their everyday lives is of particular consequence to them. Often such non-intimate inter-actions and their concomitant identities determine how and where a client will live, what training or education he will receive, the kinds of interpersonal relationships he will experience and even, on occasion, whether he will live or die. Wolf Wolfensberger's (1980) description of 'The Extermination of Handicapped People in World War II Germany' evidences how eugenic deaths were 'expertly' and 'impersonally' administered by human service professionals. The author described how this participation was socially engineered through the euphemistic reformulation of killing as a medical procedure. He also cites modern parallels to this process in such medical phrases as 'allowing the baby to die', 'death as a treatment of choice' and so on. We have recently seen cases wherein physicians have co-operated with *parents* in withholding life-saving medical intervention from retarded persons. These decisions are often made by people who have short-term, 'people work' relationships with clients, usually helping professionals, who are by training and by virtue of job demands predisposed to a 'fault-finding' type of identity-making with the retarded.

A more inclusive usage of 'fault-finding procedures' was suggested by Harold Garfinkel (personal communication, 1974). I adapted it to refer to those ways pathology or deviance often get labelled. That is, by evaluating behaviour through its pragmatic relevance to the service worker. Thus, specific faults located with particular children may vary depending on the context within which interaction occurs. For example, parents and medical personnel do not generally describe clients similarly, partially because the social organisation of interaction in the clinic is substantially different from that of the home. That is, their task is one in which some standard of normal structure (function, affect, intellectual or sensory motor development) is employed to locate deviations or pathologies whose identification, in turn, form the rationale of a plan for treatment or remediation. By definition the clinical relationship is personally indifferent, objective and, to use anthropological language, 'etic'. The term 'etic' is used in anthropology to contrast with the word 'emic'. The former refers to an outsider's perspective on a culture (an analytic perspective which is, from the point of view of those within the culture, often extrinsic to subjects' concerns). 'Emic' refers to the native's perspective in doing the activities of the culture (it is a naturalistic perspective, intrinsic to the actions of cultural members). In the present context it will be maintained that clinical criterion and the assumptions upon which they are built are 'etic' perspectives on the client's situation. Part of the strength of phenomenological forms of observation, as the reader will see, lies in their abilities to provide the researcher access to the 'emic' view of the client. This will be a major proposal and focus of this chapter. Interaction in the clinic is short lived, even when we find short serial contacts over the course of years, and rarely involves intimacy of any sort. Further, the relationship occurs within a clinical setting, literally out of the everyday world of the client (i.e. his ward or other daily living situation). Given the definition of the clinical situation, the periodicity and location of such interaction, it is not surprising that *essentially pejorative* identities of chronically impaired persons are produced. Nor is it unexpected that these identities are not resonant with those produced by persons who are related to the client in a long-term, holistic and intimate way.

In ten years' experience, I have rarely met a client whose clinical identity did not seriously underestimate abilities which were taken as part of his or her everyday identity by friends, researchers or other intimates. It is important that we understand those forms of social interaction which systematically produce underestimations of competence, as well as those which afford more positive, capable identities for the retarded. Since the world of the clinic, and its associated forms of evaluation, are relatively well known to us, it will be helpful to illustrate, through case data, how current assessment procedures fail to identify abilities which emerge in more ordinary, everyday relationships.

Three Vignettes Displaying Ironies Between Clinical and Everyday Identities

Bobby

Robert, or, as he preferred to be called, Bobby, was a fifty-year-old man with Down's Syndrome who lived at a board and care facility I visited regularly. The following is a pertinent excerpt from a previous work about my experiences with Bobby.

> I first got to know Bobby through his clinical records. Of course, he had a fairly substantial file which accompanied him wherever he lived, and which summarized his career in human service contexts. His record was a kind of clinical biography — describing his contacts with various helping professions, their assessments and descriptions of Bobby as well as any remedial procedures offered to correct Bob's deficiencies. *These texts, what they did and did not contain*, were testament to the clinical identity which Bobby had been given by clinicians. Nowhere was Bobby discussed in terms of his having any sort of competence and human value; instead an exclusively fault finding perspective was employed. These descriptions pointed to a series of encounters during which clinical standards of normality had been used as criteria against which constitutional faults of the client were identified. This method afforded Bobby an essentially *devalued*, *incompetent* and *hopeless* identity. Consider the following excerpts from Bobby's file:
> 'Down's Syndrome . . . diabetes with peripheral vascular disease . . . edema of lower extremities.'
> *Communication assessment:* '. . . speech or language therapy is not recommended as prognosis for improvement is poor . . . client can communicate basic needs but can not express complex ideas and understands very little . . . difficult to communicate with . . .'
> *Cognitive assessment:* A quick test of intelligence yielded a mental age of approximately 2-8 years. Clinician concludes that Bobby is 'severely mentally retarded with severe brain damage'.
> *Occupational therapy:* 'Time and effort in this area are not suggested as prognosis for improvement is poor . . . maintain client in a protected environment as he can never function independently' (see Goode, 1983).

While these excerpts are out of context, *it is not* that I left out all the 'good' things they said about Bobby. There were none. The contents of clinical files typically display only lists of faults about chronically damaged persons, especially someone as 'low functioning' as Bobby.

Thus the clinical picture of this client was consistent with the faulting orientation described above, and Bobby was afforded a clinical identity of extreme disability. His file was testament to serial encounters of short duration, in clinical settings, which employed objective instruments of evaluation to determine 'Bobby's capabilities' (in the possessive). For example, communicative competence was determined through a verbal interview and administration of standard clinical instruments. Performance in the interview and on the assessment instruments was the basis for an assessment of language disabilities and potential for remediation (in this case, that he could communicate very little, could not express complex ideas and had a very poor prognosis for improving skills). Without in any way impuning the adequacy or professionalism of the clinical persons who made this determination, they were, for reasons made clear below, incorrect in extending their assessment beyond the walls of the clinic.

Those who knew Bob well differed in their judgement about his communicative competence — including myself once familiar with him. Although a full discussion of this familiarisation process is not possible in this present context, I was part of a research team which visited his board and care quite regularly (see Goode, 1983). My involvement and familiarity with him grew over time. As participant-observer, I was able to see him within his peer group and in a variety of situations. In this way, I had access to slices of his everyday life and was able to observe Bobby's abilities and disabilities as they were ordinarily displayed by him on a daily basis. By the time I had got to know Bobby as a friend, I was not shocked when his peers reported that Bobby talked as well as you or I but 'you [the researchers] just didn't understand him'. As far as the general population of the facility was concerned, Bobby had 'no communication problems' and 'talked fine'. His intimates thus assessed his communication abilities in a different manner and with divergent conclusions from clinical persons. The better I got to know Bobby, the more I trusted his peer-group's assessment — my own intimacy with Bobby being the key determinant in viewing him as a person who could think and express his thoughts.

Why was there such a divergence between clinical and peer-group identities afforded Bobby? Part of the reason had to do with how assessments are organised in clinics, but this disjuncture was also due to 'real' differences in how Bobby performed in clinical versus home contexts. With his friends at the board and care facility Bob was more relaxed, more assured, more knowledgeable about the affairs going on around him, more willing to volunteer remarks and literally pronounced utterances more clearly and forcefully. Within the 'strange' world of the clinic, and we have videotaped these incidents, he was tense, lacked confidence, was frustrated at not being understood, did not participate and, when he spoke, enunciated poorly and failed to project his voice. Of course these differences in his behaviour were quite understandable, given the unfamiliar ground — and the fact that strangers who could not understand him were giving the tests! Some of his fear of the place was also motivated by his prejudice about 'hospitals', places which, as anyone who is familiar with de-institutionalised clients knows, are often regarded with awe and fear. This belief also contributed to his deficient behaviour within the clinical situation, hence contributing to the negative assessment staff made about him.

While some decrease in competence upon entering unfamiliar institutional territory would be expected for any of us, the differences between the everyday life at the board and care facility and the world of the clinic were so substantial that the consequences of moving from one place to the other were overwhelming. Bercovici (1980) makes use of the concept of subculture in describing 'community placements' which, she maintains, are discontinuous with and largely cut off from the wider society. If the tables were turned, and clinicians found themselves briefly visiting Bobby's world, *they* would be lost. Bobby would have to guide *them* and help them understand its procedures and organisation, and they might begin to appreciate just *how* differently organised those worlds are. When Bobby went to the clinic, he did not experience the situation in the same way you or I might. It was more like visiting another culture.

There were yet other reasons for the negative clinical identity and underestimation of Bobby's competence. In some areas, communication assessment for example, the very logic of the procedures contributed to 'Bobby's' incompetencies. In one interview he was asked to communicate with a stranger without aid from one of his more verbal intimates. The task, as he and I knew, was problematic if not an impossibility under the circumstances. While I can recall how little I understood of Bobby's speech when I first met him, I can also remember, after getting to know him better, sitting in during a clinical interview and getting incredibly frustrated at the inability of the interviewer to understand what were to me clear and sensible utterances from Bobby. To identify with Bobby's position one need only imagine that every time he would open his mouth, persons would take the utterances as gibberish.

But, the interview proceeded on the basis that *everyman* should be able to demonstrate his abilities to communicate to *anyone* else given any appropriate opportunity (i.e. that language skills are independent of cohort and situation). While the assumption that 'communication is nothing personal' is generally non-problematic for many forms of clinical work, it may be inappropriate, if not seriously misleading, when we deal with 'unusual communicators' such as the retarded, mentally ill, neurologically handicapped or, for a non-pathological example, even very young children. With such persons, communication may be an extremely personal affair, as we all realise as everyday societal participants. We know this to be true of the early communications of a child, that mommy is the person who can translate 'problematic' utterances validly. If the language evaluation professional who assessed Bob were to visit her sister's home and encounter problematic communications from her eighteen-month-old niece, she would *not* have concluded incompetence on the child's part. Instead, she might have turned to her sister and asked, 'What's Mary saying?' In so doing she would be acting upon what Schutz (1970) called society's 'stock of knowledge', which all societal members possess and which, in this case, allows them to understand that communication with some persons is acutely sensitive to the degree of intimacy between those communicating. This commonplace knowledge, the 'it takes two to tango' theory of communication, is one which professional language evaluators are trained out of believing, or, at least, they are trained not to allow such a belief to penetrate professional practice. It is a kind of professionally produced amnesia for the everyday social structures.

The clinical model of communication both *anonymises* it (sees it as cohort independent) and *constitutionalises* it (sees communicative competence as an attribute of a person rather than part of a concrete communicational system). Both these transformations, from a sociological point of view, mitigate against the possibility that a person such as Bobby will be assessed as communicationally competent. Supplanting interview procedures with those of 'objective measurement' does *not* substantially alter the situation. The tests are built on the same assumptions as the interview — that they capture cohort independent, constitutional communicative abilities which a person 'has'. Neither technique, interview nor objective test, addresses the client's abilities to participate in intimate, cohort specific communication networks such as those engaged in by Bobby and his peers at the board and care facility.

Breta

The radically different social organisation of extra-clinical settings and the correspondingly different identities afforded to developmentally disabled individuals within those contexts was nowhere more problematic than in the relationship between clinical and familial identities of children. Parents of developmentally disabled children were probably the first to discover the systematic clinical underestimation of everyday competences in the family context. Till recently, the majority who pointed this out were regarded as 'uncooperative', 'unrealistic' or even 'delusional' (see Goode, 1980). In many places they are still so regarded today.

Yet, from the point of view of a trained observer who has had opportunities to see children in clinical situations and at home, part of the unwillingness of the professional to accept parental testimony about their children's competence at home may stem from the clinician's lack of understanding concerning the organisation of family affairs with such persons. Many times clinical professionals employed their own determination of the child's abilities as an objective criterion against which parental claims were measured. When there was a conflict in assessments, parental intimacy, rather than being seen as a reason for trusting the parents' knowledge of the child, was construed as an obstacle to parental objectivity. When very significant divergences of opinion occur, the pejorative labels applied to parents, cited above, became entrées in case documentation. They were ways, sometimes, to discredit parental knowledge because it was contradictory and arrived at subjectively.

This was the case when I worked with a family which had a deaf-blind, alingual, non-ambulatory, retarded daughter. Betty Jones's ideas about her daughter, Breta, had already been described as 'very unrealistic' by both clinical and educational staff. By the time I arrived on the scene as an 'in-home ethnographer', there was already a lively conflict about who was correct in their assessment of Breta, parents or human service professionals.

From clinical or educational vantage-points, Breta was profoundly flawed and without chance for significant positive change. Because of prenatal exposure to rubella virus, she had been born with Rubella Syndrome (pre-natal rubella embryopathy) whose specific sequelae in her case included bilateral cataracts (blindness); inner ear abnormalities and central nervous system (CNS) damage resulting in deafness; CNS damage involving mental retardation; motor area damage resulting in cerebral palsy (tongue thrust, pincer grasp, 'parachute position' ambulation with the aid of a walkette), and congenital heart defects, as well as other mal-formations. Largely due to these multihandicaps, Breta, who was twelve when I met her, had no oral or gestural language, almost no self-help skills (she *was* able to control nature's call reliably unless ignored for too long a period), and required virtually twenty-four-hour custodial care. Nor was she, by conventional standards, a pretty child to look at, with or without her leg braces, bilateral hearing aids and thick glasses. She had a rather disturbing habit of transferring massive amounts of saliva to objects before touching them more thoroughly. It was presum-ably this practice which lay at the heart of one teacher's reference to Breta as 'slug-like'. This teacher was, in fact, quite fond of Breta and worked with her fairly effectively. While he genuinely cared, the identity he afforded her was a product of his classroom interaction with her. His ambivalence was partly due to how much lower functioning she was in relation to other class members. All professionals involved in her case considered her to be very low functioning with poor prognoses in sens-ory motor, social or cognitive areas.

Betty did not see her daughter quite this way, although she was aware of how Breta was construed by persons who employed medical, develop-mental or common-sense criteria of judgement. The first day I met her she said something to the effect that, 'I know you won't understand this but we think Breta's beautiful, really.' She had been correct; I did not understand what she had meant, at least not until I had been in the home for some time and Breta had begun to 'grow on me'. In her own way, Breta was beautiful — though it was the kind of beauty which could be seen only when you knew who she was. Using the language of *Le Petit Prince* (Saint-Exupéry, 1943), it was a beauty one could 'see with the heart' while remaining 'invisible to the eye'. This observation from literature turns out to be true regarding parental judgements about retarded children; one can only further wonder whether Saint-Exupéry's proposal about 'invisibility' applies in the case of clinicians who see with the eye. Perhaps important and intimate aspects of human interaction are invisible in the light of rationalism and science. If true, this could certainly help account for why parents and clinicians are often in con-flict over the basic questions of who a child is and what he can do — one illumines his vision with the heart, the other with the light of science.

This should not be taken as a way of saying that what a parent sees with his or her eyes is not real. Quite the reverse: intimate or even 'hyperintimate' knowledge of a person does not invalidate perceptions, even when they contradict details of the clinical picture. Betty claimed, for example, that 'Breta can communicate with me completely. Honestly,

there's nothing that Breta can't tell me.' If we employ the clinical identity of Breta as a way to judge her claim, then Betty was being at least
'unrealistic' if not 'delusional'. Although sympathetic to the family,
even I had trouble with her proposal when I first encountered it. I
found it hard to take seriously since I could not even imagine what she
meant by it.

After six months' observation in the home, not only was I able to
imagine what she meant but, to a degree, had been able to document it
empirically. I employed a phenomenological procedure of suspending
judgement based upon scientific or common-sense ideas, and tried to
take Betty's claims at face value, to relate them to the actual conditions
which I observed. Within such a research attitude details of their inter-
subjective understanding were described. These were 'local' phenomena,
in the sense that they did not extend to extra-familial members, and
were based upon years of mutually built routines and shared experiences: conceptions of temporal organisation of daily activities; knowledge about the lay-out of rooms and the home; procedural definitions
of daily activities such as dressing, bathing, pottying, playing, etc. (i.e.
agreements about who was to do what to whom and when); evaluations
of the propriety of certain behaviours; idiosyncratic incidents of bio-
graphy (trips, broken limbs, changes of residence, etc.); and many other
items of information.

To maintain that Betty and Breta shared definitions of routine, particular and general items of information and so forth was not to say they
had identical versions of them or that these items were shared sym-
metrically. For example, there was a mealtime routine (more exactly
mealtime routines – differing for breakfast, lunch and dinner) which
was ordinarily followed. During meals both Betty and Breta knew what
was expected of the other and, while Betty clearly bore the brunt of
the labour, for the affair to be successful both participants had to do
their part. In fact, it was one or the other's failure to do so which had
alerted me to the existence of a mealtime routine in the first place.
During such incidents Betty might complain that Breta 'usually' does
not spit out her spaghetti, or Breta might begin to 'stamp' her feet
when she did not get her milk on time or in the correct cup. After a
time it was clear that both Betty and Breta orientated to such routine
procedures and that, within them, communication in the form of requests and responses were not only possible but, seemingly, were un-
equivocal.

The reader may think, it is one thing to assert there were family
routines, shared biographies and a fine web of intersubjectively shared

knowledge which allowed Breta and her mother to communicate effectively; it is another thing to establish empirically that Breta possessed
such knowledge. After all, the child evidenced no symbolic communication, therefore one could not ascertain what she knew but only attribute
knowledge to her. One could never 'really' know what she did or did not
understand. This sounds troublesome, but it is no more so than 'normal'
communication. We all know more than we can say, in fact, *knowing
something and the ability to communicate knowledge are not at all
identical phenomena.* For example, one may be able to ride a bicycle
without being able to say how one does so. At home, the basis for attri-
bution of knowledge to Breta was found in the details of family life and
how Betty's claims about Breta related to actual observed instances of
family interaction. On such a basis, there was considerable evidence to
back up Betty's assertions. There were even naturally occurring 'tests'
of their validity.

'Tests' refer to those instances when, *acting upon* the belief that
Breta knew and adhered to routines, for instance, would result in pre-
dictable, pragmatic consequences. If the 'proof of the pudding is in the
eating', then Betty's claims were very often pragmatically valid. Once,
when I was having trouble giving Breta her milk during one of my initial
attempts at mealtime, Betty turned to me and remarked, 'Oh, you're
using the wrong cup, that's why she's making such a fuss.' And, as was
usual, after supplying me with the correct cup, the problems with Breta
ceased. Such incidents were prototypical of my experience in the family,
occurring literally hundreds of times during my tenure in the home.

Through such experiences I began to regard Betty as the reigning expert on Breta-related affairs in the family. When ambiguities of interpretation occurred, or problems in handling Breta, more often than not I
could obtain a satisfactory explanation from her. She was also very open
and frank about what she did not know about her daughter. There were
still mysteries which remained, mysteries about which Betty would sometimes say, 'We'll never know about [for example] what Breta dreams,
or thinks about her friend Diane, or hears with her hearing aids.'

Despite such gaps, Betty knew her daughter better than anyone else
— at least in terms of her behaviour in intimate, holistic relationships
such as those in the family. Seeing her in this way obverted the clinical
stance towards Betty's claims as noted in Breta's files. It transferred
her 'delusions' into defensible observations made about qualitatively
different social relationships than those of the clinic. If she was in
'error', it may be in the sense that she, like clinicians, extended her
identity for Breta beyond the confines of the family context within

which she experienced her daughter's capabilities. However, through her testimony, our appreciation of Breta's potentialities under familial circumstances can be radically upgraded.

Christina

Some retarded persons may experience minimal or even no intimacy as a part of their everyday lives. Many of these people, such as the severely and profoundly retarded who live in State Hospitals or other large institutions, are often surrounded by those who maintain flawed, faulted identities of them. Sometimes there is no possibility for retreat from such definitions, or for support or otherwise positive affiliations with intimate others. Such persons' likes and dislikes may be ignored or unappreciated. Unlike Johnny, in our first field note, they may find nobody to be their 'mommy during the day'. They may become clinical, custodial or pedagogic 'objects' in the sense which Goffman (1961) described person-objectification during the course of institutional 'people work'. To further his observation, it is organisation of people work which forms the social context out of which identities for retarded clients emerge. Often, the retarded person is seen as 'relevant' in so far as he is seen as helping or hindering daily staff routines. This form of identity-making substantially parallels those described above.

Such was the situation with Christina, another deaf-blind Rubella child but who resided in a State Hospital ward. Chris's clinical profile was similar to that of Breta, with the exception that Chris had no motor involvement and was able to ambulate, grasp and eat normally. She had been institutionalised at the age of six and was eight when I met her. I worked fairly consistently with her, 'one-to-one' for over three years — needless to say getting to know her quite well during this period.

Within the hospital, Chris was afforded three distinct organisational identities, entailing specific versions of her competencies and incompetencies. One 'version' of Chris was produced by custodial personnel on the ward, who talked about her in terms of her abilities (or lack thereof) to perform those tasks which they required of her during eating, bathing, dressing, pottying, playing, etc. Another identity was afforded Chris by clinical staff at the hospital who were charged with examination, diagnosis and remediation of her condition and health in general. These staff employed a mechanistic-medical model (in which Chris, like Breta, was construed in a deeply pejorative way) coupled with a people work identity (in which Chris was described as difficult to examine, diagnose or cure). Finally, Chris's teachers described her somewhat differently, although in equally negative terms — as unable to be taught, lazy, stubborn, without an attention span, etc.

Describing three distinct identities within a 'single' institution shows that, in claiming that identities were products of social contexts, 'context' is not intended in the sense of a social organisation as large or diffuse as a State Hospital. There were, instead, distinct contexts *within* such an institution. 'Sociogenic or socially constructed identities' refer to conceptions of persons which are produced in face-to-face, micro-level interaction through that interaction's organisation. In so far as clinics, wards and classrooms were separate places, staffed by separate persons and organised according to different routines and rhetorics, it was entirely possible to find divergent, interactionally-based descriptions of Chris's capabilities and disabilities within a single institution such as a State Hospital.

There was a common factor to these identities — they were pejorative. Clinicians, custodians and teachers had some form of the task of 'normalising' Christina as their basic *raison d'être* during interaction with her. Since, almost by definition, a child like Chris was bound severely to hamper any remedial efforts in whichever context one chose to observe, it was sociologically sensible that faulted, though differentiable, identities for Christina were produced in the clinic, school and ward.

While we can make sociological sense of such negative descriptions, they were not very sensible from Chris's 'point of view'. I use the phrase 'point of view' guardedly, since time does not permit for a discussion concerning my entitlement to speak authoritatively about Chris's deaf-blind, alingual perspective (see Goode, 1979). She did have a valid outlook, if one made the effort to discover it, which I did. I designed observational methods which would maximise the possibility of empathy and intimate knowledge of her. These included: simulated deaf-blind experiences; long-term direct observation (at one point spending over 24 hours by her side); mimicking her behaviours; allowing her to structure interaction; and videotaping our interaction. These changes in the organisation of our relationship, and its documentation, allowed me to produce a competent identity for Christina.

Negative assessments of Chris's competence stood in various relationships to those I made through long-term intimate and even extra-ordinary forms of observation. Sometimes clinical assessments were inaccurate — that is, as with Bobby or Breta, they were incorrect in detail. For example, the clinical descriptions of visual and auditory acuity clearly underestimated Chris's sensory abilities as evidenced in daily, on the ward, activities. Other times, the objective, fault-finding descriptions of

Chris were technically accurate — for example, the description of her walking as 'non-purposive', 'atethoid', 'spastic' with 'an overly wide gait' — though contradicting the actual subjective experience of the phenomenon for her. Chris enjoyed her admittedly abnormal form of walking immensely and, with her welfare in mind, it is questionable whether there ought to have been a remedial 'walking programme' — which, of course, there was. Finally, from the perspective of the face-to-face interaction of which we were part, there were competencies which were completely ignored in formal assessments or 'on the job' assessments. I referred to these as 'deep' or 'generic' competencies (see Goode, 1979).

Without getting too much into the details of Chris's case, what differentiated her from Breta or Bobby was the perspicuous absence of others who, through intimate and affiliative interaction, knew about, and might even defend, a more competent identity of her. Thus, while Betty had to endure regular conflict with human service professionals regarding her daughter's identity, within her home she could treat Breta commensurate with those competencies and faults which she 'actually' evidenced in the home environment. Bobby, to an even greater degree, was for all practical purposes free from the influence of the pejorative identity and incompetencies granted him by clinicians in his daily activities. He simply had nothing to do with their world and the documents testifying to his clinical identity were filed in the board and care facility offices, unconsulted by staff.

Christina, on the other hand, had no choice but to live out human service worker and professional visions of her life. She was treated in accordance with the negative characterisations which she was assigned in various social contexts within the hospital. Without intimate others, she was surrounded by persons who treated her as less than she was or could become. In so far as she was excluded from the competency granting social relationships, which both Bobby and Breta were allowed, her life was socially denigrated through institutionalised forms of help giving.

Conclusion

While time does not permit a detailed drawing out of procedural clinical implications for each case, these materials do suggest certain policy changes regarding human services to persons who are severely cognitively and/or physically damaged in chronic and irremediable ways.

All cases evidence a repeated fact — that the availability of such persons' behaviour in institutional service settings is such that we may be seriously misled about these clients' capabilities in more familiar intimate relationships. The objectivity of clinical procedure 'constitutionalises' and 'decontextualises' competence and produces, from a sociological vantage-point, distortions not only of individual client capabilities and potentialities, but of the very nature of ability itself. I have suggested that we can understand why this occurs in terms of the social organisation of the clinical enterprise and its discontinuity with the organisation of intimate, long-term helping relationships. There are a number of dimensions to this observation.

Clinical encounters are essentially unaccepting of the chronically, irremediably damaged person. The *sine qua non* of clinical work is the location of faults and their amelioration. With persons like Bobby, Breta or Christina, such attempts are going to be frustrated by the very nature of their disabilities. A clinical logic, which may be useful when dealing with acute, traumatic illness of 'normal' persons, proves misdirected and iatrogenic when applied to this type of client. The kinds of clients described in this chapter are not seen as people who 'have' irremediable problems, they are seen *as irremediable problems*. There is a world of difference between 'being' and 'having' a problem.

While fault-finding is also evident in non-institutional contexts of interaction with severely disabled people, it does not basically characterise long-term relationships. These, generally, do not seem to lead to an essentially faulted identity for the client. It would seem, drawing here upon a considerable amount of experience with chronically damaged clients in public settings, human service institutions, and other interactional contexts wherein intimate contact was not evident, that *fault-finding procedures are almost always employed by non-intimates; pejorative identifications, within some frame of reference and vernacular, are almost always the outcome of such encounters*. Considering the ubiquitousness of the phenomenon, one must recall Wolfensberger's (1980) description of Western culture's punitive and denying response to deviants and deviancy. He argues that the 'comfort culture', coupled with our concern about our own (ultimately to be realised) handicaps and imperfection, provide the bases for socially organised, institutionalised fault-finding as a form of 'help giving'.

Fault-finding mechanisms serve as dis-identification devices, whether used by lay persons or professionals, often as ways to combat the self-implicative quality to any human disabling. They can be ways to deny an essential truth with which persons in this culture seem ill-equipped to come to terms — that is, that 'the presence of the handicapped person

condemns me' (Wolfensberger, personal communication, 1980). The most generic change these case materials suggest is not procedural *per se*, but concerns the way we are to think about, and thus 'help', the chronically damaged. In my encounter with the man with hydrocephaly, the doctor's description and my own were but two sides to the same coin. Both served to create psychological distance between ourselves and the 'patient'. In our own respective fashions, we failed to encounter his presence in an ethically or humanly valid way. Yet, if we do not begin human services with an *acceptance of human imperfection and those who are imperfect*, then we may continue to try unrealistically to overcome it or to deny it. Under such circumstances we will continue to practice interventions which will ultimately be iatrogenic in effect — euphemistically masquerading, even to ourselves, as help-giving in the forms of 'assessment' and 'therapy'.

We have seen that those who achieve intimacy with deeply imperfect persons *do* accept them and their viewpoints about basic human concerns. Such intimacy leads to a recognition of the client's subjective experience of life, even when this is discontinuous with, or even denies, our own experience and common-sense knowledge. As Kielhofner (1983) suggests,

> that they [highly disabled persons] cannot accommodate the usual definition of competent performance challenges those who serve them to *construct* social versions of their competence as a starting point for therapy. Such a *relativity theory* of competence would ask: What would be a good performance for someone with this radically altered brain or body? The question lies both in the perspective (however limited or deviant) of the individual and the ability of someone else to recognize and appreciate performance from that same perspective.

Kielhofner thus offers an important implication for human services to chronically damaged persons, one which these materials support. Our conceptions of clients, and those procedures we use to enhance their competences, must begin with an acceptance of their subjective experience. For many human service professionals and workers, this acceptance itself presents the single greatest challenge to valid and efficacious help-giving. To achieve it often requires that they resist common-sense and professional interpretations of client actions. While this is possible, if not common, among intimates, it is almost entirely absent in more formal helping forms. Moreover, the whole notion of subjectivity is not seriously considered in many of the helping professions for the developmentally disabled. They tend to discredit client subjectivity in favour of more 'objective' approaches to assessment. In so doing they ignore J.-P. Sartre's warning in *Being and Nothingness* (1965). He writes, 'The environment can act on the subject to the exact extent that he comprehends it; that is, transforms it into a situation. Hence, no objective description could be of any use to us.'

Finally, this writing displays the importance of observational method for an understanding of human services to the chronically disabled. From a sociological perspective, both client behaviours and the ways they are interpreted are primarily *social* phenomena. When people cognise during performance, or reflect upon the character of their own or others' performances, they do so within a socially ordered situation and employing a socially generated cognitive apparatus to order that situation. While our judgements are social in origin, we seem to ignore this consensual basis for thought and action. We reify our service activities, that is we take it that, when we assess a client's capabilities, we are objectively and validly capturing her 'actual' self. Instead, we ought to consider how our consensual agreements about how to interpret performance help create that 'actual' self. It is the very rare professional who can do service while, at the same moment, maintaining a critical cognisance about what she is doing. The relevancy of certain forms of sociology, notably ethnographic and phenomenological description, is that they can reveal that which is less than obvious to practitioners – that the client they 'find' before them rests as much upon the social organisation of their relationship with her as it does 'her' (the client's) physical and/or psychological characteristics *per se*.

Such an awareness is as important as it is difficult to achieve. It represents a way to combat our tendency to set ourselves up as human service 'professionals' who can arbitrate 'fairly' about what is or is not realistic or reasonable to claim about human interrelations or about what a person can or cannot do. While current professional helping ideologies claim to be grounded upon empirical examinations of the material organisation of human behaviour, it is ironic that we have set ourselves up in a pontificating stance regarding what will be allowed to be claimed as actual or real. We professionals know so little about the material organisation of the everyday lives of these persons, or about how they make sense of their lives or attempt to master their world.

One recommendation to be drawn from these studies is to refrain from discrediting claims and experience on the basis of their degree of fit to scientific models of phenomena. Perhaps we ought especially to begin to listen to those who know the chronically, irremediably damaged intimately and, in some senses, 'better' than we. 'Before there was argumentation, there was action. [*Im anfang war die Tat.*] In the beginning was the deed. And human action had solved the difficulty long before human ingenuity had invented it' (Friedrich Engels, 1892).

References

Bercovici, S. (1980) '"Educating" retarded adults: An attempt at "normalisation"?' in J. Jacobs (ed.), *Phenomenological Approaches to Mental Retardation*, C.C. Thomas, Springfield, Illinois.

Blatt, B. (1970) *Exodus from Pandemonium*, Allyn and Bacon, Boston.

Bogdan, R. (1976) 'The judged not the judges: An insider's view of mental retardation', *American Psychologist*, *31*, 47-53.

Edgerton, R. (1967) *The Cloak of Competence*, University of California Press, Berkeley, California.

Engels, F. (1892 [1970]) 'Socialism: Utopian and scientific' in *Karl Marx and Friedrich Engels: Selected Works*, International Publishers, New York.

Garfinkel, H. (1967) *Studies in Ethnomethodology*, Prentice-Hall, Englewood Cliffs, NJ.

Goffman, E. (1961) *Asylums*, Anchor, New York.

Goode, D. (1979) 'The world of the deaf-blind' in H. Schwartz and J. Jacobs (eds.), *Qualitative Sociology: A Method to the Madness*, Free Press, New York.

—— (1980) 'Behavioral sculpting: Parent–child interactions in families with retarded children' in J. Jacobs (ed.), *Phenomenological Approaches to Mental Retardation*, C.C. Thomas, Springfield, Illinois.

—— (1983) 'Who is Bobby?: Ideology and method in the discovery of a Down's Syndrome person's competence' in G. Kielhofner (ed.), *Health Through Occupation: Theory and Practice in Occupational Therapy*, F.A. Davis, Philadelphia.

Jacobs, J. (1969) *The Search for Help: A Study of the Retarded Child in the Community*, Brunner-Mazel, New York.

Kielhofner, G. (1983) 'Rose colored lenses for clinical practice: From a deficit to a competency model in assessment and intervention' in G. Kielhofner (ed.), *Health Through Occupation: Theory and Practice in Occupational Therapy*, F.A. Davis, Philadelphia.

Langness, L. (1982) 'Mental retardation as an anthropological problem', *Werner-Grenn Working Papers in Anthropology*.

Merleau-Ponty, M. (1962) *The Phenomenology of Perception*, Routledge and Kegan Paul, London.

Polanyi, M. (1958) *On Personal Knowledge*, Harper and Row, New York.

Saint-Exupéry, A. (1943) *Le Petit Prince*, Harcourt Brace Jovanovich, New York.

Sartre, J.-P. (1965) *Being and Nothingness*, Citadel Press, Secaucus, NJ.

Schutz, A. (1970) *On Phenomenological and Social Relations*, University of Chicago Press, Chicago.

Wolfensberger, W. (1980) 'The extermination of handicapped people in World War II Germany', *American Journal on Mental Deficiency*, *19*, No. 1.

NOTES ON CONTRIBUTORS

Deborah Bart, Doctoral Candidate, Graduate School of Education, University of Rochester, Rochester, New York, USA.

Len Barton, Senior Lecturer, Education Department, Westhill College, Selly Oak, Birmingham, England.

Bob Bogdan, Professor, School of Education, Division of Special Education, Syracuse University, 805 S, Crouse Avenue, Syracuse, New York, USA.

James Carrier, Lecturer, Department of Anthropology and Sociology, Box 320, University of Papua New Guinea, P.O., N.C.D., Papua New Guinea.

David Goode, Associate Professor, Wilkes College, Department of Sociology, Wilkes-Barre, Pennsylvania, USA.

Joan Gunn, Assistant District Health Planner, Medical District 17, United States Department of Veterans Administration, Chicago, Illinois, USA.

Alan Hurst, Senior Lecturer, School of Social Studies, Preston Polytechnic, Preston, Lancashire, England.

Judy Kugelmass, Director, Special Children's Centre, Ithaca, New York, USA.

John Quicke, Lecturer, Division and Institute of Education, University of Sheffield, Sheffield, England.

Louis Rowitz, Professor, School of Public Health, University of Illinois at Chicago, Post Office Box 6998, Chicago, Illinois, USA.

Mårten Söder, Research Student, Arbetslivscentrum, Box 5606, S-114, 86, Stockholm, Sweden.

Sally Tomlinson, Senior Lecturer, Department of Educational Research, University of Lancaster, Bailrigg, Lancaster, England.

AUTHOR INDEX

SUBJECT INDEX